T0323956

Galvano Della Volpe

NLB

Logic as a
Positive Science

Translated by Jon Rothschild

British Library
Cataloguing in Publication Data

Della Volpe, Galvano
  Logic as a positive science.
  1. Science – Philosophy
  I. Title
  501   Q175

ISBN 978-0-86091-031-2

First published as
Logica come scienza positiva
© Editori Riuniti, 1969

This edition first published 1980
© NLB, 1980
NLB,7 Carlisle Street, London W1

Typeset in English Times by
Red Lion Setters, London WC1

Printed in Great Britain by
Redwood Burn Ltd.,
Trowbridge and Esher

Contents

Contents

Translator's Preface

Logic as a Positive Science represents the fruit of more than two decades of the philosophical work of Galvano Della Volpe. Its publication was first announced in 1947 under the title *Critica del 'Conosci te stesso'* (Critique of 'Know Thyself') and in 1948 as the 'second edition' of *Critica dei princípi lógici* (Critique of Logical Principles), a study of Kant and Hegel first published in the early 1940s, before Della Volpe became a Marxist. As late as January 1951 an article in the journal *Pensiero critico* announced it yet again, this time as *Introduzione materialistica alla logica* (Materialist Introduction to Logic). But this article was published many months after its submission to the journal, and the first edition of *Logica come scienza positiva* had in fact appeared in August 1950.

Its publication established Della Volpe as a major, though always controversial, philosopher whose 'school' was to polarize theoretical discussion in the Italian Communist Party, which he had joined in 1944. In 1956 a second edition of the work appeared, 'entirely revised', as Della Volpe put it. This second edition was indeed heavily altered. The three chapters and one appendix of the first edition had become four chapters and three appendices in the second. In the critical edition of Della Volpe's works (*Opere*, edited by Ignazio Ambrogio, volume 4, 1973) annotation of the textual changes in the second edition compared with the first runs to more than 40 pages of small type.

In the last years of his life Della Volpe was reportedly at work on a third edition, which was uncompleted at his death in 1968. In 1969, however, the second edition was re-issued under a new title. The change was accompanied by this statement from the author: 'But a more satisfactory and definitive title (for the next reprint) would be

Logic as a Historical Science, since the immediate reasons for the original title (the polemic against the idealist notion of logic as the "science of the pure concept") no longer apply. Such a change, of course, would not be merely formal, since it would involve the (consistent) application of the historical-dialectical criterion to logic itself, or the general theory of dialectic.'

Because of this publishing history, the work has come to be known under two different titles, although the second edition of *Logic as a Positive Science* in the *Opere* does not differ from the separately issued *Logic as a Historical Science*. NLB has chosen to issue it under its original title, for two reasons. First, the book is probably more widely known in the English-speaking world under this title; second, although Della Volpe may well have come to believe that the polemical considerations that motivated his original choice of title no longer pertained, it remains the case that the book itself *was* inspired, in good part at least, by just these considerations, and is structured and presented accordingly. The original title thus accurately expresses the content of the work, which was not changed by the posthumous alteration of the title.

The text here has been translated from the second, definitive edition of the entire work, including the three appendices. But it does not contain three separately published essays that were appended to the posthumously issued *Logic as a Historical Science*.

Della Volpe is notoriously difficult to translate, and the *Logic* is arguably his most involved work. The intrinsic complexity of the subject matter is compounded by a number of stylistic devices. Chief among these are his frequent practice of quoting other philosophers in their original language and paraphrasing long passages as a preliminary to criticism. My aim in the present translation has been to minimize stylistic and terminological barriers to understanding. Sentences have accordingly been recast and shortened, paragraphs frequently divided. Parenthetical citations of sources have been brought down into footnotes. No quotations have been left in the original language unless that language was English. References have been changed to accord with English versions of translated works wherever they were available.

All quotations from Kant and Hegel have been taken from the latest English translations, which are indicated in the footnotes. Terminology has occasionally been altered to bring usage into conformity with Della Volpe's. I have indicated these changes where they were important, but have not done so where they seemed trivial. One general change that has been made throughout is that Hegel's term *Begriff*, nearly always translated as 'Notion', has been rendered as 'Concept', in accordance with an argument put forward by Walter Kaufmann. Where Della Volpe has paraphrased rather than quoted, I have used the English translations as a guide, and have therefore diverged slightly from the Italian text in some cases, although not significantly. The frequent bracketed interpolations within quotations are Della Volpe's, and not the translator's.

The central concern of *Logic as a Positive Science* is to establish a scientific logic free of any aprioristic speculation. Della Volpe argues that there can be no specifically philosophical logic, or method of producing true knowledge. On the contrary, there is only one logic and one method: that of modern, experimental science. The establishment of this proposition is, according to the dictates of his method itself, part and parcel of a description of what that logic is, and how it is distinct from and superior to any other. Della Volpe maintains that the liberation of philosophy from idealist speculation is itself a historical process, and critical consideration of that process is integral to the constitution of a genuinely scientific logic and methodology.

Della Volpe's own point of departure was a study of two of Marx's early writings: 'Critique of Hegel's Doctrine of the State' and the 'Economic and Philosophical Manuscripts' (1844). He maintained that Marx's initial criticism of Hegel established the basis of philosophy as science, the heart of the critique being Marx's exposure of the 'mystification' inherent in Hegel's dialectic. While the criticism was primarily negative in these early writings, it attained its first positive expression in the 1857 introduction to *A Contribution to the Critique of Political Economy*, the first comprehensive statement of Marx's scientific method in economics. Della Volpe saw his own task as the generalization of the method expounded therein. At the same time, he viewed Marx's work as a culminating point in a philosophic evolution stretching back to ancient Greece. The cardinal moments in that evolution were a sequence of historic critiques: Plato of Parmenides, Aristotle of Plato, Galileo of the scholastics, Kant of Leibniz, and Marx of Hegel.

But Della Volpe does not present his argument chronologically.

He begins with Kant, then moves to Hegel, then back to Plato and Aristotle, and thence to Marx and Galileo. This departure from historical sequence is partly a consequence of the method itself (as Della Volpe explains in his final chapter) and partly a result of the genesis of his *Logic*, which grew out of his early criticism of Kant and Hegel. It may therefore be of some help to restate the structure of the *Logic* chronologically. What follows is not intended as an interpretation of the work, and still less a commentary on the many controversial aspects of Della Volpe's assessment of the history of Western philosophy. It is, rather, an attempt to set out a guiding framework, and to explain some of the terminology used in the work.

For Della Volpe, the starting-point of science is the ability of human beings to make meaningful *judgements* expressed in language. In the history of Western thought, the judgement has typically been considered a linkage between a subject and a predicate joined by a copula, the verb 'to be' in an appropriate grammatical form. (For example, 'Socrates is mortal'.) In this sort of judgement, a relation is asserted to hold between a particular (the subject, 'Socrates' in this case) and a universal (the predicate, 'mortal' in this case).

Philosophical consideration of this relation goes back to Parmenides, with a reference to whom the *Logic* begins. Before Parmenides, all Greek philosophers had assumed the reality of change in the world and had attempted to explain it, although in conflicting ways. Parmenides challenged all the prevalent theories, arguing that both change and difference were illusory. His basic premise was that it is impossible either to know or to speak about that which does not exist: that which is for thinking and saying must exist, for it can exist, whereas nothing cannot. In other words, the object of thought can exist, while nothing cannot exist, so the object of thought cannot be nothing. Since 'that which is not' is unthinkable and unknowable, change is impossible, for any change would involve a transition from that which is to that which is not, and change could not be described without using the unintelligible expression 'that which is not'.

Since all change is impossible, so are growth and decay, and likewise distinctions within what exists. Being is therefore a continuous and homogeneous whole. With this reasoning Parmenides established an absolute duality. On the one hand we have being, oneness (or unity), that which is rational; on the other, not-being, the many (or multiplicity), the irrational. The question of the relationship between the two poles of this duality is not merely logical, but *gnoseological*—that is, it concerns the conditions, origins, and limits of any theory of knowledge. Parmenides's conception leads to a denial of the reality of the world of the senses, the variegated (multiple) reality that we perceive. To be distinct, each of the elements of this reality would have to be itself and not others; therefore, in order to describe it we would have to think simultaneously of being and not-being, which has already been declared impossible. This demonstrates that the multiple is not; it does not belong to true reality, but is mere appearance. We may therefore add two terms to the duality: reason to the first pole (being, the rational, unity) and the senses to the second (not-being, the irrational, multiplicity). The terms of this Parmenidean duality run through Della Volpe's entire work.

Parmenides's dualism was inherited by Plato, who grappled with its implications in formulating his theory of knowledge, mainly in his later dialogues. In the *Meno* Socrates remarks that in daily life fallible human opinion often serves as well as true knowledge. The Greek term for an opinion of this kind—*doxa*—actually refers to any statement about appearances, or the sensible world. Translations of Plato therefore render it 'judgement' as often as 'opinion'. The problem broached by Plato in his theory of knowledge was this: some human judgements are true, others false; but even the true ones differ from knowledge (*episteme*, as opposed to *doxa*) in that they are subject to criticism. Thus arises the Platonic problem of the 'true *doxa*', which may be formulated thus: how can human beings talk about the world, make judgements, etc., in a meaningful sense? And what is the difference between a 'true *doxa*' and knowledge?

In the two dialogues in which he considered these questions most fully—*Theaetetus* and *The Sophist*—Plato took up some of the implications of the duality of Parmenides. The latter held that what is not is not and cannot be mentioned. If that is so, then there can be no statement that something is not so-and-so (e.g. 'man is not a bird'). Thus no statement can be negative. But that very statement is itself negative and therefore falls under its own proscription. Parmenides's duality is therefore self-destructive and must be reformulated. The real question, says Plato, is not 'how can there be negative things?' but rather 'how can things be truly or falsely denied?'. For example, if we deny something of Theaetetus (e.g.,

'Theaetetus does not fly'), we are not saying something about 'not-Theaetetus', but are associating a 'not-something' with a 'something'. But to associate a not-something is, implicitly, simultaneously to associate a 'something'. If we say that Theaetetus is not a fish, then there must be something else in the genus in which fish is included that he *is*. To deny one predicate of a subject is to affirm another of it, and vice versa. Hence, contrary to Parmenides, negation is an essential part of thought.

These considerations led Plato to a theory of classification. The sensible world, Plato held, had in some way to be related to ideas, and the key to that relationship lay in the connection between unity and multiplicity; the idea is the unity of the multiple elements that 'participate' in it. When we say, for example, that 'Socrates is mortal', we are stating that the subject (the particular, the multiple, the sensible) *participates in* (or forms part of) the predicate (the universal, unity, the ideal), which in turn *pervades* the many particulars. Thus, Socrates is mortal, and Theaetetus is mortal too. Both 'participate' in the genus (*eidos*, which also means 'form') 'mortal', which thereby 'pervades' both Socrates and Theaetetus. To err—or to utter an untrue *doxa*—is to associate a subject with an *eidos* in which it does not participate.

How, then, do we make these associations of subject (particular) with predicate (universal) correctly? Plato's answer is given in his process of dialectical division, or *diairesis*. The procedure is described by the Eleatic Stranger, one of the characters in *The Sophist*. A notion, he says, can be defined by considering it part of a wider group and then dividing that group (or genus) into two components, one of which must be the required notion. If we take, for example, the genus 'living thing', we may subdivide it into the species 'animal' and 'plant'. We then consider 'animal' a genus and divide it into the species 'rational' and 'irrational'. So we continue until we arrive at the thing we are seeking to define (for example, 'king' or 'fisherman' or whatever). At each step of this process, the 'higher genera' pervade the lower, while the lower participate in the higher. The idea of 'king', for example, will then be the *unity* of all the genera that have participated in its deduction through the process of diairesis. The entire procedure is based on pairs of oppositions that are mutually exclusive. In other words, all diairesis is permeated (pervaded) by the essential dichotomy 'sameness-otherness' (or 'tauton-heteron', tauto-heterology). Discourse about the world thus becomes possible through the replacement of the Parmenidean duality of being and not-being by the dichotomy of sameness-otherness, Platonic tauto-heterology.

The next step in Della Volpe's historical lineage is Aristotle's critique of diairesis. Aristotle argued that Plato's process was logically flawed by *petitio principii*, for he has assumed as a premise exactly what was to be demonstrated. In dividing, we have to select one of two contraries within each genus. But to make the selection we must already have in mind the character of the thing to be defined. In defining 'man', for example, we decide to divide the genus 'animal' into the species 'rational' and 'irrational' only because we already know that man is rational. The lower genera thus serve as criteria for the division of the higher, while the process of diairesis claims to *deduce* the lower genera from the higher. In other words, subject and predicate are reversed, the predicate (universal) *determining* the subject (particular).

But for Della Volpe, Aristotle's critique was not merely logical, but also *ontological*, because Aristotle criticized Plato for confusing the category of substance with other categories, ascribing substantiality to all the categories. Thus, Plato claims to be deducing some (substantial) forms from other, higher ones. But actually he has *presupposed* the lower (substantial) forms in every case, and has thus presupposed all of empirical reality, even while striving to deduce empirical reality from a realm of substantial forms (or ideas) standing beyond it. Hence the *ontological*, and not merely logical, *petitio principii*.

It was in this critique that Della Volpe detected the 'materialist genius' of Aristotle—but also the flaw that prevented him from fully resolving the problem of logical discourse. The materialist insight was Aristotle's recognition that the substance of a genus or species is *not different* from the substance of any member of that genus or species. When we say, for example, 'Socrates is a man', we are not postulating two substances, 'Socrates' and 'man', and asserting that these two substances are somehow associated such that one 'participates' in the other and is 'pervaded' by it. Rather, our point is that the substantiality of 'man' *is* the substantiality of 'Socrates'. 'Man' stands for an entity, but that entity is just the subject of which it is predicated. The contrariety 'man/not-man', Aristotle holds, exists 'potentially', but not 'in actuality', for actuality, or the process of becoming, 'separates contraries' such that in the real world we have not 'man/not-man' but either 'man' *or* 'not-man'. Hence Aristotle's expression 'entelechy (actuality) separates contraries', and hence also his principle of non-contradiction in its original, materialist sense: nothing can be both A and not-A. The individual thing, which Aristotle called 'first substance', *has no contrary*.

But, Della Volpe further argues, Aristotle's critique of Plato was inadequate. He continued to agree with Plato that real knowledge had to be certain and permanent, and therefore necessary and not subject to change. For Plato this meant that the object of knowledge itself had to be unchanging, and therefore not sensible, not 'of this world'. Aristotle on the contrary held that the human intellect is *dianoetic*: it achieves knowledge discursively, by discriminating and conjoining concepts grounded in reality. But since he continued to believe that knowledge was knowledge of *real* universals, he had to find some way of ascribing reality to universals without reintroducing Plato's forms, which he had already rejected. He did this by cleaving the category of substance into first and second substance. First substance was individual men and things, while second comprised the genera and species to which these individuals belonged. The sense in which these genera and species are 'secondary' is that without first substance they would not exist (since the substantiality of 'man' *is* the substantiality of 'Socrates'). But genera and species can also serve as subjects of other attributes, indeed sometimes the same attributes as are predicated of first substance, as when we say not only that 'Socrates is mortal', but also 'Man is mortal'. Since second substance is still substance, the universal—or, in Aristotle's terminology, the 'essence' of an individual—retains subsistence. We are now free of Plato's subsistent *forms*, but are afflicted by Aristotle's *substrate-essences*. Plato's position that the empirical world of the senses is *derivative* of a subsistent world that exists independent of it has thus not been integrally rejected. The logical and ontological primacy of the predicate (universal) over the subject (particular), which was absolute in Plato, still remains in Aristotle, and indeed became entrenched, through the writings of subsequent 'Aristotelians', in the tradition of Western philosophy.

This tradition, under which the empirical world was considered either squarely illusory or at best a shadowy reflection of a 'higher reality', was not to be shaken until the beginning of the rise of modern science during the Renaissance. The pivotal figure for Della Volpe here is Galileo, the theorist of the experimental method leading an assault on the 'a priori discourse' of the scholastic physicists. Galileo's primary methodological contribution was his liberation of the natural sciences from a priori speculation through the doctrine that physical theories had to be formulated so as to *correspond to observed facts*, or, in the terminology of the period, to 'saving appearances'. Theories had to be continually tested, and altered or discarded if they failed to 'save appearances'. Moreover, in Galileo we also find the germ of the modern idea that one theory is 'confirmed' through the *disproof* of its rivals.

The first thinker to give philosophical expression to this spirit of modern science was Kant. The rationalist tradition had typically considered sensations as 'confused ideas', and on this basis had erected a hierarchy according to which the senses, which offered us merely 'indistinct representations', were inferior to the intellect. The senses were therefore regarded as insignificant in the generation of knowledge, which was the task of 'pure reason'. Against this tradition, and in particular in opposition to Leibniz, one of its most prominent exponents, Kant asserted the *positive contribution* made by the senses to knowledge. Implicit in this view was Kant's real revolution in philosophy: recognition of the reality and positivity of the multiple, and therefore the indispensability of *both* the senses and the intellect in affording us knowledge. Della Volpe considers this innovation the very apex of Kant's achievement, and accordingly calls it the 'cardinal critique of Leibniz'. But Kant failed to apply his critical exigency consistently. He insisted on a rigid distinction between analytic judgements—in which the predicate enunciates something already inherent in the concept of the subject; for instance, 'all squares have four sides'—and synthetic judgements —in which the predicate is not implicit in the concept of the subject; for instance, 'this flower is red'. His consequent search for the possibility of synthetic judgements a priori led him away from what Della Volpe regards as the crucial point: that *every judgement* entails a synthesis of distinct elements that stand in reciprocal functionality with one another.

After consideration of the important but incomplete contribution of Kantian criticism, Della Volpe evaluates Hegel's conception of logic, which he regards, in disagreement with the bulk of the Marxist tradition on the matter, as a *regression* from Kant and a return, in effect, to an updated form of Platonic mysticism. It is here that we find the unifying theme of the work. Della Volpe draws a methodological parallel between Aristotle's critique of Plato's diairesis and Marx's critique of Hegel's dialectic. Both Hegel and Plato dissolve the material world into the abstract, lending the predicate (universal, unity, the rational) priority over the subject (particular, multiplicity, the irrational). Inevitably, then, in dealing with the real world, of which their own philosophy is a part, they are compelled to postulate reality gratuitously, as a *manifestation of the idea*. The dissolution of the empirical world is thus paralleled by the transformation of the ideal into reality—the process called hypostatization. This procedure—dissolution of the empirical datum into abstract and indeterminate idea and then attribution of substantiality to the idea, which then functions as subject—is the characteristic of all a priori thought, and all instances of it are marred by the ontological *petitio principii* that Aristotle detected in Plato and Marx in Hegel. Moreover, it was just this flaw—although he did not express it as such—that Galileo attacked in the method of the scholastics. Many critics have argued that the flaw in Hegel's dialectic is that his various abstractions are so indeterminate that his dialectical concepts are empty. In Della Volpe's view, the problem is not that they are empty but that they are as full as can be, but with a *vitiated* content, for the very act of a priori abstraction is necessarily followed by the surreptitious attribution of substantiality to the idea.

In effect, then, we have a single conclusion: Marx's critique of Hegel stands in the tradition of Aristotle's critique of Plato and implicitly inaugurates a more general materialist critique of all varieties of a priori, speculative thought. And since the early Marx's critique of Hegel also parallels Galileo's critique of the scholastics, we may draw a corollary of this conclusion: Marx did for philosophy and the 'moral' (or human) sciences what Galileo did for the natural sciences.

This entire argumentation is presented in the first three chapters of the *Logic* and constitutes the prelude to the generalization of Marx's method, the exposition of the materialist doctrine of judgements, which is presented in the fourth chapter. Della Volpe begins his presentation by re-examining the flaw in Hegel's treatment of the senses, or, as Hegel himself put it in his *Phenomenology of Spirit*, of 'sense-certainty'. Hegel had argued that what was actually perceived by the senses was not particular objects, but 'universals as such'. As against this, Della Volpe insists (with Kant) on the positive role of the senses, and on the particularity of the object sensed. Thus, he maintains, the real judgement of knowledge takes shape as a synthesis of distinct elements. It must take account both of the ineradicable positive character of the multiple (which constitutes the instance of *matter*) and of the equally indispensable instance of reason (unity). Without the former we have an indeterminate abstraction (such as Hegel's generalization of the state in a particular epoch into the Essence of the state as such); this sort of abstraction, in the light of the earlier critique, produces not a genuine judgement of knowledge, but a hypostasis. Without the latter element, however, we have merely the unintelligible multiplicity typical of empiricism, which impedes the formation of *hypotheses* (as opposed to hypostases). Implicit in this synthesis is Aristotle's 'materialist insight' that whatever exists is determinate and non-contradictory and that to think is to think of some determinate object. It follows that from the standpoint of materialism, the subject and predicate (particular and universal) stand in synthesis in *every judgement.* Contrary to empiricism, the predicate is not *inducted* from the subject; contrary to rationalism, the subject is not *deduced* from the predicate. The judgement is simultaneously analytic (this is the function of the subject) and synthetic (the function of the predicate). Therefore, matter and reason, subject and predicate, analysis and synthesis, particular and universal, are reciprocally functional and equally indispensable in the formation of the materialist judgement, which is therefore a *determinate* (as opposed to indeterminate) abstraction and a *hypothesis* as opposed to a hypostasis. It is this principle of the formation of judgements that Della Volpe calls 'tauto-heterological identity'.

Finally, the argument is concluded by specification of the method through which such judgements are properly formulated. Science begins, Della Volpe writes, with the concrete material of reality, or more accurately, with specific and concrete *problems* that have arisen historically. This he calls the 'historical-material instance'. The subsequent determinate abstractions, forged as syntheses of the kind described earlier, must be formulated in the light of the historical antecedents of the present problem; this he calls the 'historical-rational instance'. Consideration of this instance enables us to formulate hypotheses as 'means' (in the mathematical sense) of the antecedents of the given consequence. But the concepts thus generated—determinate and historical abstractions—are then precisely hypotheses and nothing more. They are not absolute, like a priori hypostases, but must be tested against reality, through a return from abstraction to concrete reality. In the natural sciences this return to the concrete is the *experiment*; in the social sciences it is the Marxist criterion of practice.

The reciprocal functionality of matter and reason, induction and deduction, subject and predicate, is thus paralleled by the reciprocal functionality of theory and practice, and is embodied in the methodological circle of concrete-abstract-concrete. These principles, taken together, constitute, for Della Volpe, the sole real logic, methodologically identical for all the sciences, natural or 'moral'.

This fellow [the Jesuit Scheiner] goes about thinking up, one by one, things that would be required to serve his purposes, instead of adjusting his purposes step by step to things as they are.

GALILEO

He [Hegel] does not develop his thought from the object, but instead the object is constructed according to a system of thought perfected in the abstract sphere of logic.

MARX

To the precious memory of Pilo Albertelli

I

Critique
of Kantian Logic

1

The critical problem of not-being, in the classical, Parmenidean sense of the term[1]—that is, the problem of multiplicity broached alike by Kant in his sharp rejection of Leibniz's negative concept of the senses and by Marx in his critique of Hegel's dialectic, 'mystified' by the theological 'interpolation' of content, or multiplicity—must be posed once again if present philosophical difficulties are to be resolved.

The task of this study will be to demonstrate that no acceptable solution of the problem of the 'logical' principle, or of the *thinkable*, is possible without an integral and critical grasp of the connection between this question and that of the specific and positive nature of the *sensible*, a typical synonym for multiplicity, or not-being. Indeed, one may say that they constitute a single, complex problem: the recurrent issue of the relationship between *oneness*, or 'being', and *multiplicity*, or 'not-being', from the standpoint of 'truth', or *logos*.

An implicit premise of our inquiry will be the self-evident principle of the *semantic nature of thought*, or truth: the proposition that no thought, consciousness, or reason worthy of the name can exist without that system of meaningful signs *par excellence* which are words, language. This principle is now generally accepted by philosophers

---

[1] See, for example, fragments 2, 4, and 8: '...thou couldst not know that which is not...nor utter it' (fragment 2); '...thou shalt not cut off what *is* from clinging to what *is*...' (fragment 4); 'it [what is] was not in the past, nor shall it be, since it is now, all at once, one, continuous;...nor will the force of true belief allow that, beside what is, there could also arise anything from what is not;...' (fragment 8). The original Greek, with English translation, may be found in G.S. Kirk and J.E. Raven, *The Presocratic Philosophers*, Cambridge, 1957, pp. 269, 275, 269.

and linguists alike. Humboldt, for example, maintains that we domi-
nate our representations and command 'clear thought' only through
the use of words as 'signs' of these representations. Indeed, in his
view 'there is nothing in man's innermost being so profound, deli-
cate, and vast that it does not pass into language'. Marx, speaking
with his full modern authority as a materialist, tells us in *The
German Ideology* that 'the immediate [concrete] reality of thought is
language' and that 'the problem of descending from the world of
thought to the real world is converted into the problem of descending
from language to life'. Benedetto Croce acknowledges that 'an unex-
pressed image, which does not become words . . . even if only
murmured to oneself, . . . is something that does not exist'. For
Saussure, thought in itself is a 'nebula' in which nothing is distinct
until the emergence of language. Finally, for Ludwig Wittgenstein,
the postulate of the possibility of linguistic signs is that of the 'deter-
minacy of meaning' itself, or the sense of how things are (even if not
of *what* they are!). It should thus be understood that the logical and
gnoseological values that form the object of this study must always
be regarded as logical-semantic values.[2]

The first historical-ideal guideline for an assessment of the critical
dimension of our problem can be extracted from an examination of
Kant's general position in logic—in particular, the impasse into
which he was led by his conception of transcendental logic and its
relationship to formal logic. Kant was unable consistently to apply
his supreme critical criterion—the real Copernican principle of his
work—namely that the bond between the senses and the intellect[3]

[2] For the problem of the relationship between logical-semantic values and so-called
aesthetic-semantic or 'artistic' values, see chapter IV, note 41. For the critical connection with neo-positivist semiotics, see Appendix 3.

[3] *Translator's note:* The German term *Verstand*, to which Della Volpe is referring
here, is conventionally translated into English as 'understanding'. This usage prevails
universally in all the standard English translations of Kant and Hegel from which
quotations have been taken throughout this text. In each case, however, I have
replaced 'understanding' by 'intellect', for two reasons. First, 'intellect' corresponds
more closely to the common Italian rendering of *Verstand* as *intelletto*, and is therefore more closely attuned to Della Volpe's usage. Second, Della Volpe's general
position, like that of Lucio Colletti in his *Marxism and Hegel* (NLB, London, 1973),
strives to revalue *Verstand* as against *Vernunft*, or 'Reason'. The Hegelian tradition
in particular depicts Reason as superior to mere Understanding (Intellect), which is
identified with common sense and natural science. Della Volpe's revaluation of
Verstand is therefore better rendered by translating it as 'intellect', rather than the
more neutral 'understanding'. The same usage was followed by Lawrence Garner in
his translation of Colletti's *Marxism and Hegel*, for the same reasons. (See his
explanation, p. 9n.)

which constitutes 'knowledge' can only be a relationship of *specifically distinct* elements. This concept was inherent in Kant's refutation of Leibniz's rationalist dichotomy between the two. (This refutation runs through all Kant's critical work, from his Inaugural Dissertation of 1770 to his posthumously published writings.)

Let us begin by examining some of the most significant formulations of this refutation. First of all, in a note to §7 of the *Anthropology*, which introduces us to the Apology of the Senses, Kant writes: 'A great error of the Leibniz-Wolff school was to assert that the senses comprise solely indeterminate and the intellect determinate representations, and thus to see a purely formal (logical) rather than real (psychological) difference in consciousness between the two, a difference affecting merely the form and not also the content of thought. In this manner, the senses were regarded merely as *lacking* (in clarity of partial representations)—that is, as lacking distinctness. In reality, the senses are something very *positive*, an *indispensable addition* to the intellect in according us knowledge. Leibniz is the real culprit, for, faithful to the Platonic school, he upheld the existence of innate and pure intellectual intuitions, called ideas, which are said to be momentarily obscured in the human mind, but which, once analysed carefully and clarified, allegedly give us knowledge of objects as they are in themselves.'[4]

In the *Critique of Pure Reason* we read: 'The concept of sensibility and of appearance would be falsified, and our whole teaching in regard to them would be rendered empty and useless, if we were to accept the view that our entire sensibility is nothing but a confused representation of things, containing only what belongs to them in themselves, but doing so under an aggregation of characters and partial representations that we do not consciously distinguish. . . . The philosophy of Leibniz and Wolff, in thus treating the difference between the sensible and the intelligible as merely logical, has given a completely wrong direction to all investigations into the nature and origin of our knowledge. This difference is quite evidently transcendental.'[5] And further: Leibniz 'allowed sensibility no mode of

---

4 *Kants Schriften*, Academy edition, vol. VII, pp. 140-141.

5 *Translator's note:* Kant's *Critique of Pure Reason* appeared in two editions, with substantial modifications between the first and the second. The first edition is conventionally identified as A, the second as B, and references are generally to a standard pagination in the original German edition. 'Critique A 115', for example, would refer to page 115 of the first edition. All citations from the *Critique of Pure Reason* in this work are taken from the translation by Norman Kemp Smith (Macmillan, London,

intuition peculiar to itself, but sought for all representation of objects, even the empirical, in the intellect, and left to the senses nothing but the despicable task of confusing and distorting the representations of the former.'[6] In Kant's posthumously published writings he frequently repeats that Leibniz's distinction between the senses and the intellect is a distinction 'merely of degree' (of consciousness) and not of kind; it is 'non-specific'. Kant maintains, on the contrary, that 'an intuition and a concept are representations wholly distinct in kind'.[7]

Let us further note that this cardinal critique of Leibniz (as we shall henceforth call it) dominates not only Kant's 'theory of knowledge'—for the critical conception of the object as 'object of experience' (*Objekt der Erfahrung*) has meaning only if Leibniz's distinction between *confused* and *distinct* cognition is replaced by the *specific* differentiation of the conditions of knowledge, senses-passivity (emotion) and intellect-spontaneity (function)—but also his 'aesthetic theory'.

It is quite clear that this critique explicitly constitutes the decisive element of the 'succinct result' of the analytical portion of the critique of the intellect advanced in Kant's polemic against Johann August Eberhard. An investigation of this article, briefly entitled 'On a Discovery', will therefore carry us squarely into the tangled pathways of Kant's logic.

The daily enrichment of my knowledge through ever wider experience, Kant argues, teaches me that I can extend my knowledge beyond a given concept. But if it is asserted that I can extend my knowledge beyond given concepts even without experience, that I can formulate synthetic judgements a priori, which require *more than* what is contained in the given concepts, then there must be some foundation for this *more*, for this addition. I can only scoff at those who, like Eberhard, hold up the principle of sufficient reason (that is, the principle of non-contradiction) in this regard, and tell me that this *more*, which I think of a priori as belonging to the concept

second impression with corrections, 1933, reprinted 1978). Smith's translation marks the standard page references to both German editions in the margins, and indicates the changes Kant made in the second edition. In the subsequent notes, both the standard reference and the page reference to Smith's translation are given. 'Critique A 43-44, pp. 83-84', for example, which is the appropriate reference for the quotation above, indicates pages 43 and 44 of the first edition of the Critique, which may be found on pages 83-84 of Smith's translation.
  [6] Critique A 276, p. 286.
  [7] *Fortschritte*, Vorländer edition, pp. 105-106.

of a thing but which nevertheless is not implicitly contained in it, is simply an *attribute*. For I still lack the *foundation* for what I register, apart from what is intrinsic to my concept, which I already know. In short, I lack the foundation of that more, that attribute, which necessarily belongs to a thing but nonetheless *is not contained* in the *concept* of the thing.

'Now', Kant continues, 'I found that the extension of my knowledge through experience rests upon empirical (sense) intuition, in which I encountered much that corresponded to my concept, but could learn of still more as connected with this concept that was not thought in it.' Yet I easily understand that if there is to be an a priori extension of my knowledge beyond a pre-existing concept, then a pure intuition a priori is required, whereas in the preceding case an empirical intuition was sufficient. The problem is that I must seek such an intuition, and it remains difficult to discover how this is possible.

'But now I am instructed by the critique to remove all that is empirical or actually sensible in space and time and thus to annul any empirical representation of things, therefore to negate all things *qua* empirically represented, and I then find that space and time remain, ... the intuition of which precedes all concepts of them and of the things in them. Given the nature of these original modes of representation, I can only regard them as merely subjective (but *positive*) forms of my sensibility (not merely as the deficiency of the clarity of the representations obtained through this sensibility), not as forms of things in themselves, therefore only as forms of objects of sensible intuition, and hence of mere appearances.'[8] In this manner, Kant continues, it is evident how synthetic knowledge a priori arises in mathematics and natural science, since these a priori intuitions make 'possible' the characteristic *extension* of such knowledge, and the synthetic unity which the intellect must impose on the multiplicity of intuitions in order to conceive of the object of these intuitions makes such extension actual and 'real'.

From this concise summary of the critique of the intellect, however, Kant also derives the following formulation of the principle of

[8] Henry E. Allison, *The Kant-Eberhard Controversy: An English translation together with supplementary materials and a historical-analytic introduction of Immanuel Kant's 'On a Discovery According to Which any New Critique of Pure Reason Has Been Made Superfluous by an Earlier One'*, Johns Hopkins University Press, Baltimore and London, 1973, pp. 150-151.

synthetic judgements in general: 'they are possible only under the condition that an intuition underlies [*untergelegte*] the concept of their subject, which, if the judgements are empirical, is empirical, and if they are synthetic judgements a priori, is a pure intuition a priori.' He then continues: 'Every reader can easily see for himself the consequences of this proposition, not only for the determination of the limits of the use of human reason, but even for an insight into the true nature of our sensibility (for this proposition can be demonstrated *independently* of the derivation of the representations of space and time, and can thus serve as a basis for the demonstration of their *ideality*, even *before* we have deduced it from their inner nature).' Finally, if we ask whether the foundation of the predicate in synthetic judgements a priori is to be sought in the subject itself, on the basis of the principle of non-contradiction (in which case the judgement will always be purely analytic, contrary to those who, like Eberhard, invoke the principle of sufficient reason), or whether it cannot at all be derived from the concept of the subject (in which case only the attribute is synthetic), we can only respond: 'Neither the name [and the being] "attribute" nor the principle of sufficient reason distinguishes analytic from synthetic judgements. Rather, if by synthetic judgements are meant judgements a priori, then according to this label nothing more can be said than that their predicate is in some way grounded in the *essence* of the concept of the subject, and is therefore an *attribute*, not, however, *merely as a consequence of the principle of [non-]contradiction* ....The *Critique* clearly demonstrates the ground of this possibility—namely that there must be a pure *intuition* underlying the concept of the subject, which makes possible, yes, which can alone make possible, the a priori connection of a synthetic predicate with a concept.' In sum, the problem of how to 'proceed in order to go with my concept beyond this concept itself, and to assert more of it than is thought in it' will never be solved if the conditions of knowledge are considered 'merely from the side of the intellect', as is done in 'logic'. 'The senses', and indeed the 'faculty of a priori intuition', must also be taken into consideration. And 'he who imagines himself to find consolation in the classifications which logic makes of concepts (since it, as it must, abstracts from all objects of these concepts) is wasting his work and his efforts'.[9]

---

[9] Ibid., pp. 152-153.

For our purposes, two points are important to note in this dense and concise 'result' of Kant's critique.

1. Kant is concerned to establish the 'true nature' of the senses, namely their 'positive' character and therewith their *equality of rights* with the intellect. He goes so far as to portray the senses not only as preceding and founding the intellect, but also as relatively independent and transcendent with respect to the solution of the particular problem of the spatio-temporal a priori itself (and of the consequent 'a priori synthesis'). Kant's anti-dogmatism attains its apogee in this profound and unequivocal assault on the cardinal dogma of Leibnizian-Wolffian gnoseology: its *negative* conception of the senses, with all the metaphysical consequences.

2. Kant's solution of the cardinal logical problem of synthetic judgements a priori is nevertheless fundamentally ambiguous, for he has contaminated the new with the old. He attempts to satisfy the concern cited above in a manner not radically different from the traditional abstract logic of judgements, merely renovating the idea that attributive judgements are syntheses of *concepts*—a legacy he had inherited from a scholastic and rationalist logic that was inherently metaphysical and at odds with Aristotle's more profound logic and ontology. The ultimate consequence is that synthetic judgements a priori are only judgements of the type 'substance is permanent', in which the synthetic conjugation of the 'predicate' with the 'subject' is supposedly effected on the basis of a priori intuition. The result is a logical deformity, a formalistic-transcendental cross between Leibnizian and Kantian postulates. All that is left are the *principles* of the *pure* intellect, constituents of *pure* natural science, with their lamentable abstract formalism.

Thus Kant does not approach the problem of *experience*, and implicitly the problem of the senses and their positive character, in an entirely critical manner, despite his profound concern to do so. This, as we know, is not *his* problem; his problem is that of 'possible experience'.

But before proceeding to an examination of those sections of the Transcendental Deduction that deal with the problem of experience, even if only indirectly, we must first consider Kant's general position in logic—his awkward stance between the old logic and the new. Kant simultaneously maintains both the principle of analytic judgements—namely the principle of identity and non-contradiction, which he formulates thus: 'no thing may take a predicate which contradicts it'—and the principle of synthetic judgements a priori, according to which 'every object is subject to the necessary conditions of the synthetic unity of the multiple in a possible experience'. We shall see that these considerations are not unrelated to the aims of our theoretical inquiry.

Let us leave aside Kant's doctrine that all analytic judgements (those that consist of pre-existent concepts and thus require 'no recourse to experience') are a priori in character. This conception is a conspicuous remnant of rationalist gnoseology,[10] but for the moment it is of no great interest to us. Let us instead examine how Kant adapts the new synthetic a priori to the old logical, metaphysical framework. He even speaks of a '*transcendental* validity of the principle of non-contradiction',[11] despite his repeatedly stated conviction that this principle 'belongs only to *logic*', inasmuch as it applies to knowledge 'merely as knowledge in general, irrespective of its content'[12]—in short, despite his propensity to reduce traditional logic to perfected formal logic[13] of a purely formalistic character.[14] Let us see.

Kant grants, of course, that the principle of non-contradiction may yet be of some positive use, in the sense that it helps not only to avoid mistakes and errors that result from contradictions, but also to

---

[10] See Hans Vaihinger, *Kommentar zur Kants Kritik der reinen Vernunft*, Stuttgart, 1922, vol. I, pp. 281-282.

[11] *The Kant-Eberhard Controversy*, p. 112. The text reads as follows: 'Now, since no one contests the transcendental validity of the principle of contradiction, he [Eberhard] seeks first to establish that of the principle of sufficient reason, and therewith the objective reality of the latter concept, secondly, the reality of the concept of simple being; without, as the *Critique* demands, requiring them to be verified through a corresponding intuition.' The passage is cited, together with Critique A 291-293, by H.J. De Vleeschauwer, *La Déduction transcendentale dans l'oeuvre de Kant*, Paris, 1934-1937, vol. III, p. 423.

[12] Critique A 151, p. 190.

[13] Cf., for example, Critique A 52-57. See also Gottlieb Benjamin Jäsche's preface to the first edition of his *Kants Logik*: 'Kant's judgement on this point is beyond doubt . . . : that logic must be regarded as a separate, self-sustaining, and self-grounded science . . . .He has recognized and used the principle of contradiction as a self-evident law requiring no derivation from a higher principle. But he has circumscribed the use and validity of this principle, banishing it from the domain of metaphysics, where it seeks to shore up dogmatism, and confining it to the pure, logical use of reason, where alone it is valid.'

[14] This has been pointed out by one historian of logic, Heinrich Maier, *Die Syllogistik des Aristoteles*, Tübingen, 1896-1900, vol. II/2, pp. 386-387.

ascertain the truths characteristic of analytic knowledge, of which it is the supreme principle. He also concedes that the 'fact that no knowledge can be contrary to it without self-nullification makes this principle a *conditio sine qua non*' of our cognition. But he then concludes by explaining that 'it is only with the synthetic portion of our knowledge that we are concerned; and in regard to the truth of this kind of knowledge we can never look to the above principle for any positive information, though, of course, since it is inviolable, we must be careful to conform to it'.[15] What is the truth of *this kind* of knowledge? In order, Kant replies, for any knowledge to have objective reality, that is, to refer to an object (*Gegenstand*) and thus acquire genuine significance and value, the object must be *given* in some way, otherwise the concepts are empty. But: 'That an object be given (if this expression be taken not as referring to some merely mediate process, but as signifying immediate presentation in intuition), means simply that the representation through which the object is thought relates to actual or possible experience ... . The *possibility of experience* is, then, what gives objective reality to all our a priori modes of knowledge. Experience, however, rests on the synthetic unity of appearances, ... Accordingly, since experience, as empirical synthesis, is, in so far as such experience is possible, the one species of knowledge which is capable of imparting reality to any non-empirical synthesis, this latter [type of synthesis], as knowledge a priori, can possess truth, that is, agreement with the object, only in so far as it contains nothing save what is necessary to the synthetic unity of experience in general.'[16]

Thus the *truth* of synthetic knowledge a priori—that sort of truth on which the principle of contradiction sheds no light and for which this principle cannot be the decisive criterion (*Bestimmungsgrund*)—lies in the accordance of this knowledge with that specific object of its own which is the phenomenal object, the *Gegenstand*. In the same manner, the truth of analytic knowledge a priori can only lie in the accordance of such knowledge with *its* object, not the *Gegenstand* but the *Objekt*, or possible logical object (possible in the pre-critical sense). Commenting on the dependence of the truth of analytic judgements on the principle of non-contradiction, Kant writes, for example: 'The reverse of that which as concept is contained and is thought in the knowledge of the object [*Objekt*] is always rightly

[15] Critique A 152, p. 190.
[16] Critique A 156-158 and B 195-197; pp. 193-194.

denied. But since the opposite of the concept would contradict the object, the concept itself must necessarily be affirmed of it.'[17]

Further on in the *Critique of Pure Reason*, we read: 'The object [*Gegenstand*] of a concept which contradicts itself is nothing, because the concept is nothing, is the impossible, e.g. a two-sided rectilinear figure (*nihil negativum*).'[18] If we compare this case to that of the *ens rationis*—for example, certain new forces of nature which, although they can be conceived without contradiction cannot be classed as possible, since 'empirical examples are lacking'—we may conclude that the *ens rationis*, the concept without object, is distinguished from the *nihil negativum*, the pure nothing or not-being, in that 'the former must not be classed among [real] possibilities, because it is a mere fiction (though not self-contradictory), while the latter is contrary to all [logical] possibility, inasmuch as the concept nullifies itself'. In the end, however, 'both . . . are empty concepts'. Elsewhere, in the posthumously published works (*Fortschritte*, p. 157), Kant repeats that 'anything of which even the simple thought is impossible (in other words, the concept of which is self-contradictory) is itself impossible', but that anything of which the concept is possible 'is not possible merely on that account'. Consequently, 'the first sort of possibility may be called logical, while the second may be called real'.

Hence, to establish synthetic knowledge a priori—in other words, such necessary and instructive knowledge as that of a geometric figure, to take Kant's own example, a knowledge that is concrete (even if only with the formal concreteness of mathematics, which is, of course, not the same as the natural concreteness of phenomena)— what is needed is first of all a concept that is not self-contradictory. For as we have seen, a concept that is self-contradictory is just as *empty* as a concept that lacks an intuition and thereby violates the principles of possible experience. What is needed, in sum, is a *dual* possibility, *logical* and *real*. The *transcendental* validity of the principle of non-contradiction finds striking confirmation here. However, even Kant's previous admission is quite significant, that this principle is the *conditio sine qua non* of any knowledge and therefore can never be violated, even when we are dealing with synthetic knowledge a priori, for which it is merely *insufficient* (since it does not furnish a *Bestimmungsgrund* for it). We may add that

[17] Critique A 151-152; p. 190.
[18] Critique A 290-292; pp. 295-296; cf. A 596 note; p. 503.

Kant holds to this idea so tenaciously that in section 5 of his introduction to the *Critique of Pure Reason*, which deals with mathematical knowledge, he allows that a synthetic proposition can be
evaluated on the basis of the principle of non-contradiction provided
it is preceded by another synthetic proposition from which it can be
deduced, but never of itself. In other words, as several commentators have correctly pointed out, Kant holds that mathematical
judgements (among others) proceed in conformity and harmony
with the principle of non-contradiction, but not by virtue of it, for
this principle merely regulates, in a negative way, the mutual
relationships of propositions. Moreover, in the *Fortschritte*
(pp. 154-155), Kant declares outright that metaphysics relies on
analytic judgements (and the principle of non-contradiction) for its
means (*Mittel*) but relies exclusively on synthetic judgements for its
goal (*Zweck*)—a statement perhaps intended to mean that the analytic judgements in question serve as 'links in the chain of method',
like the axioms of mathematics which, according to the
introduction, rest on the principle of non-contradiction. Kant maintains, however, that although these axioms are valid for simple concepts, they are admissible in mathematics only if they can be
represented by intuition. Even so, this is a final confirmation that
Kant continues to uphold the old concept that *Denken* (thought), as
logical possibility, and *Erkennen* (experience), as real possibility or
transcendental thought, stand on the *same level*.

Kant's grave concessions to formal logic emerge clearly in all the
passages we have cited so far. Indeed, they admit the fundamental
principle of formal logic into the very heart of transcendental logic.
Only the most noteworthy of these concessions are of real interest to
us here.[19] They are: a) blind acceptance that analytic judgements are
a priori even when the concept of the subject is empirical, since Kant
dogmatically maintains that it is the apodictic character of the connection of the predicate to the subject, on the basis of the principle of
non-contradiction, that renders these judgements a priori in general;
b) maintenance as valid in a 'transcendental logic' of the traditional
differentiation of judgements according to quality and quantity as
well as according to relation, even while the modality of the

---

[19] See, for example, Vaihinger, pp. 281-287; Norman Kemp Smith, *A Commentary
to Kant's Critique of Pure Reason*, London, 1930, pp. 36 ff., 176-186; De
Vleeschauwer, vol. II, pp. 49-53, 71-72, 87-88, and 127-128.

judgement 'in no way contributes to the content of the judgement'; c) underlying the 'metaphysical' deduction of the categories, a deliberate conception of the intellect as a function that lends unity simultaneously to diverse representations in a *judgement* and to the simple synthesis of diverse representations in an ˙ *intuition*—'a unity . . . which is the pure intellective concept and, like the intellect itself, in the very act by which it gives rise to concepts, through an analytical unity, likewise introduces a *transcendental content* into its representations through the synthetic unity of the diverse that is to be found in intuition in general'.

The most serious consequence of this repeated attempt to absorb the supreme principle of traditional logic into the sphere of the transcendental is Kant's fundamental definition of the synthetic judgement a priori as a synthesis *sui generis* of *subject* and *predicate* within which the 'underlying' intuition is the 'third term', the *mean*. Here we are forewarned that even though the synthetic process does not proceed according to the principle of non-contradiction, the traditional type of synthesis (of concepts) is nonetheless maintained, to the point that Kant asserts that in a certain sense the predicate depends on the essence of the concept of the subject and is therefore an *attribute*. The result is a hybrid, Leibnizian-Kantian formula, the counterpart of the assertion that the *Gegenstand*—the concrete object—of a *self-contradictory concept* is a *nullity* (the relevant example being drawn from concrete mathematical knowledge).

What are we to conclude? For the moment, just this. Kant indeed caught a glimpse of a new conception of thought, and of the intellect; he realized that the human intellect is 'discursive' and can achieve knowledge only 'through universal concepts', in the precise sense that it is not a faculty of intellectual intuition 'but merely a faculty of the connection of given intuitions in an experience' (*Prolegomena to Every Future Metaphysics*, §§57 and 34). In other words, Kant anticipated the concept of *cognitive* intelligence as synthesis of category and pure intuition. But despite energetic efforts, he did not succeed in even glimpsing the nature of the true *hierarchical relations* between this new thought, or aspect of thought, and the old.[20] He therefore lost sight, as we shall see, of the specific

[20] As we have seen, he succeeded only in contaminating logical possibility, or possible objectivity, with real possibility, or possible experience, a contamination that is manifest in his reduction of the formal synthesis of category and intuition to a *sui generis* conceptual synthesis.

nature and function of the old, *dianoetic* (Aristotelian!) principle of logic, and the authentic, transcendental nature and function of the new principle of possible experience. The new concept of dianoeticity, or *discursiveness*, thereby eluded him.

2

But it is by examining the Transcendental Deduction that we can first begin truly to gauge the most serious consequences of this sort of *formalization*, or intellectualization, of transcendental logic—consequences that are grave, and even fatal, for any attempt to resolve the problem of experience adequately. Here we shall plumb the means by which Kant established and actually used his synthesis a priori as a new gnoseological instrument.

In §19 of the Deduction (second edition of the *Critique of Pure Reason*), Kant states that a judgement is merely the manner in which given modes of knowledge are attributed to the objective unity of apperception. The judgement 'bodies are heavy' thereby ceases to be a perceptive judgement, a subjective connection forged by association, and instead becomes an objectively valid relation, a genuine *judgement* (the *judgement of experience* of the *Prolegomena*, §§18-22), since the copula 'are' serves to 'distinguish the objective unity of given representations from the subjective'. It therefore 'indicates their relation to the original apperception, and its *necessary unity. It holds good* even if the judgement is itself empirical, and therefore contingent'.

This does not mean, Kant cautions us, that the representations 'body' and 'heavy' necessarily belong (*gehören*) to each other 'in empirical intuition', but rather that 'they belong to one another *in virtue of the necessary* unity of apperception in the synthesis of intuitions'. In other words, these 'two representations ... are combined *in the object*, no matter what the state of the subject may be'. In short, as he says elsewhere (*Critique*, B 130), '*the concept* of body is posited in the category of substance'. To put it another way, the intuitive object corresponding to body—'its empirical intuition'—is determined as *substance*, or as the bearer of predicates, by virtue of its permanence in time. 'Heavy' itself is therefore an empirical intuition perceived as a *property* of the previous empirical intuition. Kant likewise resolves that 'the empirical intuition of body must always be

16

considered in experience as subject and never merely as predicate'. In other words, the criterion that allows *subject* to be distinguished from *predicate* is established by pure intuition; it is not left to the will of abstract intellect, as in formal logic, under which the position occupied by the *concepts*, whether subject or predicate, is of merely quantitative importance.[21]

But this sleight of hand through which the empirical and contingent character of the judgement 'bodies are heavy' is conjured away, magically transformed into the purely necessary by its contact with the unity of apperception, raises the problem of the *judgement of experience* cited by Kant himself in a note to §22 of the *Prolegomena*. Here, after concluding that in judgements of experience the synthetic unity of perceptions is represented as necessary and universally valid, Kant asks how this proposition, that judgements of experience contain *necessity* in the synthesis of the perceptions, can be reconciled with another that he repeats again and again, that 'experience, as knowledge a posteriori, can render only *contingent* judgements'. Here is his answer: 'When I say that experience teaches me something, I always mean only the perception that lies in it, e.g. that heat always follows illumination of a stone by the sun, and thus the proposition of experience is, so far always, contingent. That this heating *necessarily* follows from the illumination by the sun is, indeed, contained in the judgement of experience (by virtue of the concept of cause), but I do not learn this through *experience*; on the contrary, experience is only generated when the concept of the intellect (of cause) has been added to the perception.'[22] And how does this 'addition to perception' come about? Kant postpones consideration of this question to his treatment of the transcendental faculty of judgement in the *Critique of Pure Reason*.

His response, however, not only leaves the problem unresolved, but even aggravates it. He argues that experience in one sense—immediate experience—can be reduced purely to the information imparted by perception and is thus wholly contingent. But experience in another sense—mediated and therefore necessary experience—has nothing whatever to do with immediate experience, except that it constitutes an enigmatic *addition* (of the pure concept) to perception.

[21] Cf. De Vleeschauwer, vol. III, p. 83.
[22] *Prolegomena to Any Future Metaphysics That Will Be Able to Present Itself as Science*, translated by P. Gray Lucas, Manchester University Press, 1953, reprinted 1978, p. 64.

Ultimately, experience in the second sense thus appears as a sort of *regeneration* of experience in the first sense. Before evaluating the intricate problems posed by this response, however, let us examine whether it can be integrated into the relevant doctrine of the *Critique of Pure Reason*, particularly into the most fully developed version of the transcendental deduction, §26 of the second edition, which is entitled 'transcendental deduction of the universally possible employment in experience of the pure concepts of the intellect'. This section of the Critique is permeated by the best of Kant's treatment of the transcendental faculty of judgement, the schemata ('key to the employment of the categories'), through which he attempts to illuminate this enigmatic addition to perception.

Paragraph 26 (cf. §24) of the *Critique of Pure Reason* deals with the problem of the *representation* of space—that is, of 'space represented as an object [*Gegenstand*]' as required, for example, by geometry. It is here that Kant finally clarifies the concept of a priori intuitive diversity as a priori formal intuition, a concept that had first been put forward in the Transcendental Aesthetic (where a priori diversity consists rather in the *forms* of sensibility). He attempts to show that space and time are not merely static sensible forms, but genuine intuitions; as such, they are simultaneously *in synthesis with* and *distinct from* the intellective concept. 'Space and time and all their parts', he states in §17, 'are intuitions, and are, therefore, with the manifold which they contain, *singular* representations, of which they constitute the *form*', or formal element. Hence: 'they are not mere concepts.'[23] 'But space and time', he continues in §26, 'are represented a priori not merely as *forms* of the sensible intuition, but as themselves *intuitions*, which contain a manifold [diversity], and therefore are represented with the determination of the [intuitive] unity of this manifold .... Thus *unity of the synthesis* of the manifold, without or within us, and consequently also a *combination* to which everything that is to be represented as determined in space and time must conform, is given a priori as the condition of the [empirical] synthesis of all *apprehension*—not indeed in, but with these intuitions.'[24]

With, not in [*mit, nicht in*]! Of course. For otherwise, if the synthetic unity of apperception were given in the intuitions themselves,

---

[23] *Critique of Pure Reason*, p. 155.
[24] Ibid., pp. 170-171.

the unity constituted by the representation of space and time would be merely an apperceptive, *intellectual* unity. Space and time would then be concepts and not *intuitions*.[25] Now, since formal intuition (= figurative synthesis = productive imagination) is broken down into the various schemata (number, permanence, succession, etc.), which act as mediators between the senses and apperception, the intuition-schema can be qualified as both sensible, because its intellectual unity is *not in* it (otherwise it would be spontaneity and not receptivity), and intellectual, because this unity nevertheless *accompanies* it, is *with it*.

Kant explains the presence within us of formal intuition—a priori diversity or a priori given—through the theory of *original acquisition*. The formal foundation of the possibility of sensible intuitions, he argues, is the specific *passivity* of the subject. Under the impetus of the emotions, this passivity develops as a *pure* multiplicity, which is the *form* of the empirical manifold.[26] Drawing primarily on the cardinal critique of Leibniz, which is generally overlooked by commentators on these passages, Kant writes: 'The infinite difference between the theory of sensibility as a special mode of intuition, which has its a priori form determinable according to universal principles, and the theory which views this intuition as a merely empirical apprehension of things in themselves, which (as sensible intuition) is only distinguished from an intellectual intuition by the clarity of the representation' could be no more clearly exhibited than it is by Mr Eberhard himself, contrary to his own intention. 'From the incapacity, the weakness, and the limits of the faculty of representation (the exact expressions which Mr Eberhard uses) one can derive no extension of knowledge, no positive determination of the object.'[27] Instead, there must be a 'positive principle', to wit: 'The ground of the possibility of sensible intuition is neither of the two, neither *limit* of the faculty of knowledge nor [indeterminate] *image*. It is the

---

[25] Cf. De Vleeschauwer, vol. III, pp. 283 ff. and Martin Heidegger, *Kant und das Problem der Metaphysik*, Bonn, 1929, p. 138, which brings grist to his mill: 'The analysis of the transcendental aesthetic in the logic, however, becomes more questionable once it becomes clear that the specific object [*Gegenstand*] of transcendental logic, pure thought [*Denken*], is also rooted in the transcendental imagination [*Einbildungskraft*].' Even these few lines clearly manifest Heidegger's tendency to *smother* thought, along with what is 'specific' in it, in the transcendental *imagination*.

[26] In this regard, see Vaihinger, vol. II, pp. 91 ff. and De Vleeschauwer, vol. III, pp. 243-244, 247-258.

[27] *The Kant-Eberhard Controversy*, p. 134.

merely particular *receptivity* of the mind, whereby it receives representations in accordance with its subjective constitution, when affected by something (in sensation).' What is innate is only this 'first formal ground, e.g. the possibility of a representation of space', but 'not the spatial representation itself'. Impressions are always needed to lend cognitive power to the representation of an object, which is always 'its own act'. Thus: 'the formal intuition, which is called space, emerges as an *originally acquired* representation (the form of objects in general), the ground of which (as mere receptivity) is nevertheless innate, and the acquisition of which long precedes determinate concepts of things that are in accordance with this form. The acquisition of these concepts is an *acquisitio derivativa* (derived acquisition), as it already presupposes universal, transcendental concepts of the intellect. These likewise are acquired and not innate, but their *acquisitio*, like that of space, is *originaria* and presupposes nothing innate except the subjective conditions of the spontaneity of thought (in accordance with the unity of apperception).'[28]

The enigmatic 'addition' of the intellective concept to the 'perception' or sensation, through which Kant intends to resolve the problem stated in the note to §22 of the *Prolegomena*, is thereby resolved. He maintains that this addition is made possible by the mediation of the formal intuition, that is, by the schemata. But the schema, let us recall, constitutes only 'a universal procedure of imagination', a simple 'relation' by which to provide 'an image for a concept', since it is the product of the transcendental imagination, the synthesis of which 'has as its goal not *any particular* intuition, but only *unity* in the determination of the senses'.[29] Kant therefore fails to resolve the problem of the *contingent character* of the judgement of experience, which thus remains merely an assertion of self-evident, absolute, and abstract universality and necessity. The perception is not derived from the intellective concept, even if the latter is synthesized with the formal intuition, because of the formal character, the abstract universality, of the latter (which is schema, i.e. 'relation'). The *informative* aspect of the real *content*—namely the particular, empirical, or sensible—is thereby lost, and with it the 'richness' of reality. Indeed, reality itself threatens to fade from view. What remains, in the end, is the instructive value of the

[28] Ibid., p. 136.
[29] Critique A 140-142, pp. 182-183.

conceptually synthetic character of the categories, mediated by the underlying formal intuition: the instructive value of the principles of pure natural science. In other words, there remains only insistence on the *necessity* of the instructive element, but *not the instructive element itself*. Indeed, the regenerating synthesis of the empirical and accidental itself tends to eliminate it, along with its properties. The problem of *experience*—and implicitly of the *positivity of the senses* required by the cardinal critique of Leibniz—remains unresolved, for it is not broached in a completely critical manner.

At the same time, it is nevertheless undeniable that both Kant's conception of the unity-distinction relationship between formal intuition and category (in other words, the with-not-in character of the latter with respect to the former) and his conception of original acquisition, provided they are viewed apart from their dogmatic pre-suppositions and appurtenances, mark the most advanced point he reached in the direction of our problem. Indeed, both these conceptions are deeply inspired by the cardinal critique of Leibniz, as the relevant passages themselves make clear.

With the first conception Kant means to establish that the only synthesis a priori admitted by the positivity of the senses is one in which formal intuition really forms the *matter* of the categorial *form*. Hence, as formal matter, it is *specifically* distinguished, within the synthesis itself, from its co-element, the pure concept. Commentators like Vaihinger (*Kommentar*, vol. II, p. 93) and De Vleeschauwer (*La déduction transcendentale*, vol. III, p. 258) miss the mark when they argue that the only difference between formal intuition and category is that the former 'operates only in unconsciousness' and the latter 'in consciousness'. Concepts like these lead to a collapse into abstract, intellectualist psychology and gnoseology, or into rationalist, Leibnizian logic, which in this case amounts to the same thing. (Vaihinger explicitly appeals to the 'terminology of the past century'.)

With the second conception—that of original acquisition—Kant strives to satisfy the same exigency, this time by suggesting that this sort of formal synthesis can consist only in an original act of acquisition in the sense of an act of identification of heterogeneous elements like necessity and contingency, or being and not-being. Kant speaks of the 'innate' subjective conditions, or formal foundations, of original acquisition (which here appears as a twofold original acquisition, that of pure intuition and that of the pure concept) in order to

express—through defining the senses and the intellect as two faculties, one passive, the other spontaneous and active (for this is what
Kant means by 'innate')—his profound concept that there is a *transcendental* difference between the elements of the synthesis, viz. the
senses and the intellect. It is true that this is a quite improper mode of
expression. But the impropriety does not necessarily affect the substance of the problem Kant has noted, since these 'innate' conditions
or foundations are annulled in the *act* of original acquisition. The
latter is the only real transcendental principle that is required to weld
the senses and the intellect into the unique synthesis of heterogeneous elements—'original' and 'acquired', or, to put it another way,
necessary and contingent. The facile appeal of various critics to
Leibniz is therefore erroneous, here as elsewhere.[30]

Having reached this point in our examination of the set of problems
Kant posed in the *Critique of Pure Reason*, it is appropriate to cast a
glance at the related problem of the Analytic of the Beautiful in his
Critique of Judgement, which is also dominated by the cardinal
critique of Leibniz. We shall then be in a position to draw the final
conclusions required for our inquiry.

Let us examine, then, the results that Kant's 'critique of aesthetic
judgement' affords us in further determining the positivity of the
senses, or of feeling in general.

We may begin by noting that Kant approaches the problem of
'feeling' in the narrow sense, as distinct from the problems of knowledge and will. After establishing in the *Critique of Pure Reason* that
everything in our *knowledge* that belongs to pure intuition contains
only simple 'relations', he remarks that the feelings of pleasure and
pain, as well as of will, remain excluded, *for they are not at all
knowledge.*

Then, criticizing the Leibniz-Wolff concept of beauty as 'perfection perceived in a confused manner', he states that it is a mistake to
think that the difference between the beautiful and the good lies
solely in their logical form—the former being a *more confused*, the
latter a clearer, concept of perfection—the two being identical in

---

[30] Vaihinger (vol. II, p. 95) asserts outright that 'even in this portion of the
Entdeckung [Discovery], Kant has only further developed Leibniz's doctrine of the
"virtual existence" of certain concepts'. The cardinal critique of Leibniz implicit in
these passages has eluded Vaihinger completely. Likewise De Vleeschauwer, vol. II,
p. 26 and vol. III, p. 243.

content and origin. For: 'then there would be no *specific* difference between them, but the judgement of taste would be just as much a cognitive judgement as one by which something is described as good—just as the man in the street, when he says that deceit is wrong, bases his judgement on confused, but the philosopher on clear grounds, while both appeal in reality to identical principles of reason.'[31] For the Kant critical of Leibniz, however, the beautiful consists in 'a formal subjective finality', a finality that is 'without end', precisely because it dissolves into the feeling of an 'immediate delight in the object'. It is a pleasure that 'does not depend' on the 'representation or concept' of the object's 'utility or perfection'. 'Disinterested' pleasure in an arabesque, a sea shell, or a piece of music without words, for instance, is 'free' or 'pure beauty', whether artistic or natural (§15). Hence the judgement of taste is 'simply contemplative'. It is 'indifferent as to the existence of an object [*Gegenstand*], and only decides how its character stands with the feeling of pleasure or displeasure'. And this *contemplation* is not 'directed to concepts', since the judgement of taste 'is not a cognitive judgement (neither theoretical nor practical), and hence also is not grounded on concepts, nor yet *intentionally directed* to them' (§5). The judgement is said to be aesthetic precisely because its determining principle is not a concept, but 'the feeling (of the internal sense) of the concert in the play of the mental powers as a thing only capable of being felt' (§15). It is the 'quickening of both faculties (imagination and intellect) to an indefinite, but yet, thanks to the given representation, harmonious activity' (§9). Aesthetic judgements are synthetic, since they 'go beyond the concept and even the intuition' of the object, and add to it 'something which is not even a cognition at all, namely the feeling of pleasure (or displeasure)'. But this, of course, is never 'knowledge' (§36).

Furthermore, the aesthetic judgement is a priori, because it is universal and necessary, its 'subjective' universality being grounded in the presence, identical in all subjects, of the subjective conditions of the faculties of imagination and intellect—hence the communicability and universal validity of the judgement of taste. In short, a 'judgement to the effect that it is with pleasure that I perceive and

---

[31] *The Critique of Judgement*, translated by James Creed Meredith, Oxford at the Clarendon Press, 1952, reprinted 1978, §§15 and 16, pp. 71-72. Subsequent passages from the *Critique of Judgement* are also from Meredith's translation, in which Kant's paragraphs are clearly numbered.

estimate some object is an empirical judgement. But if it asserts that I think the object beautiful', then it is, on the contrary, 'an a priori judgement'—i.e., it is unrelated either to 'concepts' or 'perceptions' of objects (§§37, 38).

Finally, the subjective, aesthetic finality expressed in the feeling of the beautiful or the sublime is a rule not of nature but of our simple faculty of reflective judgement of nature. Similarly, it is alone the other sort of finality—objective or logical—that is fundamentally expressed in the idea of reason: in organic bodies the part and the whole are mutually cause and effect and therefore designate the fulfilment of a non-finalistic, non-mechanistic or experimental causality. In sum, both sorts of finality are *regulative* and heuristic but are not constituent principles. They are of no value in understanding nature or things, but they are indispensable in satisfying the supreme aspiration of human reason for unity. This aspiration is not satisfied by the *unity of experience*, which explains only the sensible or phenomenal object *in general*, but is eluded by the 'particular laws' and the infinite 'specific forms' of nature.

What does this theory of the beautiful offer us in the way of genuine identification of the positivity of feeling? It does point to the positivity manifested by feeling, by the particular, in 'free beauty' as the product of a *purely contemplative* judgement. But even if we ignore the intrinsic difficulties of a *judgement* that is *mere intuition* (and that dissolves into a kind of hybrid judgement in which the predicate is a feeling!), this positivity of aesthetic feeling is still severely limited by the systematic position occupied by the aesthetic judgement. Indeed, since it is not knowledge, the latter does not participate in the structure and constitution of the world of experience, however purely 'phenomenal' it may be, but is merely a rule of subjective human reflection. Here it is confirmed yet again that the real particular and contingent, genuine sensibility or feeling, does not participate directly and positively in 'knowledge', in the sort of *immission into being* that is knowledge. (Its intellectual projection, however, its shadow, namely formal intuition conceived as a transcendental schema, does participate.)

Here as elsewhere, the desideratum of the cardinal critique of Leibniz is satisfied only in appearance. Indeed, from the vantage point of this third of his Critiques, we can view the entire itinerary of 'feeling' in Kant's philosophy. It is rejected by the theoretical *Critique of Pure Reason* on the grounds that it 'is not a representative faculty of things'; it is admitted to the *Critique of Practical Reason*, but only to be conjured away under the label of 'the feeling of respect for the law', a feeling so pure as to be 'neither pleasure nor displeasure';[32] finally, it is restored in the *Critique of Judgement*, in the form of that contemplativeness which is pure beauty, although even here it remains devoid of reality. It is, one may say, rather a history of impotence.

It is nevertheless evident that the notion of a feeling, a 'pleasure or displeasure', that is simultaneously *disinterested*—i.e. one to which any concept, purpose, or will is alien—yet *universally valid* can be highly fruitful, provided it, and all its potential, can be liberated from the deadening rationalist framework in which Kant envelops it.

I would argue that in a certain sense the *formal matter* which the *formal intuition* must constitute in its innermost being as co-element in the *synthesis a priori* that is *original acquisition* (§26 of the Transcendental Deduction) may be reducible to this universal contemplative—or disinterested—pleasure.

Could it be that such a reduction—and the consequent transvaluation of this formal matter or formal intuition into the matter or intuition *tout court* that is that feeling as 'disinterested'—may perhaps set us on the road to resolution of the problem of judgements of experience, to the establishment of the concrete concept as a sort of *formal intuition* that can only be the *empirical concept*, and to the attainment of the distinctive and essential simultaneous contingency and necessity of the judgement of experience? If so, we shall finally achieve complete satisfaction of the requirements of the cardinal critique of Leibniz.

3

We are thus led back to the problem of judgements of experience, and to the problem of experience itself, compelled to settle accounts with the entire problematic of Kantian logic.

I have said that Kant did not approach the problem of experience in a fully critical way, that this was not *his* problem. Exactly what do I mean by this? To answer, let us press Kantian dogmatism to its

---

[32] On this point, see my book on Hume: *La filosofia dell'esperienza di David Hume*, Florence, 1933-1935, volume II, chapter II.

ultimate limits. To begin with, his hypothesis of the 'thing-in-itself', dogmatic expediency though it is, does prove fruitful.[33]

With this hypothesis Kant ascribes the ultimate foundation of the judgement of experience to the extra-mental, to Being, to the absolute *Objekt*. The judgement of experience itself is therewith transmuted into a non-objective, phenomenal (i.e. human) value. But we must note *what this really implies*.

If we keep in mind that ultimately the 'thing-in-itself' signifies nothing other than the *extra-mental existence of a multiplicity of things that stimulate our senses*, then we must realize that Kant's positive gnoseological conception of sensibility never went beyond acknowledgement of the *passive* character of sensibility and the related pure formal *given* (diversity of the a priori intuition, the schema). But we must also understand that this formal given, which is not a product of the spontaneity of the intellect, has a twofold aspect and value. On the one hand, it sets a *limit* to the rationality of the human world, but at the same time it is always rational *for itself*. Ultimately, then, it is semi-rational, or in other words *semi-irrational*. The intellectualist narrowness that typifies Kant's conception of the discursiveness of thought as *'possible* experience'—that is, the human, self-evident gnoseological a priori—may thus be seen as a repercussion in the theory of knowledge of his metaphysical disparagement of irrationality or particularity. This explains why ultimately Kant has grasped only the shadow of the particular: the forms or 'subsumptive schemata' of the intellect. So little is the intellect affected by its synthesis with what these schemata are supposed to mediate and guide (the multiplicity and singularity of 'perception') that it deploys itself in the various categories purely in accordance with the exigencies of the *logical* table of judgements.[34]

In sum, Kantian phenomenalism is typically intellectualistic in that it succumbs to the dogmatic concept of the relativity of the irrational. In the end, Kant has replaced Leibniz's fideistic and dogmatic

---

[33] 'When Kant assumes', Lenin acknowledged, 'that something outside us, a thing-in-itself, corresponds to our ideas, he is a materialist. When he declares this thing-in-itself to be unknowable, transcendental, other-sided, he is an idealist.' (*Materialism and Empirio-Criticism*, Collected Works, volume 14, p. 232.)

[34] It is only in passing—in the *Fortschritte*, p. 102, for instance—that Kant is struck by the idea of quite another 'metaphysical' deduction of the categories, when he says: 'that unity of consciousness required to connect the diversity of intuitive representations of objects in space and time to diverse functions is given by the categories.'

intellectualism with a more cautious and 'critical' variety: subjectivism, or more precisely—*phenomenalism*.

Indeed, if we strip Kant's irrational or formal given—which is, incidentally, irrational only for the human intellect, or *intuitus derivativus*, but not for the divine intellect, or *intuitus originarius*—of its character of relativity (and therefore of negativity) and if we insist that once all remnants of theological and dogmatic realism are expunged, the irrational—or not-being—can only be *positive* (hence the need to abandon all varieties of phenomenalism for materialism!), then we are left with none other than unadulterated irrationality-particularity as *feeling* (pleasure and displeasure), or sensibility in general. In other words, we are left with something very much like the *disinterested but universal feeling* that also satisfies the instance of being, or the rational.

This sort of formal feeling would then be the only critically admissible irrationality—and at the same time the only critically admissible rationality. And that would reveal the only critically acceptable significance of Kant's thing-in-itself, containing the sensible or material *positive* we have been seeking: *disinterested feeling*.

Having come this far, how can we now *logically* conceive this synthesis of the irrational and the rational, of *feeling* and *reason*?

We can get some indication of what this synthesis may be if we recall the formula cited above—not simply a pure feeling, but a pure formal feeling. For the rest, we shall seek the *specific* distinction between sensibility and reason—or, ultimately, between the irrational and the rational—within one and the same ontological category: the 'human', rejecting Kant's dogmatic hypothesis that there is some other variety that should somehow compete for this specific distinction.

How, then, does the logic of this synthesis take shape? What validity do traditional logical principles, ancient and modern—the principle of identity and non-contradiction and the principle of dialectical contradiction—assume in the ambit of this logic?

Let us begin by examining what our treatment of Kant's logic teaches us in this regard. It is my view that what must be contested in Kant is not his assertion that the principle of non-contradiction retains a transcendental validity (for here as elsewhere he is generous with us), but rather his *conception of that validity*. The negative consequences of his conception may be summarized as follows. Kant eventually loses sight of the true structure of the transcendental—and therefore of the critical conception of oneness, or unity—precisely because he indiscriminately places logical possibility and real possibility on the same ('transcendental') footing. He does so by means of the dubious principle that the concept (in the undifferentiated sense of category and concept-essence) is empty either when intuition is lacking or when it is self-contradictory. As we have seen, the immediate consequence of this principle was a formalization and intellectualization of synthetic judgements a priori, with the significant corollary of a *rigidification* of formal, categorizing discursiveness into discursiveness of a logico-formalist type. He thereby misses the *dynamism*—or *functionality*—or unity, which is the principle of the categories, and thus also loses unity itself, and with it actual multiplicity.

It should also be noted that the conception of unity as apperception or transcendental ego did not serve to prevent this improper intellectualization and abstract restriction of unity. Rather, it compounded it with transcendental psychologism (a noun that destroys the adjective, and against which Fichte protested in his *Darstellung* of 1801).

Unity, or oneness, is not self-consciousness precisely *because*, as Kant glimpsed, it must be the *synthetic unity of multiplicity*. (Nor, we would add, is it self-consciousness for the reasons adduced by one important Italian critic of Kantian and post-Kantian idealism, as we shall see.)

The transcendental validity of the principle of non-contradiction, if it needs justification, must be sought in a direction different from that taken by Kant. This principle must not be permitted to rigidify the instance of unity as such (its character as a functional category) with an *immediate* presence. But at the same time, it must be demonstrated that this principle is required by the very instance of unity (which, precisely in order to reveal itself as such, has to multiply). In a certain sense, Kant's conception of this principle must be turned upside down; it must be shown that it satisfies the instance of multiplicity, of the material or sensible, *no less than that of unity, or the rational*. Ultimately, the complex and concrete logical principle (within which the dialectical principle itself is reabsorbed) must be discovered within it. Indeed, rather than 'logical principle' we would prefer to say *ontological principle* or *principle of experience*, since the term 'logical principle'—which evokes such concepts as 'thinking subject', 'knowing subject', and similar and related notions from which they are distinct—tends to restrict us to the sphere of the abstractly formal gnoseological and epistemological distinctions of 'spiritual forms', which we believe must be overcome if we are really to arrive at concrete being—multiple oneness—in its unalloyed coherence, free of any remnant of scholastic abstraction. This point will be clarified in the course of our inquiry. For the moment, let us strive merely to adumbrate the twofold instance of multiplicity and unity satisfied by the principle of non-contradiction once it is properly understood (namely, as we shall see, as the principle of *tauto-heterological identity*).

Let us now turn to two points we have hitherto neglected: analytic judgements and synthetic judgements a posteriori.

One critic, Pantaleo Carabellese, has emphasized that Kant's analytic judgements (and his synthetic judgements a posteriori too) are marred by the absolute presupposition of the concepts on which they are founded, which are considered already fixed and therefore *unformed*, intuited concepts. Pre-critical 'possible objectivity' or 'logical possibility' thereby persists, particularly in these 'base-concepts' of analytic judgements; indeed, they are intended to afford us the essence of the real. This is why Kant can say, Carabellese observes in his commentary on the *Prolegomena* (Bari, 1925, p. 23), that 'it is necessarily and eternally true that all bodies are extensive, whether they exist or not, etc.'. These base-concepts of synthetic judgements a posteriori—destined to be extended by experience—are *not* previously posited by experience. But if, as Kant has taught, the concept is a formation, and if the formative act is the judgement, then 'there cannot be judgements that presuppose their concepts in absolute manner'. Or better: there are no *fixed* concepts intuited by the intellect; there are no purely (abstractly) *intellectual* concepts; there are no *essences*.

Our examination of the problem of the formation of the concept (or the problem of 'knowledge' as synthesis or judgement) has thus necessarily led us to the related problem of what Carabellese calls 'empirical objectivity'. We would prefer to call it the problem of the *empirical concept*, i.e. the *empirical character of the concept* as an inescapable feature of any judgement, and thereby a feature of any 'knowledge'. In short, we have arrived at the problem of the *contingency* of judgements *in general*. Indeed, the contingency that was previously shown to be characteristic of judgements of experience—a contingency frustrated by Kant's intellectualistic conception of a priori synthesis—now appears, if we pursue the truth glimpsed by Kant that the concept is a formation, a synthesis, a judgement, as a characteristic of *every* judgement, and consequently of all 'knowledge'.

Indeed, if we discard the intellectually intuited, presupposed concept, what remains is a concept which, gestating as judgement, is born through a syn-thesis. And a synthesis, to be genuine, requires *specifically* distinct elements. It is therefore not only the so-called intellectual (or rational) factor that contributes to the birth of the 'concept', but equally the sensible or, broadly speaking, aesthetic factor. Any *conceptus*, or conception, thereby acquires an irreducibly empirical and contingent character, and the distinction between analytic and synthetic judgements collapses therewith, for all that remains is the judgement as a syn-thesis of critically distinct elements. The second difficulty (which was not a problem for Kant), that of a posteriori or perceptive synthetic judgements—in other words, the problem of how an intuition is added to a given concept—will itself be resolved by resolving the difficulty it shares with analytic judgements: the aspect of presupposition characteristic of given concepts. Indeed, the first difficulty is transmuted into the second by virtue of the principle of the formation of the concept. The entire problem of *experience*, or of judgements of experience, is thereby posed as that problem which accompanies the aporias, unnoticed by Kant, of analytic judgements, synthetic judgements a posteriori—and even synthetic judgements a priori.

We thus apprehend this problem primarily as that of the contingency of judgements of experience—or of judgements *tout court*, as we may say from now on. We do so by inverting our focus of interest. Later we shall look at the other problem, Kant's principal and prevalent interest, which is actually but another aspect of the same problem: that of the *necessity* of judgements.

We now begin to perceive how the principle of non-contradiction can properly come into play as a concrete logical principle.

Carabellese has called attention to a difficulty that 'often goes unnoticed, and even more often unresolved, even today': 'Why is it that we all talk of the *same* things? Why do we combine in the *same* manner what are necessarily subjective and diverse empirical elements? Empirical objectivity nevertheless remains objectivity. That certain something which is *horse* for me is *horse* for everyone else too. The categoriality (i.e. formal correspondence to the categories) of the concept does not account for the correspondence of the content.' In other words, formal correspondence to categories does not suffice to account for *empirical* objectivity. For the moment we will limit ourselves to responding to the question this way: precisely *because* they are empirical—that is, subjective and diverse—the elements that we combine in the concept of horse are combined in such a way—in the *same* way by everyone—that they constitute the unity *sui generis* that is the empirical concept of 'horse'. And is it not precisely a concept like that of horse which is *subject to the principle of identity and non-contradiction*, as a principle of *discrimination or determination*? Kant's 'pure intellectual' and Hegel's 'dialectical' concept are certainly not subject to this principle as such, as presumed functional categories serving the purpose of *unification*. Does this not already herald a connection—paradoxical though it may be—between the principle *par excellence* traditionally assumed to be merely 'formal' or analytico-rational, and the *content*? Can the principle of non-contradiction then play this sort of role in the determination of the object, the *Gegenstand*? Is this principle logically and gnoseologically valid after all—although not in the sense Kant believed when he formulated the principle that a concept is empty either if intuition is lacking or if it is self-contradictory and thus indifferently scrambled category and concept-essence? But if we take care to avoid this error and recognize, exactly on the basis of the Kantian principle of the formation of the concept, that even the supposed concept-essence is necessarily empirical, do we not perhaps discover that the principle of non-contradiction retains its full force, *along with* the empirical concept, the empirical character of the concept, into which the supposed essence (possible objectivity) has to be transformed?

In the light of these questions, let us re-examine Kant's reasoning in his consideration of the judgement 'bodies are heavy'.

If, as Kant claims, the 'empirical' intuitions of body and heavy do not acquire any of their consistency and positivity as particular, empirical representations in the intuition considered as pure 'subjective state', how can their validity be posited in accordance with synthetic unity? If we exclude the schemata, as an admittedly imaginative but nonetheless *general* procedure, we actually find this positivity of the empirical or particular only in the intuition as *subjective* state or *pure* intuition—namely in its character of 'disinterestedness' or contemplativeness. Now, does not the static character, the undialectical character, typical of contemplativeness bear some relation to the typical static and undialectical character of *intellectual* discourse, which generally obeys the principle of identity and non-contradiction? Through what sort of concepts other than those like 'body', 'horse', etc., which correspond to 'empirical representations', can this principle remain in force?

All these questions, of course, which postulate acceptance of the principle of non-contradiction, have real meaning only if it is duly noted that they require most of all that this principle be properly interpreted. Our interpretation, based in part on the innermost logical-ontological significance of its original, anti-Parmenidean formulation by Aristotle, has little to do with the traditional Parmenidean, scholastic, or (last but not least) rationalist formulations of it still upheld by those who have no choice but to maintain this principle since they do not accept Hegel's outright rejection of it. In their hands, of course, it is not always merely a formal principle of reasoning. The traditional, rationalist interpretation, re-echoed by Kant himself (with the consequences examined above) explicitly regards this principle as the *principium rationis par excellence*—that principle which, as the principle of abstract, analytic reason, satisfies the instance of *unity* and *necessity* characteristic of the rational as such. (But it does not, in their view, satisfy the instance of *multiplicity*.)

A recent example of this sort of interpretation may be found in Heidegger's *Vom Wesen des Grundes* (Halle, 1931, pp. 4 ff.). He, unlike us, has no difficulty expunging the principle of non-contradiction from the search for what is truly 'ground', since he accepts that principle in its Leibnizian formulation as the *principium rationis*.

But that is not all. Heidegger concludes by acknowledging the 'transcendental character' of the 'principle of identity and non-contradiction', but by this he means that it refers to 'something more primordial', which is none other than temporality. Here one can only observe that Heidegger finds it easy to discard the conception of 'truth as judgement' precisely because he considers only the traditional judgement, as a 'nexus' of concepts (sustained by the related principle of identity). But he was interested in the Kantian problem of the formation of the concept only indirectly, through the doctrine of time, of the transcendental aesthetic. His preconceived hostility to the 'gnoseological' was certainly of no use to him, as is shown by his contention that a pure intuition can never serve as 'original', or ante-predicative, truth. For the moment, it is sufficient to note that here again Heidegger takes the easy way out, for by such intuition he means the 'simple representation drawn from every nexus'. In sum, he fails to overstep the usual limits of the most dogmatic and thread-bare gnoseology and logic.

But let us return to our own inquiry. In due time we will examine the genesis of the 'principle of contradiction' in the work of Aristotle. In particular, we shall see that this principle is organically dependent on Aristotle's fundamental ontological principle of 'first substance'. This, we believe, will open the way to the discovery and characterization, in the course of gnoseological analysis, of the irrational-particular—the critical concept of not-being—which we have approximated through the hypothesis of disinterested feeling as the material co-element of a syn-thesis of heterogeneities.

As for Carabellese and the question of empirical objectivity, for the moment we may add this to the interrogative replies listed above: it is not at all certain that this problem can be solved by his negative concept of feeling as the 'implicit', in other words, the 'unexplained explicable'—a concept in which the rationalist 'confused idea', target of Kant's cardinal critique of Leibniz, obviously persists, even though Carabellese, when he considers empirical objectivity, is no more interested in the fact that there is an objectivity called 'horse' than in the fact that this objectivity is nevertheless empirical, and in what this means logically. We are moved to doubt when he says (in his commentary on the *Prolegomena*, p. 23) that 'with the empirical analytic judgement *we do not say that what exists exists*' (in other words, if I have understood properly, Carabellese's view is that the empirical judgement *in no way* concerns *existence*, the *concrete*), but rather that 'that which exists (otherwise the empirical content would not mean anything) is made this way or that'. It thus seems clear that the Rosminian Carabellese also unduly undervalues the empirical concept (even while posing the problem of empirical existence) and holds in substance to the common distinctions between perception (as knowledge of the concrete) and empirical concept (as abstract knowledge), as if the two were quite different things. (This distinction becomes caricatural in the Crocean-Hegelian reduction of the empirical concept to a *pseudo-concept*.)

But this approach leaves us with a semi-psychological view of the problem of perception and experience and makes not the slightest headway in the development of a real logic of experience, which must take account simultaneously of the necessity (indigenousness) and contingency (acquisition) of judgements.

Let us conclude this aspect of our investigation.

The preceding examination of the thing-in-itself has shown that Kant's phenomenalism is intellectualist, for, like any phenomenalism, it entails a *negative* conception of the irrational or material, inadequate to the exigency inherent in the cardinal critique of Leibniz. But it must be added that this intellectualism of Kant's phenomenalism suggests that the world of experience itself is *unreal*; indeed, this idea is already implicit in the *irrationality* of the formal given that Kant regards as underpinning that world. We can now glimpse a hitherto obscure aspect of the ultimate objective of our inquiry: in the end, the problem of the *contingency* of judgements is transformed into the problem of whether judgements have any genuine reality.

Here again, we must seek confirmation in an instance that lies concealed in the architecture of the system. It is true, as we have seen, that Kant conceives of the thing-in-itself as a pluralism of monads (otherwise his conception of the divine intuitive intellect would lose all reason for being). In this sense, the pre-critical rationality of the thing-in-itself is undeniable. But it must also be kept in mind that this is still *pluralism*, and that the instance of the *multiplicity* of being (the absolute *Objekt*) is thus evident nonetheless. The negative conception of the irrationality of the world—of the formal given— therefore expresses *not only* the instance of the rationality of that which is *not* of this world—the 'in-itself'—but also the *lack*, in the world, of that *concreteness*, namely multiplicity and particularity, which is nonetheless described as belonging to the thing-in-itself.

Now, although we can—indeed, we must—abandon the pure rationality (the 'in-itself') of the transcendental discovered by Kant, we cannot and must not simultaneously abandon the suggestive instance of plurality or concreteness, which Kant attributes to this very same 'in-itself'. We cannot do so because the lesson of the transcendental will not allow it, precisely because the transcendental brooks no *pure rationality*. It thus turns out that proper consideration of Kant's conception of the formal given—in other words, the semi-irrational (or un-reality)—can alert us to avoid the phenomenalism and intellectualism into which he himself fell because (in addition to everything else) he *indifferently* lumped together in the 'in-itself' the instance of both unity (rationality) and multiplicity. He consequently believed that his ('formal') given and the ('innate') passivity related to it were more than sufficient to account for the *specificity* of the senses, the synthesis of which with the intellect was supposed to generate 'experience', which was intended as and could only be 'possible' experience—in the abstract. In retrospect, then, we examine Kant's thing-in-itself in order completely and definitively to satisfy the exigency Kant himself posed in his cardinal critique of Leibniz.

In thus abandoning the Kantian conception that the negative irrational equals un-reality, we also abandon his mere phenomenalism. Conversely, in proceeding to the study of the *positive* irrational-particular, we proceed to the study of actual reality or existence as an aspect of judgements themselves. We thereby set out to satisfy the critical instance so explicit in the 'matter' and 'nature' to which Marxist (historical) materialism appeals.

Even in approaching the problem of existence from this direction, however, we find no lack of fruitful hints from Kant.

Let us take an example. In his critique of the ontological proof of the existence of god[35] Kant discusses the 'hundred thalers' argument. ('A hundred real thalers', he posits à la Hume, 'do not contain the least coin more [in their concept] than a hundred possible thalers.... My financial position is, however, affected very differently by a hundred real thalers than it is by the mere concept of them (that is, of their possibility).') He concludes this argument by saying that the concept of the object is not in the least augmented by its connection with the world of experience; on the other hand, 'a possible perception has been added' to the experience of the mind. This conclusion, in which the full intellectualist weakness of Kantian phenomenalism is apparent, this time in connection with the problem of *existence*, is, in a certain sense, *much less* informative than the very first essay in which he dealt with the problem of existence. There he stated that the representation of a unicorn, for example, is a 'concept of experience',

[35] Critique A 599-601, pp. 505-506.

i.e. the 'representation of an existing thing'. Hence, 'to demonstrate the correctness of the proposition that such a thing exists, one must look not at the concept of the subject, for in this one finds only the predicates of possibility, but at the *origin* of the knowledge I have of the thing: I have seen it myself or I have learned of it from others who have seen it'. ('The Only Possible Ground of Proof of God's Existence'.)

The freshness of the Humean empiricist inspiration that comes through in the concluding words[36] is so striking that we may disregard the pre-critical theory in which these conclusions are framed— the theory of existence as the 'absolute position' of a thing, the existence of which, since it is neither idea nor relation, is a predicate not of the thing but of 'the thought one has of the thing', exactly because existence is 'at the origin' of this thought, which means beyond it. In discarding this pre-critical theory we likewise discard the dogmatic realism that reconnects it to the 'critical' theory of the thing-in-itself. We do so in order to retain only the suggestion that it is possible to identify *existence* with that *particular sensation* ('I have seen it'), or *pure feeling*, which will be of value in the solution of our problem: to establish the contingency and existentiality of judgements, wholly lacking in the abstract *possible* perception presented in the famous text of 'critical' phenomenalism cited above.

Our own analysis thus leads back to a sort of crystal-pure feeling quite close to aesthetic feeling. (A German critic has noted the affinity of Kantian aesthetic feeling and the 'subjective state' mentioned in §22 of the *Prolegomena*, with which the 'I have seen' may be identified.) Now, if we understand this pure feeling as the disinterested and simultaneously formal feeling in the syn-thesis, then it can serve, at least hypothetically, as the equivalent of the *existence* we have been seeking, since we have already identified, also hypothetically, the critically understood irrational-particular with disinterested feeling.

Thus, once we appropriately modify one of Hume's fundamental formulae (he identified that feeling which is *belief*, or assent to existence, with the 'elementary act of judgement' that 'lays the basis' for

---

[36] Hume had said that belief, or *assent to existence*, 'adds no new idea' to those that compose the object, otherwise the mind could attach the idea of existence to any fiction. Therefore, he maintained, the difference between the simple idea of the existence of an object and actual belief in it must reside solely in the 'manner in which we conceive the idea, that is, in the feeling or sensation we have of it'; this difference cannot be found either in the attributes or in the totality of the idea.

'reasoning about things in fact'), it remains only to formulate our final hypothesis: that *existence*, as disinterested feeling, is none other than the *foundation of judgements*, or of reasoning *tout court*.

For the moment, this hypothesis, which follows from the entire preceding critical analysis, can serve at least to cast suspicion not only on Croce's conclusion that existence is always a 'predicate' and on the simplistic remnants of dogmatic realism in Hume and Kant, but also on Carabellese's identification of existence and feeling on the grounds that he, like Leibniz, views the latter as the 'unexplained explicable', not substantially different from the Hegelian Gentile's 'feeling' as 'indeterminate oneness'. Finally, our concluding hypothesis also casts doubt on Baratono's abstractly empiricist identification of existence and sensibility. He disregards any relation between what he ambiguously calls 'sensible form' and the logico-conceptual; his 'sensibilist occasionalism' thus eventually leads back to Crocean aestheticism. For us, however, the disinterested feeling that is existence must, on the contrary, be material—as co-element of a synthesis.

How, then, can a *logic of existence* be fashioned?

If, as we have seen, our efforts aim at establishing that the principle of non-contradiction satisfies the specific instance of multiplicity or contingency no less than that of oneness or necessity (contrary to the traditional attitude), then we must also conclude that it satisfies the instance of *existence itself*, as a synonym of multiplicity, contingency, the irrational-particular, or however one puts it.

Thus, that existence which, *under the old logic of rationalist 'identity' as applied even by Hume and Kant, is 'contingent' since its negation (its not-being) is not contradictory or absurd* is, under our logic, contingent (i.e. is precisely existence), *exactly because its negation is contradictory, or absurd.* And the 'logical' contingency which the old doctrine followed by Kant holds to be characteristic only of certain predicates in certain judgements ('right-angled' with respect to 'triangle', for example) is, on the contrary, characteristic of every predicate as such—in short, of every judgement. This is so because, contrary to what Kant always thought, the principle of non-contradiction, which is the 'logical' foundation of every judgement, coincides exactly with the 'real' foundation, the 'thinkable *given*'. In other words, it coincides with *existence*, with its characteristic static-ness-contemplativeness of 'disinterested' feeling, the ultimate *foundation* of judgements.

To summarize: we propose to integrate Hume's and Kant's solutions to the problem of existence (i.e. the contingency or existentiality of judgements) by *transforming their common logical foundation*, namely the non-contradictory or non-absurd character of the negation (of existence, of the 'fact') into the contradictory or absurd character of the negation. In so doing we strive to avert both Hume's ultimate conclusion of a contingency that negates true validity or necessity and Kant's conclusion of a validity or necessity that, since it is *self-evident*, even if only gnoseologically, frustrates true contingency.

The first section of our study thus concludes with this transformation of the criticist *solution* of the traditional Eleatic aporias into the problem-hypothesis of the being of not-being (of unity-multiplicity) as the problem of the contingency or existentiality of judgements.

II

The Platonic-Hegelian Dialectic and Aristotle's Analytics

Our *critical* approach to the problem of being and not-being is organically linked to our approach to the question of the logical principle. If we are to make further headway, then, we must consider Hegel's modern, 'dialectical' solution of this problem. This will inevitably lead us to the solutions proposed by Plato's dialectic and Aristotle's analytic.

It is therefore requisite to test the internal coherence and validity of Hegel's logic in the light of the exigencies formulated in the preceding chapter.

We shall broach this subject by examining Hegel's conception of the senses, or of feeling in general. His concept of logic, along with its limitations, can be understood after we grasp his concept of aesthetics.

To start with, let us look at Hegel's view of the nature of not-being, multiplicity, or particularity as presented in the first two chapters of his *Phenomenology of Spirit*, which deal with the 'dialectic of immediate certainty'.

The concrete content of 'sense-certainty' (of supposed 'immediate knowledge' or cognition 'of the immediate' or 'of what simply is'), Hegel writes, appears at first as the 'richest' and 'truest' knowledge, since it is thought that it, unlike the abstract intellect, has not yet 'omitted anything from the object, but has the object before it in its perfect entirety'. In reality, however, this 'certainty' turns out to be 'the most abstract and poorest truth'. 'All it says about what it knows is just that it *is*.' In other words, its truth contains solely the 'sheer being of the thing' in the general, Parmenidean sense, and not at all, as it claims, a particular and well-defined being.

Indeed, this certainty, for instance, says: This, Here, Now. To the question, What is the Now? we may reply, for example, 'Now is Night'. At noon, however, this sense-certainty 'has become stale'. It is true that the Now that is Night is 'preserved, i.e. it is treated as what it professes to be, as something that *is*; but it proves itself to be, on the contrary, something that is *not*. The Now does indeed preserve itself, but as something that is *not* Night; equally, it preserves itself in face of the Day that it now is, as something that also is not Day, in other words, as a *negative* in general. This self-preserving Now is, therefore, not immediate but mediated; for it is determined as a permanent and self-preserving Now *through* the fact [*dadurch*] that something else, viz. Day and Night, is *not*. As so determined, it is still just as simply Now as before, and in this simplicity is indifferent to what happens in it [*bei ihm herspielt*]; just as little as Night and Day are its being, just as much also is it Day and Night; it is not in the least affected by this its other being. A simple thing of this kind, which *is* through negation, which is neither This nor That, a *not-This*, and is with equal indifference This as well as That—such a thing we call a *universal*. So it is in fact the universal that is the true [content] of sense-certainty.'[1]

But if the universal is the real truth of sense-certainty, and if language, 'the work of thought', expresses only this truth, then it is 'impossible' ever 'to say' any sensuous existence that we 'mean': 'because the sensuous This that is meant *cannot be reached* by language, which belongs to consciousness, i.e. to that which is inherently universal. In the actual attempt to say it, it would, therefore, crumble away.'[2] I mean 'this' bit of paper, which appears to be quite different from 'that one'. And yet, in so doing I speak of 'actual things, external or sensuous objects, absolutely singular entities, and so on'; in other words, I 'say of them only what is *universal*'.

I get, then, the experience of what is really 'sense-certainty' by pointing, for example, to this bit of paper as 'a "Here" which is a Here of other Heres or is in its own self a "simple togetherness of many Heres"'; i.e. it is a universal'. In short, 'instead of knowing something immediate, I take the truth of it, or *perceive* it'.[3]

With the *Wahr-nehmung*, the perception, we move (in the second

[1] *Hegel's Phenomenology of Spirit*, translated by A.V. Miller, Clarendon Press, Oxford, 1977, pp. 57, 60.
[2] Ibid., p. 66.
[3] Ibid.

chapter of the *Phenomenology*) from the positing of the (abstract) universal to the development of the 'dialectic of sense-certainty'. 'The wealth of sense-knowledge', Hegel declares, 'belongs to perception, not to immediate certainty, for which it was only the source of instances; for only perception contains negation, that is, difference or manifoldness, within its own essence'.

Let us examine this *wealth*, i.e. this negativity or difference.

The This, Hegel continues, has been established as '*not* This' or as 'superseded' (*aufgehoben*), and yet not as nothing, but 'a determinate Nothing, a Nothing of a content, viz. of the This'. Therefore, the 'sense-element is still present, but not in the way it was supposed to be in [the position of] immediate certainty: not as the singular item that is "meant", but as a universal, or as that which will be defined as a *property*'. In the meantime, it is noted in passing that supersession (*Aufheben*) 'exhibits its true twofold meaning which we have seen in the negative: it is at once a negating and a preserving'. Thus, the nothing, being a negation of the This, 'preserves its immediacy and is itself sensuous, but it is a universal immediacy'.[4] The two categorical determinations of *universality* and *particularity*, or oneness, appear in their *dialectical* contrast: as the universality of *thinghood* (or pure essential reality) and the particularity of the *thing* (or specific substance). The former, thinghood, is merely the *also* of the many properties (This, Here, Now, etc.), which are indifferent to one another.

But if the many properties were 'strictly indifferent' to one another, Hegel continues, there could never be determinate properties, properties of something, or true properties. In order to be such, they must therefore enter into relation with one another, 'differentiate themselves from one another, and relate themselves to others as to their opposites'. This is how the dialectical transition from the positive unity of thinghood to the negative unity of the thing comes about.

The 'moments' that, when 'taken together' by philosophizing consciousness, exhaust the nature of the thing as the truth of perception are as follows: '(a) an indifferent passive universality, the *Also* of the many properties or rather "*matters*"; (b) negation, equally simply; or the *One*, which excludes opposite properties; and (c) the many *properties* themselves, the relation of the first two moments,

---

[4] Ibid., pp. 67-68.

or negation as it relates to the indifferent element, and therein expands into a host of differences; the point of singular individuality in the medium of subsistence radiating forth into plurality. In so far as these differences belong to the indifferent medium they are themselves universal, they are related only to themselves and do not affect one another. But in so far as they belong to the negative unity [or oneness], they are at the same time exclusive [of other properties]; but they necessarily have this relationship of opposition to properties remote from *their* Also. The sensuous universality, or the *immediate* unity of being and the negative, is thus a property only when the One and the pure universality are developed from it and differentiated from each other, and when the sensuous universality unites them; it is this relation of the universality to the pure essential moments which at last completes the thing.'[5]

We shall skip over the dialectic of universality and particularity within the thing (that is, between the universality of its independent properties and the negative One), which leads to the transition from the thing to force at the level of objective essence and from perception to intellect at the level of consciousness or subject. We shall instead move directly to the conclusions of the chapter, which are important for our purposes.

The 'singular being of sense', Hegel writes, 'does indeed vanish in the dialectical movement of immediate certainty and becomes universality, but it is only a *sensuous universality*. My "meaning" has vanished, and perception takes the object as it is *in itself*, or as a universal as such [*Allgemeines überhaupt*]. Singular being therefore emerges in the object as true singleness, as the in-itself of the One, or as reflectedness-into-self. But this is still a *conditioned* being-for-self *alongside which* appears another being-for-self, the universal which is opposed to, and conditioned by, singular being. . . . These empty abstractions of a "singleness" and a "universality" opposed to it . . . are powers whose interplay is the perceptual intellect, . . . it is always at its poorest where it fancies itself to be the richest . . . .It [perceptual intellect] does not itself become conscious that it is simple essentialities of this kind that hold sway over it, but fancies that it has always to do with wholly substantial material and content; . . . But it is, in fact, these essentialities within which perceptual intellect runs to and fro through every kind of material and

[5] Ibid., pp. 69-70.

content; . . . they alone are what the sensuous is *as essence* for consciousness, . . . and it is in them that the process of perception and of its truth runs its course. . . . What the nature of these untrue essences is really trying to get [perceptual] intellect to do is to *bring together*, and thereby supersede [*aufheben*] the thoughts of those non-entities, thoughts of that universality and singular being, of "Also" and "One", of the essentiality that is *necessarily* linked to the unessential moment that yet is "necessary". But the intellect struggles to avoid doing this by resorting to "in so far as" and to the various "aspects", . . . '[6]

The characteristic difficulty of this celebrated analysis of the dialectic of sensible consciousness lies, it seems to me, in Hegel's self-evident, indifferent, and dogmatic use of the dialectical—or *logical*—instrument of *Aufhebung* to resolve two distinct problems: a) the aesthetic-phenomenological problem of the transition from the particular, immediate, or sensible This to the universal, or mediated This, which is conceived as the not-This, or the nothing with a content, precisely as a singular whole and therefore universal immediacy or sensible universality which, as the immediate or positive unity of being and negativity, is merely *universal as such*, i.e. indeterminate; and b) the *logical*-phenomenological problem of the transition from 'thought' of thinghood or universality to thought of the thing or particularity; these are thoughts, or rather categorial articulations, whose determinateness develops out of the indeterminate sensible universality or universality as such, as seen above.

The result of this *intellectualization* of the sensible is that the 'sensible particular'—in short, the particular, multiple, or discrete—is reduced simply to the 'universal as such'—in other words, to the *indeterminate*.

Thus, on the very threshold of Hegel's system, we recognize a familiar figure (*mutatis mutandis*): the Leibnizian, and generally rationalist, notion of sensations as '*confused* ideas', the target of Kant's cardinal critique of Leibniz. It is yet another instance—the most significant since Kant—of the *negative* conception of the senses or feeling (or multiplicity) whose roots stretch all the way back to Plato.

[6] Ibid., pp. 77-78.

Nevertheless, tradition has it that the dialectic of immediate certainty represents one of the most vibrant examples of Hegel's alleged hankering after the concrete.

'Since the *sensible* has been brought into the dialectical rhythm', observes the latest Italian translator of the *Phenomenology*, echoing this tradition, 'the development of the dialectic will have to be continuously productive of *content*'. (And cf. the most recent apology for the 'modernity' of the *Phenomenology* in general, namely its alleged concern for concreteness, in Kroner, *Von Kant bis Hegel*, Tübingen, 1924, vol. II, pp. 396-397.)

So, the sensible, which is 'universal as such', is 'developed' in the thoughts of thinghood, the thing, and so on. But is the 'wealth' of sensible consciousness, the *variety* to which this consciousness lays claim, really preserved in this exposition?

Hegel immediately deems this wealth 'inexpressible', that is, producible only as the pure *genericity* or universality of language, which has the 'divine' nature of 'overturning'—through the mysterious *aesthetic Aufhebung*—the 'meaning' of the particularity or discreteness of the sensible. He also explicitly presents this wealth as something 'alongside and by the way', as 'inessential' and 'ephemeral'.

Granted, this attempt to situate the sensible within the dialectical rhythm does reveal an intelligible multiplicity that would otherwise have gone unsuspected and unjustifiable. And this is a step forward, which can on no account be contested, in the search for that wealth of variety of being that the sensible requires by its nature.

But if we look carefully at how this intelligible multiplicity is presented, we discover an instance that is wholly contrary to the character of multiplicity in general, and to the intelligible in particular. Indeed, at the end of the second chapter of the *Phenomenology*, Hegel warns us sternly that this intelligible multiplicity is intrinsically insufficient and 'meagre'—precisely because of its peculiar character of *discreteness* (maintained for it by the 'abstracting' perceptual intellect). In sum, he warns that this multiplicity—if it is to be valid as *concept*—must be 'mastered' in the sense expounded in the *Logic*, that is, in the sense of the *Aufhebung* as a pure logical-dialectical process. Here we must immediately call attention to two essential passages of the *Science of Logic*. First:

'The intellect does indeed give them [its determinatenesses], so to speak, a rigidity [*Härte*] of being such as they do not possess in the qualitative sphere [that is, in the mere realm of experience]; . . . but at the same time, it *spiritually impregnates [begeistet]* them and so sharpens them, that just at this extreme point alone they acquire the capability to dissolve themselves and pass over into their opposite. The highest maturity, the highest stage which anything can attain is that in which its downfall begins.'[7]

Second: 'Thinking reason, however, sharpens, so to say, the *blunt* difference of diverse terms, the mere manifoldness of pictorial thinking, into *essential* difference, into its opposition. Only when the manifold terms have been driven to the point of contradiction do they become active and lively towards one another, receiving in contradiction the negativity which is the indwelling pulsation of self-movement and spontaneous activity. . . . when the difference of reality is taken into account, it develops from difference into opposition, and from this into contradiction, so that in the end the sum total of all realities simply becomes absolute contradiction within itself.'[8]

Here it is sufficient to note Hegel's effort to conceive the diverse, or multiplicity, as absolutely that which is 'blunt' (not intelligible), so as to 'sharpen' to the extreme—or render *intelligible*—the diversity of the diverse. In other words, by reducing diversity to 'essential' difference, he intends to reduce it to the *relation* of 'opposition', or contrariety ('the science of contraries is one and the same', Plotinus used to say). His ultimate intention, it should be noted, is to attain—precisely through the 'rigidity' or *determinateness* of being that allegedly eludes the mere realm of experience, but does *not* elude the intellect—that 'liveliness', that 'vitality', which is the concrete. But 'life can only exist in the concrete' in the sense that 'it is one', Hegel explains in the Zusatz (Addition) to §38 of the *Encyclopaedia*, for example.

Thus, the *concrete* is *oneness* (unity), the intelligible totality, or total intelligibility. But if the elements, the components, destined to lend rigidity, determinateness, or fullness to unity owe this rigidity of theirs to the very degree of maturity of the 'simplification' or unification of representative or qualitative multiplicity—that is, to the degree of their highly mature 'sharpness' or intelligibility—how can they actually be anything but the very 'downfall' (as elements or many) that 'begins', or rather coincides, with their 'maturity'? How

[7] *Hegel's Science of Logic*, translated by A.V. Miller, London, 1969, p. 611.
[8] Ibid., p. 442.

can they avoid *dissolution* into intelligible *totality*, inasmuch as they break up into extreme, *total* intelligibility?

Is not the *intellect* perhaps lost because of this *total* intelligibility? In other words, isn't the ('positivizing') intellect—the determinateness of being—simply *assumed*? Here we may recall the difficulty that arises from the 'deduction' of the very first categories of the *Logic*. This deduction itself cannot be effected by relying primarily on differentiation or determinateness, since the latter is a 'meaning'. This is the ultimate consequence, of whose gravity Hegel was unaware, of his gratuitous assumption of the intellect.

The 'determinate' or *articulated* unity to which the 'universal as such', the indeterminate—the sensible!—is supposed to lead in the course of its 'development' thus already seems to be illusory. Indeed, we may already conjecture that this conception of sensibility—still substantially romantic—which in the *Phenomenology* takes the form of the juvenile mystical conception, as romantic as can be, of 'beautiful' *undiscriminated* primordial unity[9]—is what prevents Hegel, and all Hegelians, from *grounding the intellect* (and from developing a fully *critical* concept of *reason*), since it obscures the positive nature of the relation of the intellect to the senses or feeling, to multiplicity. For the moment it is sufficient to note that precisely because Hegel begins from a romantic concept of sensibility or feeling (conceived, under the speculative category of oneness, as the 'universal as such', or indeterminate unity), he inevitably winds up with a negative—mystical!—conception of the intellect and reason as the *inexplicable* division and subsequent reintegration of oneness. This conception is unable to account for either multiplicity (the senses) or oneness (reason), for in the end it leaves us with a unity that, try as it might, can only be immobile and false. It must nevertheless be noted that this conclusion about Hegel's 'unity'—a point to which we shall return in more detail—is only the *initial conclusion*, provisional in a certain sense, of a genuinely radical critique of Hegelian (or any other) a priori reasoning. We shall draw the *final conclusion* at the end of our examination of Hegelian 'reason', when all the consequences of the 'mystifying' character of Hegel's dialectic will be revealed. Then we shall see, as Marx's brilliant critical insight pointed out, that Hegel's dialectic ultimately reduces to the *theological interpolation* of multiplicity.

9 In this regard, see my *Hegel romantico e mistico*, Florence, 1929.

From the preceding argument we already know what to think of the real intentions—and results—critics have attributed to Hegel in these two opening chapters of the *Phenomenology*. Hegel himself wrote that he wanted to redeem philosophy from an 'appalling reign of sensibility and perception, an absolute a posteriori rule' of which Kant's philosophy was unaware.[10] But the real— Hegelian —meaning of this passage emerges clearly from its context, given in the note below. What we have here is a characteristic instance of Hegel's disparagement of Kantian criticism, epitomized exactly in the charge that Kant raised the non-identity of subject and object to 'the absolute principle'. It is thus evident that Hegel intends to 'redeem' the sensible and a posteriori absolute by elevating it to an a priori that is not 'merely subjective', like the a priori in the *Critique of Judgement*! It is quite apparent that Hegel has ultimately failed to comprehend the fruitful set of problems posed in Kant's third Critique.

But let us complete our examination of Hegel's conception of the sensible, or the aesthetic in general, by looking at several exemplary passages of the *Encyclopaedia* and the *Lectures on Aesthetics*.

At the very beginning of the *Encyclopaedia* (§§5-7)[11] Hegel posits

[10] 'Here [in Kant] it becomes clear to what secondary importance the identity of subject and object has been relegated. The identity of subject and object is limited to only nine of twelve or many more pure activities of thought; for modality offers no true objective determination, but bears within itself the essential non-identity of subject and object. Outside of the objective determinations through the categories, there remains an appalling reign of sensibility and perception, an absolute a posteriori rule under which no a priori is admitted, save as a subjective maxim of the reflecting power of judgement. In other words, non-identity has been raised to the absolute principle.' (*Werke*, volume I, pp. 162-163, Berlin, 1933.) For a full documentation of this (illusory) attempt to redeem the sensible, see the very good book of Jean Wahl, *Le malheur de la conscience dans la philosophie de Hegel*, Paris, 1929, which nevertheless represents a point of view quite different from my own.

[11] Hegel's *Encyclopaedia of the Philosophical Sciences* (1830) has been published in English in three volumes by Oxford University Press. This edition includes the Zusätze, or Additions, compiled from the lecture notes of Hegel's students. The first volume, entitled *Hegel's Logic* (1975), was translated by William Wallace and includes paragraphs 1-244 of the Encyclopaedia. The second, *Hegel's Philosophy of Nature* (1970), translated by A.V. Miller, includes paragraphs 245-376. The third, *Hegel's Philosophy of Mind* (1971), translated by William Wallace, Zusätze by A.V. Miller, includes paragraphs 377-577. All quotations from the Encyclopaedia in this book have been taken from this English edition, in which Hegel's paragraphs are clearly numbered. Minor modifications in Wallace's translation have occasionally been made to bring the terminology into conformity with Miller's more recent translation of the *Science of Logic.—Translator's note*.

that 'reflection', which in general contains the principle of philosophy ('principle also in the sense of commencement'), 'transforms feeling, ordinary ideas [representations], etc. into thoughts'. But what is feeling in general? Juridical, moral, or religious feeling, for example, is 'a sentiment (and in that way an experience) of such *content* that it can spring from and rest upon *thought* alone' (§8). Thus, the 'ineffable', feeling or sensation, is not at all the most excellent and truest, but rather 'that which is the most insignificant and untrue' (§20). To support this argument Hegel recalls his theory of the sensible as 'universal as such'. Everything and anything, he writes, is an 'individual', a 'this', '*even if it is sensible,* here and now' (§20). Moreover, as far as sensible consciousness is concerned: 'the only thing worth knowing about it is that such immediate knowledge of the being of external things is illusion and error; that the sensible world as such is altogether devoid of truth; that the being of these external things is something accidental, transient, an *appearance*' (§76).

Let us, however, linger on this 'reflection' and the 'transformation' it effects. In other words, let us examine the 'origin' of philosophy in 'experience'. To start with, what does the 'principle of experience' mean to Hegel? This principle, he says, 'contains the infinitely important assertion that man, to accept any content and regard it as true, must be in contact with it [*dabei sein müsse*]; more precisely, he must find that content united and combined with the certainty of himself. He must be in contact with it, even if only through his external senses, or with his more profound spirit, his intimate self-consciousness' (§7). That what really interests Hegel here is only self-consciousness and not the 'external senses' is indicated by his attitude towards empiricism. After paying homage to 'the important principle contained in empiricism'—namely the principle that man 'must see for himself and feel that he is present in every fact of knowledge which he has to accept' (§38)—he retracts this homage (in the Zusatz to the very same paragraph) with the following, revealing criticism: 'so long, then, as this sensible sphere is and continues to be for empiricism a mere datum, empiricism is a doctrine of bondage: for we become free when we are confronted by no absolutely alien world, but rather depend on a fact that we ourselves are'.

The real meaning and value in Hegel's eyes of the widely-noted criticism of *having to be*—and with it the exaltation of the 'great principle' of empiricism: 'that which is true must be in *reality* and must be there through *perception*'—may thus be gleaned. Although he appears to demand the real and present, the concrete at which empiricism aims, Hegel actually replaces it with his own 'concrete', with his own concept of the concrete as a dialectical unity or *co-presence* (a totality) within which the intellect is gratuitously pre-supposed only to be equally gratuitously annulled, *along with* the senses or feeling, which empiricism (and Kantian criticism) consider closely and vitally related to the intellect. In other words, Hegel replaces the concrete with his *own* concept of self-consciousness, which is quite different from Kant's.

Continuing, Hegel observes that it may be said—'not that it would mean much'—that 'philosophy owes its first origin to experience, to the a posteriori'. In reality, however, thought is essentially 'the nega-tion of what we have immediately before us'; it is an 'ingrate', similar in this respect to eating, which devours its own means of sub-sistence (§12).

Nevertheless, in considering the 'initial, abstract' universality of thought—namely universality 'indifferent to the process of particu-larization', which is the 'very immediacy' of thought reflected or mediated in itself (the a priori), in which the 'ingratitude' of thought is expressed—there is a 'correct and more profound meaning to the assertion that the *development* of philosophy is due to *experience*' (§12).

Let us see.

On the one hand, the 'empirical sciences', which do not stop at the 'simple perception' of individual phenomena but elaborate the material with the aid of thought, by discovering general determina-tions and laws, 'prepare' the content of the particular so that it can be received into philosophy.[12] Thought itself is thereby compelled to proceed to 'concrete determinations'. On the other hand, the assimi-lation of this content, the persistent immediacy of which has been superseded [*aufgehoben*] by thought, is 'at the same time a develop-ment of thought out of itself' (§12).

Within the realm of experience—in conformity with the 'internal logic of the concept', i.e. 'through the *opposition* . . . of phenomena

---

[12] Cf. *Werke*, volume XV, p. 283, in regard to experience: 'The realm of experience is not pure observation, hearing, feeling, . . . the perception of the particular; rather it is a matter of finding classes [*Gattungen*], universals, laws. And since it brings these forth, it brings them together with the ground [*Boden*] of the Concept.'

that are placed together'—the external and accidental circumstances of their conditions are 'eliminated' [*sich aufheben*] and the universal comes 'clearly into view'; it is *articulated* (§16). In short, although philosophy owes '*its development*' to the empirical sciences, it is philosophy that affords the content of these sciences 'what is essential to them', namely, the 'essential form of freedom of thought', the a priori, which is the guarantee of necessity. It may thus be concluded that 'the fact [*Tatsache*] becomes representation [*Darstellung*] and reproduction [*Nachbildung*] of the original and fully independent activity of thought' (§12). The free act of thought consists in its 'occupying a standpoint in which it is for itself and thus presents itself an object of its own production'. It is for this reason that philosophy appears as 'a circle which closes with itself', with no beginning in 'the same way as the other sciences' (§17).

This conception of 'fact' or 'experience' and its relation to philosophy is just the sort of conclusion that could have been expected from Hegel's negative conception of the senses as *universal as such*, or indeterminate. If one conceives the *multiplicity* of sensation as undifferentiated or *indeterminate* unity—or universality—then one must inevitably arrive at an equally negative (and mystical) conception of the intelligible *multiplicity* of experience, or fact. In the end, what remains inexplicable is precisely the characteristic Hegel intended to attribute to reason or unity: its *conservation* of intelligible *multiplicity* (through negation).

What is the point of this conservation if multiplicity in its original shape, which is the sensible, has already been declared a *lack*, an *insufficiency* of unity or universality, the universal indifferent to particularization, the This and therewith the 'property' that is not yet really a property? *Why* and *how* is intelligible multiplicity preserved, i.e. the faculty of the intellect, the 'rigidity' or determinateness characteristic of intelligible multiplicity? And above all, *where* does this *determinateness* (which is to be conserved while negated) come from? From *the senses*, or rather from their 'development' (as is claimed in the passages quoted above)? But sensibility is—negatively—*indeterminateness*, inasmuch as it is indifferent (universal) unity. And if we are to seek the root of intelligible multiplicity in this 'sensible universal', locating the reason for the discreteness (but read: fragmentariness!) and thereby determinateness of the intellectual precisely in *indeterminate* unity or in the intelligibility characteristic of such universality, then we are halted at a conception of the intellect as the 'imperfect' unity of universality. It is difficult to see how this can serve to *reassess* the intellect (as a moment of speculative thought, as Hegel intends). What is the sense or purpose of the conservation of the mere negative that is the intellect as a fragmentary, incoherent—or *contradictory*, but in the purely negative sense of the word—vision of a unity-totality that is necessarily *presupposed* in any event?

One is then inevitably mired in a neo-Platonic position ('Hegel is not at all the German Aristotle, but the German Proclus', said Feuerbach) and winds up with precisely that monstrosity of the rational-mystical which Hegel incautiously proposes and his apologists, even more incautiously, exalt.[13]

The illusory character of this alleged process of the development of philosophy from experience or multiplicity thus becomes clear. It may already be discerned that this process leads to a unity from which no real issue is ever possible: the concept (as essential self-consciousness). This is confirmed, for instance, in the way Hegel settles accounts with Kant's critical phenomenalism in the *Science of Logic*. First he claims that Kant's philosophy halted at mere 'psychological reflex of the Concept', since this philosophy reverted to the assertion that the Concept is permanently conditioned by a manifold of intuition. On this basis, Hegel says, Kantian philosophy 'declared intellectual cognition and experience to be phenomenal

---

[13] See the Zusatz to §82 of the Encyclopaedia (*Hegel's Logic*, p. 121): '...there is ...mystery in the mystical, but only however for the intellect, which is ruled by the principle of abstract identity; whereas the mystical as synonymous with speculation is the concrete unity of those propositions which the intellect only accepts in their separation and opposition.... Thus the reason-world may be equally styled mystical—not, however, because thought cannot both reach and comprehend it, but merely because it lies beyond the compass of the intellect.' And cf. Kroner, *Von Kant bis Hegel*, volume II, p. 272 (and pp. 284-285): 'He [Hegel] is an irrationalist because he is a dialectician, because the dialectic, through its method, makes the rational irrationalism itself, because dialectical thought is rational-irrational thought. Hegel's philosophy has been called "rational mystical" [by Feuerbach], wherein its twofold character is met in the deed.' Just how illusory is this conviction that Hegel actually succeeds in reconciling the irrational, or multiplicity, with the rational, or unity (Hegel 'irrationalizes thought itself', repeats Kroner, who has naively interpreted Feuerbach's critical formula '*rationelle Mystik*' as praise of Hegel!), can already be seen from what has been pointed out above. Further on in this chapter, we shall critically examine the *negative* conception of the intellect and judgements to which Hegel remained wedded despite himself. Indeed, he wound up with a rationalist mysticism. See also the conclusions of this chapter in regard to the (fatal) original link of Hegel's dialectic with 'ancient' as opposed to 'modern' scepticism (as is required if *critical irrationalism* is to have any foundation).

content'. Hegel then adds that Kant held that without the manifold
of intuition the concept would inevitably remain 'empty and devoid
of content despite the fact that it is a synthesis a priori'. Hegel concludes that if the concept is a synthesis, 'it surely does contain determinateness and difference within itself' and that the synthesis is
'absolute determinateness' and hence 'individuality'. The concept,
Hegel writes, is therefore 'the foundation [*Grund*] and source
[*Quelle*] of all finite determinateness and multiplicity'.[14]

In this manner, however, Hegel's alleged reassessment of experience and of intellect actually collapses into a futile, presupposed
reintegration of the indeterminate—and therefore fragmentary and
incoherent—into individual and determinate unity—determinate in
the sense that it is consistent and complete (as thought about
thought, or self-consciousness). This amounts to a modern version
of a neo-Platonic dream, and it is afflicted with the insoluble difficulties of all similar dreams.

The root of these errors, as we know, is Hegel's negative and
romantic concept of sensibility or feeling as universal as such, or
indeterminateness.

Finally, the conception of the senses presented in the Zusatz to
§447 of the *Encyclopaedia*, which some critics (John E. McTaggart,
for example) have interpreted as indicating a reassessment of the
sensible, may now be revealed in its true— unequivocally negative—
significance. 'In feeling', Hegel says, 'there is present the whole of
reason, the entire content of mind. All our representations,
thoughts, and notions of the external world, of right, of morality,
and of the content of religion, develop from our feeling intelligence;
just as, conversely, they are concentrated into the simple form of
feeling after they have been fully explicated'.

This 'development of the mind through the senses', far from
having to be interpreted in accordance with the theory that the
intelligence is a blank tablet, means that 'what intelligence seems to
draw from outside is, in reality, none other than the *rational*, and
thus identical to and present in the mind. And the activity of the
mind therefore has no other purpose than to remove the apparent
externality to itself of the *implicitly* rational object, as well as the
object's apparent externality to the mind'.[15]

It is evident that in the end this *implicit* rationality of the object,

[14] *Hegel's Science of Logic*, p. 589.
[15] *Werke*, volume VII, 2, p. 311.

which is explicated or develops as the entire content of the mind, can have no meaning unless it is identified with the sensible universal described above, precisely the indeterminate or *inexplicit* universal.

In thus annulling any gap between the senses and reason, on the basis of his *negative* conception of sensibility in general, Hegel likewise annuls any real 'development' or dialectical movement (cf. the vicious circle of the senses and reason described immediately above). All that remains is the distinction—*formal*, Kant would have said—between the indeterminate or *implicit* (the senses) and the determinate or *explicit* (reason). The only remaining ontological validity is the universal. Therefore, when McTaggart concludes that 'the [dialectical] process is one of pure thought perceived in a *medium* of *sensation*, and therefore synthetic and analytic at once' (*Studies in the Hegelian Dialectic*, Cambridge, 1922, p. 47), he does not suspect that for Hegel this medium, sensation, can only be 'accidental' or 'psychological', unless 'sensation' is understood to mean 'the realm of experience'. Experience, however, with its 'products' and 'laws', leads immediately to the 'terrain of the concept' (see above, note 12). It would be better to ground the *synthetic character* of the dialectical process in some other medium!

McTaggart's only possible conclusion, embarrassing as it is, runs as follows: 'sensation, although contributing *no positive* element to the [dialectical] process, is the *necessary* condition of our becoming conscious of the nature of thought.' It is difficult to see how a purely *negative* element of the dialectical process, namely sensation, can be the *necessary* condition of our consciousness of thought, i.e. of the *validity* of such a dialectical process.

We now arrive at aesthetics, where, in the supernatural Hegelian world of absolute spirit, and more particularly in that moment of it which is art, we will finally meet the culmination of this negative attitude to the sensible or aesthetic in general.

According to Hegel, that 'knowledge' which is art is 'the concrete contemplation [*Anschauung*] and mental picture [*Vorstellung*] of implicitly absolute spirit as the Ideal. In this Ideal, the concrete shape born of the subjective spirit, its natural immediacy, which is only a *sign* of the idea, is so transfigured by the informing spirit in order to express the Idea, that the figure shows it and it alone.' This is 'the shape or form of beauty'. The natural element in the work of art is thus 'taken as the characteristic meaningful nature-form which is significant [*sinnvoll*] of spirit'. This runs counter to the principle that art is the imitation of nature, for under that conception the natural element 'is taken only in its externality'.[16]

This concept of the beautiful as the 'sensible appearance of the Idea' of the 'representation of the (concrete) concept' is of interest to us only as an attempt to systematize romantic aesthetics scientifically. This attempt sharpens to the extreme the perversion, initiated by romantic aesthetics, of Kant's critical concept of 'free' or 'disinterested' beauty, the reasoning of which we examined in chapter I.

Hegel extols Schiller for having achieved in his concept of beauty—as 'pure aesthetic oneness' within which freedom and necessity, reason and sensibility, 'disappear entirely'—a *conciliation of opposites*, metaphysical 'true unity', and *spiritual totality* which had eluded Kantian 'subjectivity and abstraction of thinking'.[17] In so doing, Hegel himself unconsciously exhibits the erroneous tendency of all romantic aesthetics, which he indeed recapitulates in its ultimate coherence and systematization. Kroner, the greatest of Hegel's relatively recent apologists, leads us (unwittingly, of course) to the origin of the error in Schiller and to its conclusive *dénouement* in Hegel. In his *Von Kant bis Hegel* (vol. II, p. 46), he draws the link between Schiller's conception that 'nature (the senses) always *unites*, the intellect separates, but reason reunites' and Hegel's *Vernunft-Identität* (Reason-Identity), and more specifically the three dialectical gradations of 'immediacy', 'mediation', and 'return to immediacy'.

It should be noted that the *romantic perversion* of the concepts of *taste* and *genius*, which the Kant of the *Critique of Judgement* inherited from the English sentimentalists, comes about precisely through the concept that the senses completely unite opposites, or that they constitute *pure unity*. Indeed, this concept represents the very apogee of romanticism. It was Schiller himself who answered the historic call, prefacing the following paradoxical admonition to the words quoted above: 'The sensationalist aestheticians, who attach more weight to the testimony of feeling than to that of reasoning, are by no means so far removed from the truth *in practice* as their opponents, although they are no match for them *in*

---

[16] *Hegel's Philosophy of Mind*, §§556 and 558.
[17] *Aesthetics—Lectures on Fine Art*, in two volumes, translated by T.M. Knox, Oxford at the Clarendon Press, 1975, p. 61.

perspicacity.[18] He then concludes, significantly, that although the senses unite, the intellect separates, and reason reunites, 'before he begins to philosophize [that is, when he is still at the level of the senses alone] man is nearer to truth than the philosopher who has not yet completed his investigation [that is, who is still at the level of the intellect]'. Indeed, truth is 'potential' in beauty.[19]

The mistake, the perversion, consists in transforming the *critical* conception of a feeling that is at once disinterested (i.e., 'without concept') and universal into the dogmatic and Platonistic conception—more typical of Shaftesbury than of Hutcheson, Hume, or Kant—of a feeling understood as *intellectual intuition*, either as 'only a *sign*, a *means*, for viewing the whole', as Friedrich Schlegel put it,[20] or as only a 'sign of the Idea', as is maintained by Hegel (who regards feeling as the 'pure unity' of Schiller's opposites).

The error consists precisely in the transformation of an aesthetic conception that strives to illuminate the *positivity* of feeling both in general and in particular—and the fruitful set of problems connected to it, as described in chapter I—into a *negative*, theological conception of aesthetics or feeling, for this conception debases aesthetics, the particular or multiplicity, by subjecting it to the metaphysical category of pure *unity* and thereby dispelling it into the vacuity of the otiose problematic of neo-Platonism.

Having thus apprehended the full importance both of the

[18] Friedrich Schiller, *On the Aesthetic Education of Man*, edited and translated by Elizabeth M. Wilkinson and L.A. Willoughby, Oxford at the Clarendon Press, 1967, p. 127 (Letter 18).

[19] Ibid., Letter 18 and Letter 25 (p. 189). Compare this with Schlegel's concept of 'chaos' (related to the 'ironic' nature of art): 'Irony is a clear consciousness of an eternal agility, of the infinitely abundant chaos . . . . Only that confusion out of which a world can arise is chaos.' (*Ideas*, 69, 71; from Friedrich Schlegel, *Dialogue on Poetry and Literary Aphorisms*, translated by Ernst Behler and Roman Struc, Pennsylvania State University Press, University Park and London, 1968.)

[20] *Dialogue on Poetry*, p. 89: '. . . things which individually excite, move, occupy, and delight our senses, our hearts, understanding, and imagination seem to us to be only a sign, a means for viewing the whole at the moment when we rise to such a view.' And: 'The intellectual intuition is the categorical imperative of theory' (*Athenaeum*, 76). And also: 'He who wants something infinite knows not what he wants. But this proposition cannot be converted' (*Lyceum* 47). See also, Novalis: 'To destroy the principle of contradiction is perhaps the supreme task of the supreme logic.' (Jean Wahl, 'Novalis et le principe de contradiction', in *Le romantisme allemand*, Paris, 1949, pp. 161 ff.) On the fundamental romantic error, see my essay 'Crisi critica dell'estetica romantica', Messina, 1941 (second edition, Rome, 1964), and also *Il verosimile filmico e altri saggi di estetica*, Rome, 1954 (second edition, 1963), pp. 9-10, 17 ff., 34 ff., 38-45.

foreshadowing in Schiller's romantic 'pure aesthetic unity' of Hegel's 'immediacy' as the first dialectical moment (the 'universal as such', or the 'indeterminate') and of Hegel's conception of art as the 'sensible appearance of the Idea' on the plane of the absolute spirit, we now have only to examine the more particular implications of Hegel's doctrine of aesthetics. *What significance does Hegel attribute to the empiricist-Kantian principle of the 'disinterestedness' of the beautiful?* Here Hegel's romantic perversion of the concepts of taste and genius will be manifested in its full paradoxical character.

Hegel writes: 'Thus, the contemplation of beauty is of a liberal kind, it leaves objects alone as being inherently free and infinite; there is no wish to possess them or to take advantage of them as useful for fulfilling finite needs and intentions. So the object, as beautiful, appears neither as forced and compelled by us, nor fought and overcome by other external things.'[21] He counterposes this to the calculation of 'means' and 'ends' and thereby introduces us into that 'realm of shadow' which is the realm of the aesthetic 'ideal'. In so doing Hegel develops Schiller's concept that since truth is implicit (or 'potential') in beauty, we no longer have to ask how to pass from beauty to truth (and reality), but rather *how to pass from 'vulgar' truth and reality to 'aesthetic' truth and reality.*[22] At the same time, he sharpens to the extreme Schiller's mistake about the validity of feeling in empiricism (and criticism), interpreting Kant's 'disinterestedness' of 'free beauty', i.e. the being of the aesthetic object *without concept in general*, as a separation of this object from the abstract intellectual concept but *not* from the *pure concept*, from the idea—of which, be it noted, the object is alleged to be the sensible appearance. But how can this be?

How indeed, since Hegel maintains that 'the world of art, then, is the expression of God only when it does not contain *any sign of subjective particularity*',[23] and since he disparages genius as

---

21 *Aesthetics—Lectures on Fine Art*, p. 114.

22 'Thus it is from the deficiencies of immediate reality that the necessity of the beauty of art is derived.' (Ibid., p. 152.)

23 Cf. on the *originality* of art: 'The genuine originality of the artist, as of the work of art, lies solely in his being animated by the rationality of the inherently true content of the subject-matter. If the artist has made this objective rationality entirely his own, without mixing it and corrupting it either from within or without with particular details foreign to it, then alone in the topic to which he has given form does he give *himself* in his truest subjective character.' (Ibid., p. 298.)

'*particular* subject' and debases artistic inspiration to an 'un-free pathos' since it is 'alien to thought'?

Thus it is that Hegel, distorting and losing sight of Kant's critical concept of the aesthetic disinterested—through which the 'subjectivity' of the beautiful as *particularity* was emphasized—eventually misses the nature of beauty itself, which remains, for him, the romantic notion of infinity ('infinite subjectivity'),[24] i.e. pure *unity*.

But then the *sensible* appearance of the idea, which is supposed to distinguish the beautiful—the aesthetic *Schein* or *Erscheinen*[25]—remains unexplained.

As a result, ultimately Hegel achieves only the scientific systematization of 'logical beauty'—the 'irony' of Schlegel, which gratefully allows poetry and art 'to rise to the height of philosophy'[26] or, to put it in Hegelian terminology, to rise to the heights of the *Idea*.

The romantic cycle is thus closed—even the most recent epigones have not added anything really essential. It culminates in the 'serene' Hegelian realm of the ideal (*das Ideal*), the realm of 'shadows' or 'spiritual forms' (*die Geister*) so far removed from everyday 'mundane prose', from weariness, from interestedness, from need—in sum, from the 'seriousness of life'.[27]

This negative aesthetic of condemnation of the immediate or particular (rather paradoxical in aesthetics), which originates in the 'deficiencies' of immediate reality (see note 22 above), consummates the negative conception of sensibility or feeling in general (of the sensible particular as 'ineffable'). This conception is

[24] '. . . at this final stage of art [romantic art] the beauty of the classical idea . . . is no longer the ultimate thing. For at the stage of romantic art the spirit knows that its truth does not consist in its immersion in corporeality; on the contrary, it only becomes sure of its truth by withdrawing from the external into its own intimacy with itself . . . beauty in the sense hitherto expounded remains for it something subordinate, and beauty becomes the spiritual beauty of the absolute inner life as inherently infinite spiritual subjectivity. . . . The true content of romantic art is absolute inwardness, and its corresponding form is spiritual subjectivity with its grasp of its independence and freedom.' (Ibid., pp. 518-519.)

[25] 'Such necessity should not be missing in beautiful objects, but it must not emerge in the form of necessity itself; on the contrary, it must be hidden behind an appearance of undesignated contingency.' (Ibid., p. 115.)

[26] Schlegel, *Dialogue on Poetry and Literary Aphorisms*, p. 126: 'There are ancient and modern poems which breathe, in their entirety and in every detail, the divine breath of irony. In such poems there lives a real transcendental buffoonery. Their interior is permeated by the mood which surveys everything and rises infinitely above everything limited, . . .' (*Lyceum*, 42).

[27] *Aesthetics—Lectures on Fine Art*, pp. 157-158.

concentrated in the criterion of the 'sensible universal' as 'universal as such' and therefore as the 'immediate unity of being and the negative', the *Aufhebung* in its *aesthetic* application. This idea is the commencement and root of every one of Hegel's mistakes, not only in regard to the nature of the senses, but also in regard to the nature of logic, as we shall soon see.

It is time, then, to examine more closely Hegel's theory of logic, and therewith of the intellect and reason, which flows from his genuinely romanticist conception. We will have to concentrate in particular on the conclusions of his theory of the intellect, for if Hegel's conception of the intellect can also be shown to be *negative*, as we have already conjectured in our discussion of his negative conception of the senses, then our proof will have been adduced.

2

What is the intellect for the anti-Schelling and, in this respect, aspiring anti-romantic, Hegel?

'The activity of dissolution is the power and work of the intellect, the most astonishing and mightiest of powers', we read in a celebrated passage of the preface to the *Phenomenology of Spirit*, in the section devoted to demonstrating that the absolute is subject.[28]

That 'an accident as such', Hegel continues, or that which is real only through its connection to something else, 'should attain an existence of its own, and a separate freedom—this is the tremendous power of the negative; it is the energy of thought'. 'Death', or that which is not-real and abstract, 'is of all things the most dreadful'. And: 'to hold fast what is dead requires the greatest strength.' But the life of spirit does not 'shrink from death'; indeed, it 'endures it and maintains itself in it'. Spirit attains its truth only when, 'in utter dismemberment, it finds itself'. Nevertheless, spirit is 'this power, not as something positive which closes its eyes to the negative, as when we say of something that it is nothing or is false, and then, having done with it, turn away and pass on to something else; on the contrary, Spirit is this power only by looking the negative in the face and tarrying with it.' This 'tarrying with the negative is the magical power that converts it into being'; it is 'the Subject'.[29]

---

[28] *Hegel's Phenomenology of Spirit*, p. 18.
[29] Ibid., p. 19.

Let us examine the real significance of Hegel's exaltation of the intellect, of the finite (or dead), as against the *intuition* of Schelling.

Why, Hegel asks in the *Science of Logic*, has the intellect been held in such small esteem compared to reason? And he answers: because of the 'fixity' it imparts to determinatenesses and consequently to finite determinations. This fixity consists in the form of their 'abstract universality'. But the intellect, while it thus determines the universal, imparts 'fixed persistence' through the form of universality to that which has 'in itself and for itself' no stability in determinateness; it gives determinateness the 'form of imperishability' that is lacking in the 'qualitative' determinatenesses, that is, in the mere realm of experience. Now, while it is true that eternity belongs to the nature of the 'pure concept', its abstract determinations are 'eternal essentialities only in respect of their form; but their content is at variance with this form'. This is so because the content is not 'determinateness itself as universal'; in other words, 'it is not the totality of the Concept's difference, or is not itself the whole form'. The form of the intellect is itself the 'imperfect form, namely *abstract* universality'. But it is also true that the fixity of the determinateness the intellect seems to establish, the form of the imperishable, 'is that of self-relating universality', which 'belongs properly to the Concept'. Consequently, the 'dissolution of the finite' is 'expressed, and infinitely close at hand', in this universality. The latter 'directly refutes [*arguiert*] the determinateness of the finite and expresses its incongruity with the universality. Or rather we can say that the adequacy of the finite is already to hand; the abstract determinate is posited as one with the universality; and for that very reason is posited as not for itself—for then it would be only a determinate—but only as unity of itself and the universal, that is, as Concept.'

Indeed, the universality that the determinations of the mere realm of experience acquire in the intellect gives them the form of 'reflection-into-self by which they are freed from the relation to other' which they otherwise have as 'limited' and from which arises the necessity of their qualitative transition and passing away. They thus become 'imperishable'. It is therefore 'the infinite force' of the intellect to split 'the concrete into abstract determinatenesses' and to plumb 'the depth of the difference', namely the 'essential' difference, 'opposition'. At the same time, this 'is the power that effects the transition' of the determinatenesses. Is it not the intellect that, through the *rigidity* of being that its (abstract) universality imparts to merely empirical determinations, *simplifies* them and thereby *enlivens* and *sharpens* them such that they dissolve into the *unity of opposites*?

Conclusion: 'The usual practice of separating intellect and reason is, from every point of view, to be rejected.' If the (abstract) Concept is regarded as lacking in reason, 'this should be interpreted rather as an incapacity of reason to recognize itself in the Concept'. The determinate and abstract Concept is *'an essential moment of reason'*. It is the 'form spiritually impregnated in which the finite, through the universality in which it relates itself to itself . . . posits itself as dialectical and thereby is the beginning of the manifestation of reason'.[30]

The intellect is therefore a 'becoming' and 'as this becoming, it is *reason*ableness'.[31]

The first striking feature of this argumentation *in favour of* the intellect—i.e. of intelligible *multiplicity*—is that Hegel sees in the fixity of intellectual determinateness only the form of *imperishability*, the immobility characteristic of the pure eternal, which is in general the *negation* of multiplicity. These eternal essentialities (eternal because of the form) he calls 'determinatenesses'. He believes this can be justified through his concept of the universality of determinatenesses; this universality is said to consist in the capacity to impart to the determinatenesses the form of reflection-into-self, or circular reflection, since it is the universality of the *essential* difference, or opposition—in other words, the universality characteristic of circulating totality in its organic parts. This totality divides from itself into itself, into its components: 'The universal as the Concept is itself and its opposite, and this again is the universal itself as its posited determinateness; . . . Thus it is the totality and the principle of its diversity, which is determined wholly and solely by the universal itself.'[32]

In other words, the intellectual *division* of the concrete into fixed or abstract determinations is merely a *totalization* (*'totalisieren'*), a quite significant term in Hegel's first system (1802), which has its pendant in the *Science of Logic*: 'differentiation is one with universality'. Hence *discernment* is *totalization* in the sense that it reduces

---

[30] *Hegel's Science of Logic*, pp. 610-612.
[31] *Hegel's Phenomenology of Spirit*, p. 34.
[32] *Hegel's Science of Logic*, p. 606.

a (presumed) intelligible multiplicity to its unitary 'source' and thus to its *precedent*, which is the Concept, in the sense of pure self-consciousness. In this way the determinate or abstract Concept is considered not only the beginning of the manifestation of reason itself, but also its *result*. It is, in short, a shadow, a pretext.

The 'concrete'—oneness—thus *exists prior to* its 'division'. It does so precisely *because* it is the sole criterion for division, for indeed division must be effected strictly in accordance with 'comprehension' of the 'depth' of differentiation, which is only the *immediate*, essential, substantial differentiation of 'opposites'.[33] It is thereby the *immediate* systematization of essentialities or intelligibles, which assumes these, i.e. the *components*, as *total* intelligibility, which means intelligible *totality*. The self-division or self-multiplication of oneness is therefore only *apparent*.

For Hegel, let us repeat, unity *exists before* division, inasmuch as it is the only possible criterion of division; or, to put it another way, inasmuch as it is self-division (and therefore self-consciousness). It is here, in this wholly apparent multiplication of unity, that we grasp the most serious consequence of the deformation of Kant's *transcendental apperception* (and the corresponding category-function) effected by Hegel's theory of the absolute as *subject*.

The belief that Hegel maintained that the intellect really 'holds fast' that which is dead is merely a tenacious illusion of orthodox exegetes. The latest Italian translator of the *Phenomenology*, for example, asserts that for Hegel the intellect holds fast 'the components removed from the organic unity' and 'thus positively prepares' that content which the power of negativity supposedly sweeps away, leading it to a higher unification (whence the positivizing intellect and the power of the negative are deemed the 'double face of the complete dialectical rhythm').

Once again, what Hegel has merely assumed, but not proved, is precisely the necessity of the 'positivizing' intellect. The original reason for this lack of success lies, as we know, in his negative conception of the senses. *It is this pre-critical concept of aesthetics—as*

---

[33] As we shall see, these formulations of Hegel's conception of the 'division' or distinguishing of the concept are strikingly similar to a passage of Plato's dialogue *The Statesman* (one of the many concerning the criterion of 'diairesis' or the 'division of genera'). We shall find, however, that Plato's problematic is far more suggestive, for he begins with the need to dialecticize the 'higher genera', which 'pervade' the lower, by making them *divisers* of the lower, 'participating' genera. He therefore dialecticizes *by classifying*.

universality as such, or the primordial unity of opposites—that renders Hegel's anti-Schelling stance futile, however interesting it may be. This negative conception of the senses confines Hegel within the narrow limits of romanticism. (And it is surely significant that Schelling-like tones pervade the philosophy of art of the Hegelian Giovanni Gentile, as I have noted elsewhere[34]).

A corollary that confirms this theory of the intellect in a particularly interesting fashion may be found in Hegel's purely negative critique of judgements as 'dualistic' propositions, since they contain a duality of subject and predicate.[35]

In the judgement 'the real is the universal', Hegel writes, 'the real', which is the subject, passes away in its predicate. The latter, the 'universal', is not meant to have only the significance of a predicate, that is, of *accident*. Indeed, 'universal' is intended to express 'the essential nature of the real'. In general, then, the subject 'cannot have *other* predicates or accidents', and its content, the predicate, is 'not a universal that can be detached from the subject and adapted to several indifferently'. It is no longer merely the predicate of the subject, but is 'the very substance, the inmost reality, and the very principle of what is being considered'. The predicate becomes the concept of the subject, which 'exhausts the nature of the subject' and thus annuls it as an isolated, *fixed* element, the so-called *basis* of the judgement. The discursive 'form of the proposition'—that is, the dualistic connection of subject and predicate in which the subject, the particular, is found in such an external relation to the predicate, the universal, that it perpetually transcends it, and vice versa (precisely because the subject can always have an infinite number of other 'possible' predicates or accidents, while the predicate is the free universal that can be attached to other subjects)—is thus replaced by the 'unity of the concept', namely the speculative or identical proposition (the *form* 'that is itself the intrinsic becoming of the concrete *content*'). This alone is *judgement* and as such has the value of *truth*.[36] This is not the case for the (dualistic) proposition,

---

34 'The force [of feeling] of which there is talk', says Gentile, 'is infinite: and it therefore fights with equal vigour in the plant and in my heart; it is the natural force of *genius*.' (*Filosofia dell'arte*, Milan, 1931, p. 272.)

35 *Hegel's Phenomenology of Spirit*, pp. 38-39.

36 It should be noted that because of this 'unity of the concept', or *form that is itself the intrinsic becoming of the concrete content*, the concept (predicate) of the subject, since it is its substance, its essence, exhausts the nature of the subject and thus annuls it as subject (or particular) and takes its place. Here we have a striking instance of

such as, for example, 'historical' propositions or those concerning 'experience' in general.

'Even an immediate intuition', writes Hegel, 'is held to have genuine value only when it is cognized as a fact along with its reasons.'[37] For example, the proposition 'a carriage is passing' would become a judgement only if it was in doubt whether the passing object was a carriage—'in short, only if it were designed to specify a conception which was still short of appropriate specification'.[38] Similarly, the statement that 'Aristotle died at the age of 73, in the fourth year of the 115th Olympiad' would 'partake of the nature of a judgement only if doubt had been thrown on one of the circumstances, the date of the death or the age of that philosopher, and the given figures had been asserted on the strength of some reason or other. In that case, these figures would be taken as something universal, as time that still subsists apart from this particular content of the death of Aristotle'.[39]

Hegel likens this 'conflict' between the dualistic 'form of a proposition' and the 'unity of the *concept*' (which 'destroys' that form) to the relationship of metre and accent in the case of rhythm, where the latter 'results from the floating centre and the unification of the two'. 'So, too, in the philosophical proposition', he continues, 'the identification of Subject and Predicate is not meant to destroy the difference between them, which the form of the proposition expressed; their unity, rather, is meant to emerge as a harmony. The form of the proposition is the appearance of the determinate sense or the accent that distinguishes its fulfilment; but that the predicate expresses the Substance, and that the Subject itself falls into the universal, this is the *unity* in which the accent dies away'.[40]

Contrary to Hegel's intention, however, this 'dying away' of the 'accent' (which is the 'distinction of the content') is actually a *negation* wholly without conservation, as is demonstrated by the above-mentioned theory, which clearly separates the *judgement*

theological 'interpolation', which consists in the substantification or hypostatization of the idea, transforming it into the subject of the judgement (with all the related consequences). As we shall see, it was Marx who first indicted the 'mystified' dialectic of Hegel for this theological interpolation. Below we shall consider the Platonic precedent.

[37] *Hegel's Phenomenology of Spirit*, p. 24.
[38] *Hegel's Logic*, §167.
[39] *Hegel's Science of Logic*, p. 626.
[40] *Phenomenology*, p. 38.

from the *proposition*, and ascribes the value of *truth* to the former alone. (This basic theory is presented again in Croce's Hegelian theory of the pseudo- judgement).

Once *analysis*, or intellectual division, is conceived as *totalization*, it is natural that the fundamental dianoetic operation which is the judgement as a dualistic nexus should itself be identified—and thus conjured away—in the *unity* of the concept. And the requisite that the subject of a judgement must have no *other* predicates, i.e. no *accident*, and that the predicate be not a mere predicate but the very *substance* that *exhausts* the subject and thereby annuls and replaces it (hypostasis!), is quite characteristic of Hegel's mentality, mystico-rationalist as it is. Once the subject is annulled as a distinct element, the very basis of the judgement is also annulled, and with it the judgement itself. In its stead remains none other than that form-content or pure conceptual unity which, as exhaustive substance or hypostasis, is *exhaustive* and self-evident *truth*: theological-mystical truth.[41]

This is a consequence of Hegel's assertion, against Kantian criticism, that *to think* is not merely *to make judgements*, but *to demonstrate*—or better, *to mediate* completely. In sum, Hegel argues, to think is to dissolve the 'judgement' into a *syllogism* in which the 'is' of the copula is 'already posited as the determinate and pregnant unity of subject and predicate', or as 'their concept'.[42] To label such a 'dialectical' unity a syllogism—to believe that the significance of the Aristotelian syllogism has been 'conserved' and 'acquires its real truth' within it—is disconcerting to say the least, especially when one recalls that it is a fundamental law of the syllogism to *exclude* any *duplicatio medii*, which invalidates the syllogism by rendering the middle term indeterminate, a result of the influence on this middle term of the indeterminateness peculiar to *negative* quality (and to particular quantity). Our intention in emphasizing this point is to call attention not only to the purely formalistic values of the syllogism, but also to the deeper Aristotelian foundations of the *dianoetic* in general, to which Hegel, unlike the critical Kant, was and remained substantially blind.

[41] Note that this theological-mystical truth corresponds to the 'immobile unity' mentioned above. Later we shall consider the related *method* of the theological interpolation, or allegorization, of the multiple, as well as its ultimate result. For the moment, we will confine our attention to the detailed documentation of Hegel's texts, in preparation for an examination of Marx's critique of this method.

[42] *Science of Logic*, pp. 629-630, 657 ff.

But if Hegel saw intellectual *analysis* as a process of *totalization*, and the *duality* of judgements as pure conceptual *unity* (= syllogism), then it is natural that he would convert the *logical principle of distinction*, the fundamental dianoetic law of identity and non-contradiction, into the *principle of unity*, the pure-rational law of contradiction (opposition).

Hegel immediately sets the tone of his treatment of logical principles with the opening admonition that if it is admitted that the law of identity 'contains only *formal truth*', a truth 'which is abstract and incomplete', then this 'correct judgement' immediately implies: a) that 'truth is complete only in the unity of identity with difference, and hence consists only in this unity', and b) that 'when asserting that this identity is imperfect, the perfection one has vaguely in mind is this totality, measured against which the identity is imperfect'.[43] In this spirit, bearing in mind the totality-truth with respect to which the law of identity (as the 'determination' of identity) is only imperfect truth (and it is *in this sense* that this principle is purely formal), Hegel proceeds to examine the foundations of this law, which he regards, of course, in its traditional, scholastic, Leibnizian version as the principle of analytic reason, of classical metaphysics. This is the source of every one of Hegel's errors, as quickly becomes apparent in his very effort to adopt the traditional standpoint of his adversaries, like Leibniz and others, who support this principle of the dianoetic. He proceeds to examine 'the experiment with the pure law of identity' which 'is made only too often'. In other words, he examines the concrete application of this principle as understood by his adversaries. Let us see.

'If, for example', Hegel writes, 'to the question "What is a plant?" the answer is given "A plant is—a plant", the truth of such a statement is at once admitted by the entire company upon whom it is tested, and at the same time it is equally unanimously declared that this statement says *nothing* . . . .nothing will be held to be more boring and tedious than conversation which merely reiterates the same thing, or than such talk which is yet supposed to be truth. Looking more closely at this tedious effect produced by such truth, we see that the beginning, "The plant is—", sets out to say *something*, to bring forward a further determination. But since only the

43 Ibid., p. 414.

same thing is repeated, the opposite has happened, *nothing* has emerged. Such identical talk therefore *contradicts itself*. Identity, instead of being in its own self truth and absolute truth, is consequently the very opposite; instead of being the unmoved simple, it is the passage beyond itself into the dissolution of itself.

'In the *form of the proposition*, therefore, in which identity is expressed, there lies *more* than simple, abstract identity; in it there lies this pure movement of reflection in which the other appears only as illusory being, as an immediate vanishing.... "A is—A"; ... an A, or a plant, or some other kind of substrate, too, is added which, as a useless content, is of significance; but it constitutes the difference which seems to be accidentally associated with it.'[44]

The futility of Hegel's effort to understand the opposing point of view in this argumentation is exceedingly characteristic. It is natural that the statement 'a plant is a plant' seems a vapid tautology to Hegel, because to him 'the same thing' means *only* dwelling on a pure, isolated *determination* or category, that abstraction known as the *category of identity*, which, if it is to cease to be 'formal' and therewith 'imperfect' truth, requires its dialectical complement, namely difference, but does not yet attain it as such. On the basis of his concept of the concept (self-consciousness as self-dividing oneness and therefore self-consciousness), Hegel thinks that the 'plant', the empirical, *cannot be anything but* a 'useless content', of 'no importance' in the case at hand.

Two consequences follow. First, Hegel disparages *category-function*, thereby repudiating the deeper spirit of criticism (understanding criticism, of course, beyond Kantian and post-Kantian gnoseological schemata). Second, he likewise disparages the *concrete formal* (not *formalistic* or 'formal' in the Hegelian sense) truth of the *dianoetic* principle of identity. In so rejecting it—on the basis of the equation: formal = incomplete = abstract)—he lumps together as abstract formalists both the metaphysical Aristotle and the Kant focusing specifically on the '*transcendental* validity' of this dianoetic principle.

Nevertheless, as far as Kant is concerned, this does not prevent Hegel and the Hegelians from believing that even here they are the legatees of the spirit of criticism—quite the contrary! 'The concrete', writes Hegel, 'and the application [of the principle of identity] are

[44] Ibid., pp. 415-416.

precisely the connection of the simple *identical* to *a manifold* that is *different* from it. Expressed as a proposition, the concrete would at first be a synthetic proposition. From the concrete itself or its synthetic proposition, abstraction could indeed extract by analysis the proposition of identity; but then, in fact, it would not have left *experience* as it is, but *altered* it; for the fact is that *experience* contains identity in unity with difference and is the *immediate refutation* of the assertion that abstract identity as such is something true'.[45] In his *Logica e metafisica* (Bari, 1911, p. 292) the faithful Spaventa notes: 'Just as identity is empty without *difference*, so difference has no significance without identity (which parallels the maxim of Kant: without intuition the concept is empty; without the concept intuition is blind).' As if the pure categorial 'determination' of 'difference' in its dialectical interplay with that of 'identity' could replace, lending them both truth, both Kant's 'intuition' and 'manifold' and the related, *critical* problem of the synthesis as synthesis of 'heterogeneities'!

Similarly, as regards Aristotle, Hegel never dreamt of asserting that 'this man' could simultaneously not be a 'man' ('that would be arrant nonsense', Bullinger protested). And it is true that for Hegel the individual itself is not the contradiction; the contradiction is rather 'in him', i.e. 'in his essence', since man is, in his essence, a contradictory union of soul and body, spirit and nature (Bullinger again). But it is also true that the individual 'sustains the contradiction of being and not-being, etc. until, in the end, his immediate sensible existence *collapses*, diverted into the flux of becoming', the same faithful exegete, Bullinger, concludes.[46]

The result, then, is to disregard just what makes the individual individual or concrete. And it is precisely through his denial of the immediate, sensible, or aesthetic in general that Hegel annuls not only the individual (in the immediate sensible existence or particular accidental subjectivity that makes it specifically individual), but also the principle of non-contradiction and related subjective or extrinsic reflection. From the standpoint of gnoseology and logic, the result is indeed a criticism that dissolves 'representative thought', or rather '*subjective* reflection', with its 'unresolved' contradiction, its

---

[45] Ibid., pp. 414-415.
[46] A. Bullinger, *Hegels Lehre vom Widerspruch: Missverständnisse gegenüber verteidigt*, Dillingen, 1884.

'external difference' (of likeness or unlikeness). Thus it is that Hegel is able to maintain, against the principle of indiscernables, that 'the difference, while falling asunder, is at the same time one and the same relation' and that it 'has therefore passed over into opposition',[47] for he has remained blind to Aristotle's principle that entelechy, or actuality, *separates* contraries. This principle becomes distorted if one believes, as Hegel did, that it refers to: 'the principle of individualization, not in the sense of a casual and merely particular subjectivity, but in that of pure subjectivity'.[48] In fact, this principle, linked as it is to the concept that the individual ('first substance' or the individuated species that is 'Socrates') 'has no contrary', provides the ontological foundation of the logical principle that 'a man' or 'a warship' can have meaning only if posited *outside* the relation of *contradiction*—which means, in a certain sense, as something *indiscriminable*.

This blindness of Hegel's to Aristotle at his most profound renders the Hegelian critique of the fundamental dianoetic principle (which, moreover, he assumes in its scholastic-rationalist version) suspect from the very outset. On this basis, we can advance, against Hegel, two hypotheses: first, that 'difference'—the *category* in general—may not be such because, as he claims, it is 'difference in its own self' or 'reflected into itself', but rather because it is 'a distinction through something external', which proposition Hegel contests; and second, that something external must coincide substantially with 'extrinsic' (because 'subjective') reflection (and related non-contradiction), which Hegel condemns. With these hypotheses we could strive to satisfy both: a) Kant's requisite expressed in the correlative concepts of category-function and heterogeneity—in the *synthesis*—of intuition and concept; and b) Aristotle's requisite (which we shall consider later) of indiscriminability or intuitivity and the foundation of the actual non-contradictory character of thought.

It is only in the light of this twofold requisite that one can accurately comprehend the frequently noted observation that when all is said and done, even Hegel was compelled, despite himself, to apply and accept the principle of identity and non-contradiction (and not

[47] *Science of Logic*, p. 423.
[48] *Hegel's Lectures on the History of Philosophy*, translated by E.S. Haldane and Francis H. Simson, London, 1955, volume II, p. 140.

in its *dialectical* reduction) in both daily experience *and* speculative argumentation.

But Hegel maintains that 'speculative thinking consists solely in the fact that thought holds fast [*festhält*] contradiction, and, in it, its own self, but does not allow itself to be dominated by it as in ordinary thinking, where its determinations are resolved by contradiction only into other determinations or into nothing.'[49]

In other words, Hegel bases himself on his critique of 'ordinary' or empirical thinking. Ordinary thinking, he says, 'everywhere has contradiction for its content' but 'it does not become aware of it, but remains an external reflection, which passes from likeness to unlikeness'. These two determinations are kept 'against one another', counterposed to each other, since ordinary thinking 'has in mind *only them* but not their *transition*, which is the essential point and which contains the contradiction'.[50] (On the other hand, a 'sharpened' idea consists in the 'understanding' and 'enunciation' of the contradiction.)

Now then, if we compare the first passage with another,[51] in which Hegel says that 'common experience itself' declares that 'at least there is a host of contradictory things, contradictory arrangements, whose contradiction exists not merely in an external reflection', then it becomes evident that the appeal to the testimony of ordinary experience weakens rather than strengthens Hegel's speculative criticism of 'ordinary' or empirical thought, since the 'contradictory things' recognized by ordinary experience constitute exactly a deficiency of truth and reality resulting from possible violation of the principle of non-contradiction. The positive value of this principle thereby emerges, and it does not appear that these 'contradictions' can be immediately resolved, to say the least, through 'transition' and *dialectical* 'contradiction'. Hegel's appeal to ordinary experience thus demonstrates the opposite of what he sought to prove. And ordinary thought, along with its requisites (its 'fondness for *things*') is ultimately a residue that the Hegelian speculative critique has been unable to absorb into its own internal laws; the critique is thereby undermined. Here as elsewhere—indeed, as always—the violence done to things by Hegel's *delirium logicum* is manifest.

[49] *Science of Logic*, pp. 440-441.
[50] Ibid., p. 441.
[51] Ibid., p. 440.

It is in this light that we must examine Hegel's treatment of the traditional logical principles. As we shall see, he distorts these by *dialecticizing* their content, by abstractly *totalizing* their logical meaning, and by reducing them all to the principle of 'absolute contradiction', the unity of opposites.

Hegel's exposition of the principle of identity and non-contradiction runs as follows: 'The other expression of the law of identity: *A cannot at the same time be A and not-A*, has a negative form; it is called the *law of contradiction*. Usually, no justification is given of how the form of *negation*, by which this law is distinguished from its predecessor, comes to identity. But this form is implied by the fact that identity, as the pure movement of reflection, is simple negativity which contains in more developed form the second expression of the law just quoted. *A* is enunciated, and a *not-A*, the pure other of *A*, but it only shows itself in order to vanish. In this proposition, therefore, identity is expressed—as negation of the negation. *A* and *not-A* are distinguished, and these distinct terms are related to one and the same *A*. Identity, therefore, is here represented as this *distinguishedness in one relation* or as the *simple difference in the terms themselves*.

'From this it is evident that the law of identity itself, and still more the law of [non-] contradiction, is not merely of *analytic*, but of *synthetic* nature.[52] For the latter contains in its expression not merely

[52] It may be enlightening to compare this with the substantially identical conception of the logical principle of a modern neo-Platonist (and pan-theist), Semën Frank, a follower of Nicholas of Cusa: 'The law of determination, through which everything that is thought assumes the character of determined content, isolated and identical to itself, is based on the law of negation and is realized through the function of negation. *A*, as determined and limited content, is possible only through its relation to *not-A*; the meaning of what we call determination lies in differentiation, in the affirmation of its being through a relation of difference: *A is* what is opposite to *not-A*. *A* appears only in its delimitation from *not-A* and consists in this delimitation. . . . The real source and condition for the existence of the isolated content is thus neither *A* nor *not-A* but their unity . . . this "primordial unity" . . . the sphere of unity, or coincidence of opposites . . .' (*La connaissance et l'être* [translated from the Russian original: *Predmet znaniya*, Petrograd, 1915], Paris, 1937, pp. 164-165.) Finally, the mystical (neo-Platonic) orientation of Hegel's approach to the logical principle may be demonstrated in a particularly convincing and conclusive manner by comparing the passages of Hegel cited above to the following passage of *De beryllo* (chapter XXV), by Nicholas of Cusa himself: 'From the first principle [the principle of identity] Aristotle in fact deduced that it is impossible for contraries to coexist. Our beryl rather sharpens our vision so as to show us the coincidence of opposites in a synthetic principle that antedates all duality, which is to say, that antedates the distinction of opposites . . . . Just as . . . the infinitely little acute angle and the infinitely little obtuse angle coincide

empty, simple equality-with-self, and not merely the other of this *in general*, but, what is more, *absolute inequality*, or *contradiction per se*. But as has been shown, the law of identity itself contains the movement of reflection, identity as a vanishing of otherness.

'What emerges from this consideration is, therefore, first that the law of identity or of [non-] contradiction, which purports to express merely abstract identity in contrast to difference as a truth, is not a law of thought, but rather the opposite of it; secondly, that these laws contain *more* than is *meant* by them, to wit, this opposite, absolute difference itself.'[53]

As for the principle of the excluded middle, it is: 'An important proposition, which has its necessity in the fact that identity passes over into difference, and this into opposition. Only it is usually not understood in this sense, but usually means nothing more than that, of all predicates, either this particular predicate or its not-being belongs to a thing. The opposite means here merely the lack [of a predicate], or rather *indeterminateness* [but Aristotelian indeterminateness— G.d.V.]; and the proposition is so trivial that it is not worth the trouble of saying it. . . . It [this principle] implies that there *is* nothing

---

in the simplicity of the right angle, which corresponds to their common lower limit, where the duality of acute and obtuse does not yet exist, the same is true for the synthetic principle, where the infinitely lower limits of contrary realities coincide. Now, if Aristotle had interpreted the principle he called privation so as to assimilate it to the principle that embodies the coincidence of opposites, calling it privation because it is somehow deprived of contrariety, then his doctrine would have been correct. But he was afraid to concede that contraries could inhere together in the same reality, and he thus barred the way to true knowledge of the synthetic principle. He clearly saw the necessity for a third principle [metaphysical, beyond form and matter] and noted that this principle was a privation, but he made it a privation without prior positing . . . .That is why no philosopher has attained the Spirit, the synthetic principle, and, according to our perfect theology, the third person of the trinity.' (Cf. *Oeuvres choisies de Nicolas de Cuse*, translated by Maurice de Gandillac, Paris, 1942, pp. 482-483.) De Gandillac, the best recent historian of Nicholas of Cusa, made an acute observation about this point (interesting in the light of our assertion), when he said (ibid., p. 483n): 'When Nicolas of Cusa speaks of a third principle that *precedes* the two others, he extends a hand to neo-Platonism, to the tradition of the One that contains the Many. But when he somehow engenders this third principle through the movement of a right angle that passes to the common limit of acute and obtuse, he suggests precisely a synthetic form of reasoning in which the third term supposes the *prior positing* of the two others, of which it is at once the *privation* and the *trans-cendence [dépassement]*, that is, a sort of *Aufhebung*' (De Gandillac's emphasis). See also, my *Eckhart o della filosofia mistica*, Rome, 1952, second part.

[53] *Science of Logic*, p. 416.

that is *neither A nor not-A*, that there is not a third that is indifferent to the opposition. But in fact the third that is indifferent to the opposition *is given* in the law itself, namely *A* itself is present in it. This *A* is neither $+A$ nor $-A$, and is equally well $+A$ as $-A$. The something that was supposed to be either *A* or not-*A* is therefore related both to $+A$ and not-*A*; and again, in being related to *A*, it is supposed *not* to be related to not-*A*, nor to *A* if it is related to not-*A*. The something itself, therefore, is the third which was supposed to be excluded. Since the opposite determinations in the something are just as much posited as sublated in this positing, the third which here has the form of a dead something, when taken more profoundly, is the unity of reflection into which the opposition withdraws as into ground.'[54]

Since Hegel has thus abstractly *totalized* the content of Aristotle's anti-Parmenidean principle of non-contradiction and thereby transformed it into his own principle of *absolute contradiction*, it is quite futile to attempt, as many often do, to gauge to what extent Hegel strayed from the principle of non-contradiction and to what extent he remained faithful to it.

Nevertheless, Hegel himself did permit a conciliatory interpretation of his principle when, for example, after repeating that 'it is ridiculous to say that contradiction is unthinkable', he admitted the 'correctness' of such an assertion in the sense that 'contradiction is not the end of the matter, but cancels itself'.[55] On the basis of such formulations, the mistaken conviction has arisen that 'for Hegel, as for everyone, an unresolved contradiction is an indication of error', as McTaggart, for example, wrote in *Studies in the Hegelian Dialectic* (p. 19). As if the Aristotelian solution of contradiction through the *elimination* of one of the terms differed only quantitatively from Hegel's solution, as is maintained by another critic, Etienne-Emile Marie Boutroux, who writes: 'the Hegelian metaphysic, *more radically dynamic*, admits that the two terms, contradictories becoming simple contraries, can both evolve and become reconciled'.[56] As if the enormous historical and theoretical

---

[54] Ibid., pp. 438-439. In *Hegel, sein Wollen und sein Werke* (p. 241), Theodor Häring observes: 'thus, the only really important meaning of the principle of the excluded middle recognized by Hegel is that everything a positive (A) and a negative moment (not-A) have represents a dialectical unity.'

[55] *Hegel's Logic*, Zusatz 2 to §119.

[56] See essay in Pierre-Eugène Marcellin Berthelot, *Evolutionisme et platonisme*, Paris, 1908, pp. 201-202.

problem of the *twofold solution* of contradiction did not exist!

That Boutroux and the other critics have failed to notice this problem is indicated by Boutroux's own comment on Hegel's solution: 'the two contradictory, or rather contrary, terms are at once *eliminated* (which is authorized by classical logic), conserved (in another form), and transcended.'[57] Here it is clear that Boutroux has failed to understand that Aristotelian logic authorizes an *elimination* of the contradictory terms which—since it is based on exclusion of the contradictory, the *abolition* of the *relation* of negativity—implies an indiscrimination or intuition (noeticness). On the other hand, the elimination of the terms authorized by Hegelian logic—based on *abolition* of any *isolation* of the terms, i.e. of that which prevents the constitution of the terms as such in their dialectical fullness as terms—involves pure relationality alone, the *essential* relation of opposites. This is why there is a radical difference between the two logics, exactly on how to eliminate contradiction.

On the other hand, Pierre-Eugène Marcellin Berthelot has intelligently recognized that 'undoubtedly the Hegelian dialectic rests on the *use* of the principle of contradiction; but for Hegel contradiction exists not between various forms of being—matter and spirit, individual and society, art and philosophy—but between *two counterposed theses*: on the one hand the thesis that any one of the essential forms of being could be either affirmed, i.e. posited as total and definitive reality, or denied, i.e. totally eliminated in the name of another of the forms of being; on the other hand, the thesis that each of these essential forms of being must be posited in and through its relation to the totality of the others.' He has further recognized that 'since . . . the first of these two theses accords with the logic of Aristotle, and since Hegel's system . . . constitutes a *refutation* of this thesis *through showing it to be absurd*, it necessarily follows that Hegel, although he rejected the special postulates of classical logic, believed he could continue to *use* the principle of contradiction in a certain sense.'[58] To recognize all this, however, is to admit the existence of a genuine and complex problem, which is barely touched on if one concludes, as the Hegelian Berthelot does, that what Hegel produced was an 'extended formal logic' ('which is the *condition* of his endeavour').

[57] Ibid., p. 202.
[58] Ibid., pp. 243-245.

Here, then, is the problem bequeathed us by Hegel's treatment of logical principles: How could he have *used* the principle of non-contradiction, precisely in the consistent formulation of his own philosophy, if his radical *negative critique* of this principle contained the slightest particle of truth? In other words, how can we reconcile the fact that 'abhorrence' of contradiction, contrary to Hegel's contention, is characteristic not merely of 'ordinary' thought, but also of 'speculative' thought, with his assertion that 'recognition of the positive side' of contradiction, i.e. attainment of 'consciousness of contradiction', is ultimately the very instance of unity or reason, satisfied only by 'speculative' thought?

It is clear, then, that the problem of unity, i.e. of reason, can be posed today only as the problematic of just this reconciliation. It can be formulated as follows. What is the meaning, if any, of the instance of consciousness of contradiction? Later, when we consider the tauto-heterological principle, the foundation of Plato's diairesis and the original nucleus of Hegel's dialectic, we shall discover that this problem has yet to be solved. Indeed, it amounts to the present-day problem of the principle of logic itself, which certainly cannot be illuminated by any 'formal' (formalistic) logic, however 'extended' or developed. But more of this in its proper place. For the moment, we shall examine more closely Hegel's theory of reason, his theory of the 'dialectic', to which we have had occasion to refer only indirectly so far.

3

If we are really to penetrate Hegel's theory of reason and grasp the full import of his negative conception of the intellect, then we must examine more closely his definition of reason as *consciousness or thought of contradiction*.

This formula tells us that reason, as consciousness of contradiction, is essential, or pure, self-consciousness, *a subject*. 'The second negative', Hegel writes, 'the negative of the negative, at which we have arrived, is this sublating of the contradiction, but just as little as the contradiction is it an *act of external reflection*, but rather the *innermost, most objective moment* of life and spirit, through which a *subject*, a *person*, a *free being* exists.'[59] Hegel identifies this

[59] *Science of Logic*, pp. 835-836.

'subjectivity' as 'the dialectical soul that everything true possesses and through which alone it is true; for on this subjectivity alone rests the sublating of the opposition between Concept and reality, and the unity that is truth'.[60] Exactly what does Hegel mean by this subjectivity? How does it differ from Kant's notions of 'subjectivity' and 'self-consciousness'? How well does the reduction of consciousness of contradiction (or reason) to this subjectivity stand up to criticism? We may begin to answer these questions by considering the process by which Hegel derives this theory of reason from scepticism about ordinary consciousness, or common sense, for this scepticism culminates in his concept of the aesthetic *Aufhebung*: his original, dialectical conception of sensation or feeling and therewith of the intellect.

Let us place the problem in its historical context. It seems clear that the question of reason must have taken shape in Hegel's mind when he related Kant's 'I think', which Hegel considered a new version of Descartes's *cogito*, to the Transcendental Dialectic—the doctrine of antinomies—more than to the Analytic. This *cogito*, Hegel held, drew its real strength from the dialectical scepticism of Plato's *Parmenides* and, more generally, from ancient scepticism about the intellect and common sense (as well as, of course, from Christian spiritual meditation, from John to Eckhart to Nicholas of Cusa).[61] He therefore inevitably saw the dialectic as the supreme problem of reason. In other words, for Hegel the supreme problem of reason was, in substance, the problem of the relationship between philosophy and scepticism.

One of Hegel's earliest philosophical essays, significantly entitled *Verhältniss des Skeptizismus zur Philosophie* (The Relation of Scepticism to Philosophy), which was written in 1802, is characterized most prominently by an intense defence of ancient against modern scepticism, closely linked to an equally intense glorification of Plato's *Parmenides* as an introduction to the dialectic of the 'higher genera' of *The Sophist*. In sum, there is an organic connection between scepticism about common sense and the dogmatism of reason.

In this essay, directed against Gottlob Ernst Schulze, a wholesale

---

[60] Ibid.
[61] For the best and most refined documentation of Hegel's Christianism, see *La malheur de la conscience dans la philosophie de Hegel*, by Jean Wahl, who sympathizes with Hegel. See also my *Hegel romantico e mistico*.

and positivist Kantian who never went beyond the 'facts of consciousness', positing their ultimate causes in an unknowable 'thing-in-itself', Hegel's primary objective was to substantiate the arguments of the ancient sceptics—the original, most ancient ten tropes or modes, as well as the later seven—as part of his polemic against '*modern* scepticism', which he considered the 'dogmatism of the common human intellect'. Ancient scepticism, Hegel argued, did not threaten philosophy, but was directed 'in a not particularly philosophical but rather popular manner, against common sense or the common consciousness which clings to the given, the fact, the finite (whether this be called appearance or intellectual concept) and sticks to this as something certain, secure, and eternal'. This sort of scepticism, he continued, shows that such certainties are unreliable, for 'they also invoke appearances and finitudes, and from their difference and the equal rights of all of them to prevail—from the antinomy thus recognizable even in the finite—such scepticism recognizes the untruth of the finite'. It may 'therefore be considered the first step on the road to philosophy, since the beginning of philosophy must be the advance above the truth that is offered by common consciousness, and the intimation of a higher truth'.

Even the final modes of this scepticism, as employed by Sextus Empiricus, are directed against reason and philosophy only in appearance, since, according to Hegel, by rendering the rational finite, and therefore antinomic, they covered it with the 'scab' of the dogmatism of limitation only in order to be able 'to pick it'. The modern scepticism of a Schulze, with its initial certainty of the facts of consciousness, therefore stands in contrast to the ancient, which, through its complete and total suspension of judgement with regard to certainty, truth, and being, does not presume to know any 'thing' or 'finitude' and has no need to slip under philosophy's feet, in order to 'trip it up', either the 'certain thing' or the thing-in-itself, the 'thing hidden behind this'.[62]

But there is more. Hegel advances three further objections to Schulze's position, of different character but nonetheless significant and relevant for our critique. Let us consider them one by one. First, to the 'subjectivist' contention of the modern sceptic, who points to

---

[62] *Werke*, volume XVI, pp. 97-106; cf. Hermann Glockner, *Hegel*, Stuttgart, 1940, volume II, p. 271, who makes the mistake of assuming that this latter remark of Hegel's refers to ancient scepticism.

the differences and contradictions among the many talented philosophers who have sought truth down through the ages, Hegel squarely counterposes this typically rationalist maxim of Leibniz: 'most sects are right in a good part of what they affirm, but not so much in what they deny'. He then concludes that, if we leave aside the contrast between 'philosophy' and 'non-philosophy', the contrast between different philosophical 'systems' is nonetheless always marked by 'agreement on principles'. In this sense, the 'old rule *contra negantes principia non est disputandum*' remains valid, since every difference or dispute expresses 'merely' the greater or lesser degree of 'abstraction' through which the principles and systems of 'reason'—or unity—are manifested. This agreement is therefore the indefectible end dictated to us by the nature of reason itself, since the latter, being 'oneness', is the 'concrete'.[63]

Second, to Schulze's contention that the spirit of the Third Academy, that of Carneades (like, moreover, that of the Second), differed from that of the sceptics, Hegel counterposes his conviction that there was no such difference, a conviction reiterated by Hegel's faithful follower Georg Andreas Gabler in his *Kritik des Bewusstseins*. It is thus clear that if we are forced to choose among the three—Sextus Empiricus, who considered Carneades insufficiently sceptical ('when we describe a thing as good or evil we do not add it as our opinion that what we assert is probable'[64]); Schulze, who argues that Sextus failed to differentiate sharply enough between Carneades (and Arcesilas) and the sceptics; and Hegel, who considers 'empty' and idle Sextus's attempt to draw a distinction, however relative, between Carneades and the sceptics[65]—Hegel is the most incorrect and Schulze, the much maligned 'modern' sceptic, the most nearly correct. What is of interest to us here is the systematic theoretical thesis that rendered Hegel so insensitive to the peculiarity and import of the theory of the 'probable' (as purely sensible evidence or 'strong inclination', as Sextus put it) elaborated by Carneades, who may be considered the precursor, and in a certain sense the inspiration, of 'moderate scepticism', as Hume, prime representative of 'modern scepticism', believed he could label his critical scepticism. That thesis is that only ancient-style scepticism

---

[63] *Werke*, volume XVI, pp. 72-73.

[64] Sextus Empiricus, *Outlines of Pyrrhonism*, I, 226, Loeb Classical Library, Greek text with English translation, p. 139.

[65] *Werke*, volume XVI, pp. 90-91, 106.

about common sense can lead to philosophy, since this scepticism is directed against the 'dogmatism of the finite', which in turn is the danger ineluctably associated with modern scepticism about reason.

Finally, Hegel objected that in his Critique of Theoretical Philosophy Schulze had introduced an abstract distinction between intuition and reason, fantasy or genius and philosophy, viewing spirit as a sort of 'vessel of potentiality', or capacity, instead of conceiving it, at bottom, as a 'totality' and therefore as 'genius' and 'talent'. This objection does indeed strike at the 'empirical psychology' to which Schulze's scepticism, with its 'cultural barbarism', gives rise; but it does not suffice to persuade us that Hegel has really shown that fantasy can be reconciled with philosophy—in other words, he has not demonstrated the 'rational-irrational character of philosophy', as Glockner has put it. In his *Hegel* (volume II, p. 276), the latter notes the Schiller-like strains that run through Hegel's text, and thus infers an internal factor of crisis of the pan-logistic dialectic, on the grounds that Schiller's concept of beauty as the 'pure unity' (or totality) of opposites is in fact a positive and essential constituent of Hegel's dialectic (as was hinted, as we have seen, by Hegel himself). This is true enough in the narrow sense that the frustration of the aesthetic that it implies (as the romantic or mystical-theological conception of feeling) inevitably gave rise to a pan-logistic dialectic, which is to say a rationalistic mysticism. But it is difficult to see how this can be interpreted as a synthesis of the rational and the irrational. (Equally baseless is Glockner's claim that the romantic-Schillerist influence is happily repugnant to Hegel's 'dialectical logicizing', as is Kroner's depiction of that same influence as the factor that genuinely contributed to the 'irrationalization' of the dialectic!)

Let us return, however, to the ancient sceptics. Hegel's sole criticism of them is that they were 'inconsistent', since they went no further than the extreme 'subjectivity of knowledge', halting at the phenomenon or emotion. ('We', Sextus Empiricus said, 'do not overthrow the affective sense-impressions which induce our assent involuntarily; and these impressions are "the appearances".' See *Outlines of Pyrrhonism*, I, 19.) The root of this error, Hegel continues, was their failure to understand that 'the extreme cannot subsist without its opposite' and that the subjective therefore 'must simultaneously be extremely objective'.[66] This leads us directly to

[66] Ibid., pp. 106-107.

Plato's scepticism in his dialogue *Parmenides*, the standpoint from which Hegel viewed the ancient sceptics.

'What more perfect and separate document and system of genuine scepticism could be found', Hegel asks, 'than the *Parmenides* in Plato's philosophy', for this document 'embraces and destroys the whole territory of knowledge by means of the concepts of the intellect'. The reasoning, for example, through which Sextus denied the truth and 'rationality' of the 'reflections-concepts' of 'whole' and 'parts', demonstrating that these 'contradict' and 'annul' each other, is but a 'superficial' repetition of *Parmenides*. This scepticism of Plato's, Hegel writes, 'is itself the negative side of the knowledge of the absolute', since it represents 'the overcoming of the principle of [non-]contradiction' and 'presupposes reason as the positive side'. This scepticism, which is 'explicit' in *Parmenides*, is 'implicit' in every 'pure philosophical system'. And, against Tiedemann, Hegel defends the neo-Platonist Ficino, who counsels that *purification* of the soul—or as Hegel says, 'freedom of the spirit'—must be the prelude to the sacred study of *Parmenides* and its mysteries.[67]

It is precisely this scepticism of Plato's *Parmenides* which, since it leads Hegel to the 'dialectic of pure thoughts' or *higher genera* of *The Sophist*,[68] illustrates the ultimate fate of every scepticism of the ancient type, every scepticism about common sense: it is swept into a dogmatism of unity and, in the case at hand, offers a foretaste of the abstractness of Hegel's rationalism, of his theory of the dialectic. Indeed, all that interests Hegel in *The Sophist* is 'pure thoughts': those thoughts 'in the consideration of which in and for themselves Plato's inquiry concentrates . . . being and not-being, the one and the many . . . .That the one is identical with itself in the other, the many, the diverse: this is what is true and *all* that is important for knowledge in what has been called Platonic philosophy'.[69] Let us phrase it more accurately: all that is of interest to Hegel is the community of the higher genera in itself, shorn of the process of dichotomous division (which he does not even mention) from which Plato derives,

---

[67] Ibid., pp. 85-93; cf. Hegel's endorsement of the mystical comment of Proclus, *Werke*, volume XIV, p. 244.

[68] 'In the *Parmenides*', wrote Hegel, 'the recombination of opposites into unity is still lacking, as is the affirmation of this unity; this dialogue, therefore . . . arrives at a thoroughly negative result. But in *The Sophist* and *Philebus*, Plato does affirm this unity.' (*Werke*, XIV, p. 230.)

[69] *Werke*, volume XIV, pp. 230 ff., 237.

albeit deductively, the empirical judgement, or *doxa*, as a classifying judgement—in sum, his 'definition' of the angler, the sophist, the statesman, and so on.

It is self-evident that some common tendency must underlie this close link between ancient scepticism and the dogmatism of reason, which we have seen in both Hegel and Plato. It is this: both tend to pose the possibility of error, or of not-being, exclusively in thought in general, absolutely *apart from the senses*. The result is that such scepticism, while it does avoid the dogmatism of the intellect and of formal logic, nevertheless is ultimately mired in the dogmatism and mysticism of reason, or even squarely in 'negative theology' (the Pyrrhonism of the mystics, Pascal, or the neo-Platonistic Jaspers). One of the criteria of ancient scepticism was 'not to assent to things that are obscure and constitute the object of scientific research', since 'this sort of reasoning turns out to be deceitful'. One must rather assent to the 'involuntary' emotion, to that which 'cannot be the object of investigation'.[70] Is this not perhaps sufficient evidence of this tendency in ancient scepticism? As for the dogmatism of reason, we have Plato's (and Hegel's) principle, formulated in *Theaetetus* and *The Sophist*, that not-being and error (like being and truth) lie not in the senses but purely in thought. Is this not sufficient evidence of the same tendency? We shall return to this problem shortly, and draw out all its consequences.

For the moment, however, we must examine how Hegel's dialectic of sense-certainty—that is, the 'overcoming' or 'annulment' of the singular which is 'meant', a conception inspired by scepticism of the ancient type[71]—inevitably led him to the abstract, dogmatic rationalism of his theory of the dialectic, and more particularly to the concept

[70] Sextus Empiricus, *Outlines of Pyrrhonism*, I, 13-22, pp. 9-17.

[71] Here it may be helpful to recall that: 1) In the passages of the *Phenomenology* concerning the aesthetic *Aufhebung*, Hegel explicitly invokes ancient against modern scepticism, and also proposes to develop Cartesian scepticism (Descartes's 'immediate' belief of subjective self-consciousness, equivalent to belief 'founded on authority'). 2) Some faithful interpreters of the *Phenomenology* have taken note of Hegel's contrast between ancient and modern (or critical) scepticism (although others have not, for example Wilhelm Purpus, *Zur Dialektik des Bewusstseins nach Hegel*, Berlin, 1908, especially pp. 18-95). One example is Georg Andreas Gabler (*Kritik des Bewusstseins*, Erlangen, 1827, p. 44, and cf. pp. 120 ff.), who formulates Hegel's most intimate thought on this matter as follows: 'The five (or even seven) later tropes of the old scepticism, which are directed against thoughts themselves and all dogmatism, are of a wholly different character, incomparably more profound than Humean scepticism.' 3) It is therefore evident that what Hegel is really combating and repudiating in attacking the positivism of a Schulze is critical scepticism in general, in

of consciousness of contradiction—or reason—as essential self-consciousness.

If we consider the three constituent moments of the dialectic (the concept, truth)—namely immediacy, which is the (abstract) intellectual moment; mediation, the 'dialectical', negatively rational moment; and the return to immediacy, the speculative, positively rational moment—it soon becomes evident that the first moment, by its very nature, compromises and frustrates the other two, thereby rendering the entire process illusory. This first moment is by nature universal immediacy (which means sensible universality); in other words, it is none other than a 'universal as such', the 'annulment' of the particular or sensible which is 'meant'. (Philosophically, the first 'phenomenological' distinctions described earlier—thinghood, thing, and so on—can only mean this identification of the senses and the intellect through an abstract intellectualization of the former, which is just what the dialectical annulment of the sensible is.) Indeed, once the first moment has been posited, how can the second, which is the moment of difference in which the immediate unity or (indeterminate) universal as such is articulated, or the third, in which the supposed difference is resolved and we return to immediacy, to immediate oneness, be possible? A universal immediacy is not and cannot be immediacy understood as it must be, as the nature of multiplicity. It can be conceived only as immediate oneness, or the indeterminate universal as such. But then the production of any difference or multiplicity (as required by the second moment of the dialectic) remains inconceivable, unless it is to be a purely formalistic multiplicity, conceived as the determination or differentiation of a *given*, gratuitously presumed unity or universal. This multiplicity, which is in fact purely formalistic, is therefore also taken as given, also gratuitously presumed. The same is true of the multiplicity,

---

favour of archaic, pre-critical scepticism. In the Encyclopaedia, for example (*Hegel's Logic*, §81, Zusatz 2), he says: 'Of far other stamp, and to be strictly distinguished from it ['the noble scepticism of antiquity, especially as exhibited in the writings of Sextus Empiricus'], is the modern scepticism already mentioned (§39), which partly preceded the Critical Philosophy, and partly sprang out of it. That later scepticism consisted solely in denying the truth and certitude of the super-sensible, and in pointing to the facts of sense and of immediate sensations as what we have to keep to.' And in §39: 'The scepticism of Hume . . . should be clearly marked off from Greek scepticism. Hume assumes the truth of the empirical element, feeling and sensation, and proceeds to challenge universal principles and laws, because they have no warranty from sense-perception.' All this should make it clear that Schulze is merely a convenient target.

constituted of the antinomies of reason, at which ancient scepticism halted. And as we have seen, Hegel shares with the latter, as with Plato, the dogma that error, not-being, or multiplicity also belongs exclusively to pure reasoning or thought. Thus it is that Hegel's remark (in *Werke*, volume VI, p. 157) that 'philosophy welcomes the *skepsis* into itself as a moment, namely as the dialectic', does not at all assure us that philosophy will be anti-dogmatic; on the contrary, it threatens the opposite, for the 'mystical synonym of speculation' (see above, note 13) can only be rationalist mysticism, dogmatism of the purest form. In the end, then, the third moment is also inconceivable, for how is it possible to *return* to immediate unity if there has been no differentiation from it, except in the most apparent, purely formalistic sense?

Let us put it another way. If reason or truth consists, as is already implicit in the precept 'know thyself', in a 'self-contemplation', a 'turning into self' that includes three moments: 1) being taken in itself; 2) withdrawal from itself and being outside itself; 3) return to itself and being taken in itself once again[72]—then how can it be concluded that the third moment is really the 'unity' of the first and second, of 'the immediate and the mediated', i.e. 'identity and difference together' (since, Hegel says, that which is withdrawn from itself is identical to that from which the withdrawal has occurred), if the *difference* that is expressed in the 'withdrawal' or 'being outside itself' is, as we have seen, merely formalistic and therefore apparent and illusory, and if in reality all that remains is identity or unity (= immediacy), namely 'being taken in itself'? Let us recall the delusions about the exaltation of the intellect as the 'activity of dividing' and about its necessity as 'positivizing' intellect.[73]

This conception, according to which the immediate and the mediated are to be understood respectively as identity, or undifferentiated unity (the 'beautiful' unity of the young, romantic Hegel), and difference, or divided unity, is not merely insufficient in itself but also suggests that this insufficiency must be connected to the theory that reason, or philosophy, is a *turning into self*, a theory that revives not only the Socratic 'know thyself', but also the Platonic 'dialogue of the soul within itself' as 'reminiscence', along with its

[72] *Science of Logic*, p. 837
[73] Below we shall compare this to the abstract *dialectical* foundation of Plato's 'division'.

entire legacy. In sum, it is related to the theory of *reason*, defined as consciousness of contradiction, as self-consciousness.

Our examination of the peculiar origin of Hegel's dialectic in *skepsis* has thus shown us how little resistant to criticism is the reduction of consciousness of contradiction or reason to 'subjectivity' as 'essential self-consciousness'. Scepticism of the ancient type leads only to mystical rationalism or rationalistic mysticism (if not to fideistic mysticism). It is a rationalism for which the truth alone is only 'the movement of itself within itself' and *reason is synonymous with self-consciousness*.

A careful comparison of the spirit of Hegel's and Plato's dialectic with that of Aristotle's quite different analytic, with the most profound suggestions of classical dialectics and logic, may now help us to conclude this examination of the concept of reason, truth, or philosophy as self-consciousness. This comparison will further illuminate the inconsistency of the concept of the dialectic as 'subject' (or as 'tarrying with the negative', as subjectivity). It will thus eventually be shown that the aporias bequeathed by the ancient dialectic, Plato's in particular (the legacy of scepticism about common sense), and inherited by the modern dialectic of Hegel can be resolved more satisfactorily by a philosophy that is rigorously inspired by a modern, critical scepticism capable of confronting, without prejudice or theological dogmatism of any sort, the most extreme aporia of all: the problem of the being of not-being.

In his dialogue *The Sophist* Plato re-examines, in a self-critical spirit, the concept of *doxa*, and therefore of multiplicity, in the light of the new problem (posed in *Theaetetus*) of a 'true doxa'—a multiplicity that actually forms part of unity instead of merely aspiring to the unity of the unattainable model idea. His starting point is the 'existence of not-being'; his intention is to resolve, by means of the process of diairesis, or classifying judgements, the aporias of his *Parmenides* concerning the one and the many, which is to say, concerning being and not-being. The goal is thus to demonstrate the capacity of the 'forms' simultaneously to 'separate' and 'blend'. Hence 'discourse' or judgement—in short, any 'assertion' or thought—is 'born of the mutual blending of the forms'.

Plato's solution of this problem consists in a number of propositions, to wit: 'not-being [is] one of the classes of being, permeating all being'; 'when we say not-being, we speak, I think, not of something that is the opposite of being, but only of something different'; 'the opposition of the nature of a part of the other, and of the nature of being, when they are opposed to one another, is no less truly existence than is being itself'; 'not-beautiful', for example, is nothing but 'a distinct part of some one class of being [the *eidos* of other] and also again, opposed to some class of being'; error, that gnoseological not-being, far from being something purely negative or contrary to truth or to being, is simply the contravention of the rules of diairesis, of 'division of things into classes'; thus error states 'things which are other than things which actually are'. Thus, for example, to say 'Theaetetus flies' is 'really and truly false discourse' only because 'things other [= *eidos* 'flies'] are said as the same [= *eidos* 'man']; in other words, 'things that are not [= 'flies']as things that are [= 'man']'.[74]

Now, this solution can be seriously assessed and evaluated only in connection with Aristotle's critique of it, which was based on his rejection of the formal process of diairesis as 'impotent syllogism'. Similarly, the full import and limitations of Aristotle's ontology, which lies at the root of this critique, can be illuminated only through comparison to the admittedly partial ontological and logical resistance Plato's solution is able to muster against Aristotle's critique.

Let us examine, then, the target of the Aristotelian criticism: diairesis, or the division of classes or beings. Diairesis, Aristotle maintains, offers us: a) a *logical mechanism* of formal dichotomy according to which one of the two differences contained in a genus must be discarded, while the other is posited and affirmed, only to be divided in its turn into two new, also mutually exclusive, differences. The process continues in this manner until it reaches the irreducible form (= *eidos*, or species), the *atomon eidos*, which is the goal of diairesis, within which the successively diairetically sundered differences are reassembled, or 'collected'. A sort of defining, since classifying, judgement is then possible. b) a *fundamental rule*: every (pervading) genus divides according to a 'fully appropriate' line of cleavage—namely in accordance with the 'natural' articulation, which is the original 'duality' of 'same' and 'other' (the pervading genera). In sum, as we saw in the case of error, division occurs 'according to species' ('part and species are not the same'!), since the

---

[74] *The Sophist*, 260b, 257b, 258ab, 257e, 253d, 263bd. The translations here are from the bi-lingual edition of the Loeb Classical Library, Cambridge, Massachusetts, and London, 1921 (reprinted 1977), translated by H.N. Fowler.

division of a genus is exhaustive only through its bi-partition into logically equivalent and therefore 'contradictory' segments (with no middle ground between the two differences).

This procedure therefore entails: 1) the 'opposition' of the differences of the (pervading) genus; 2) that the opposition in which these differences stand can be derived only from their 'participation' in the 'higher genera' of 'sameness' and 'otherness', which are the constituents of the original duality; these genera 'pervade all things'; 3) that the original duality or antinomy[75] is in fact a duality-unity, or dialectic, since the higher genera, the terms of which are 'sameness' and 'otherness', 'blend with one another'.[76]

In the most significant passage of *The Statesman* (closely related to *The Sophist* by the application and development of the method of diairesis), we are told: 'Shall we, then, join the art of the king [the *definiendum*] in the same class with the interpreter, the boatswain, the prophet, the herald, and many other kindred arts, all of which involve giving orders? Or, as we just now made a comparison of functions, shall we now by comparison make a name also—since the class of those who issue orders of their own is virtually nameless— and assign kings to the science of giving orders of one's own,

---

[75] Karl Prantl (*Geschichte der Logik im Abendlande*, Leipzig, 1927, volume I, pp. 81-82) considers it as such, as simple 'antinomy': 'Through the concept of sameness and otherness, and by means of the opposition that depends on it, this division must necessarily take shape as a bisection—a dichotomy . . . ; but against the motives of this character of opposition, it already contains the antinomy within itself.' This point of view leads Prantl to identify the 'community' of the genera purely and simply with the 'collection' of the higher differences (the *participating* genera) within every lower species, up to the final, *indivisible* species: 'it [this first concept] is not only delimited from other genera-concepts in accordance with the contrary moments of sameness and otherness, but is also divided within itself in accordance with species-concepts; the result is a constant circulation back and forth between division and collection [diairesis and synagoghé].' This opinion is generally shared by Julius Stenzel in his fundamental *Plato's Method of Dialectic* (translated and edited by D.J. Allan, Oxford, 1940). He, however, developing the concept of the community or unity of *sameness* (or being) and *otherness* (or not-being) implicit in Prantl's use of the singular ('*the* concept of sameness', etc.), acknowledges that 'every stage in division shows a being and a not-being side by side'. And: 'the value of diairesis is that it is a never-ending attempt to show the intricate relation of being and not-being.' Below we will cite Stenzel's dogmatic defence of this (diacritic) dialectic of *sameness* and *otherness* against Aristotle's critique. A. Diès misses the point (in his introduction to the French translation of *The Statesman*, Paris, 1935, p. xxi) when he concentrates exclusively on the 'sense of "distinction"', of *separation*, between that which is *same* and that which is *other*, for he thus obscures the whole question of the 'participation' of genera in genera, which is the key to *The Sophist* and *The Statesman*.

[76] *The Sophist*, 259e.

disregarding all the rest and leaving to someone else the task of naming them? For the object of our present quest is the ruler, not his opposite . . . .Then since a reasonable distinction between this class and the rest has been made, by distinguishing the commands given as one's own or another's, shall we again divide this class, if there is in it any further line of section?'[77]

Let us note straightaway one highly characteristic fact. Plato's criticism of the Parmenidean concept of absolute not-being (which is simultaneously a self-criticism) is manifested in a positive transmutation of Parmenides's negative term so as to identify it with a 'separation' of *distinction* understood as pure 'opposition' (sameness vs. otherness). In other words, there is a *totalization*. Hence the related effort to conceive of not-being or multiplicity as absolutely not obtuse or non-intelligible, but instead so sharp and intelligible that it coincides exactly with *essential* difference, which is the *relation of opposition*. This sort of effort will later acquire full self-consciousness in its modern exponent, Hegel. The effort is possible only because of the initial endeavour to make Parmenides's negative term positive simply by identifying it with an *eidos* or value, with the supreme *eidos* of 'otherness' and the corresponding 'othernesses' of the genera that 'participate' in a *descending* dialectical process. It is obvious, however, that the positivity of this negative term—not-being, multiplicity, *disvalue*, or whatever it may be called—cannot be found (if indeed it exists and must be sought) in the realm of the pure *eidos*, unity, value, or *being*. In sum, it cannot be found where it has been sought by both Plato and Hegel, as well as the sceptics, because of a common *ancient* intellectualistic prejudice. It cannot be found in pure reasoning, in thought, in the ideal.

Let us now consider Aristotle's critique, as presented in the *Prior Analytics* (Book I, chapter 31) and the *Posterior Analytics* (Book II, chapter 5).[78] This critique advances the following two charges against

---

[77] Ibid., 260e-261a.

[78] *Translator's note:* The translations from the *Prior and Posterior Analytics* below are taken from the Everyman's Library edition (Dent: London, Dutton: New York, 1964), translated by John Warrington. Those from *Metaphysics* are from the Everyman's Library edition, translated by John Warrington, 1956, reprinted 1978. In the latter book, the text is arranged in a new manner, in accordance with the recommendations of David Ross, who has convincingly characterized the traditional order of books as 'illogical'. Because of this, however, the pagination no longer corresponds to the standard referencing system. The notes below therefore indicate page numbers in this edition, as well as the standard numeration.

Plato's diairesis. 1. On the one hand, it 'begs the point at issue', since it 'takes for granted' what must be demonstrated (the genus 'king', for example). It thus falls into *petitio principii*, since it requires that the nature or species of the *demonstrandum* and *definiendum* be presupposed or known in advance in order to be able to select the *differentiae* (the 'contraries') of the genus (the 'art of giving orders', for example) into one of which this nature must fall. 2. On the other hand, it 'only proves a more general predicate [the 'art of giving orders'] than the attribute in question ['giving one's own orders'], in other words, some predicate that contains that which was supposed to be demonstrated'. To put it another way, diairesis, instead of demonstrating 'man' (or 'rational animal'), demonstrates the 'wider' notion of 'animal' (whether rational or not). It is therefore evident that it takes genus, instead of species, as the middle term, in violation of the rules of the syllogism, which require that the middle term 'always be less general, i.e. less inclusive, than the major term'. The result is that the conclusion 'nowhere follows from the premises' but is rather a question and depends 'on the respondent's conceding it'. This may be seen by considering the result of the division: animals are either rational or not rational; man is an animal; man is either rational or not rational. In a 'genuine demonstration', however, the conclusion, far from being a question, 'must arise from the premises, even if the respondent does not admit it'.

Finally, besides all this, the very purpose of diairesis is *mistaken*, for the *definition* of an essence or species as such is not *demonstrable* as a deduction.

If we leave aside the formalist technique evident in this critique—wherein Aristotle intends species purely as the middle term of a syllogism and therefore upholds his formal-verbal conception of reasoning—what current philosophical interest does it retain?[79]

---

[79] Stenzel holds that Plato's position can stand against Aristotle's critique (which he thinks is 'formally oriented'): 'The subdivisions ought, if rightly found, to stand in the relation of "being" and "not-being". (Plato's new discovery, which he considers so essential, is that "not-being" may be understood in the sense of "difference".) He must have found the demonstrative force of Division [diairesis] precisely at the point where Aristotle complained of its absence. To take the classic instance of dichotomous division: we ask, In which of the two parts must the form we seek be placed—this or "the other"? Not *that*, therefore *this*. The divider knows what the desired form *is not*, and knowing also that the alternatives are exclusive, he can recognize what it is.' (*Plato's Method of Dialectic*, p. 92.) But he fails to realize that Plato is forced into a *petitio principii* by his inability really to emerge from the 'more general' or abstract 'universal'. He fails, in short, to see that the same-other 'relation', since it is the

The value of Aristotle's criticism is surely considerable, provided we look beyond its formalistic letter and grasp its genuinely anti-dogmatic, anti-a-priori, and anti-theological gnoseological spirit. The critique is made up of two interdependent objections, which may be paraphrased as follows, inverting, for the sake of clarity, the order in which Aristotle presents them.

First, Plato unwittingly, but inevitably, concludes with a wider, more general notion than the one in question (but the 'wider' is not the 'middle term', the difference, species, or determination without which, according to Aristotle, there is neither thought nor reality). In other words, Plato is compelled to take the genus, instead of the species, for the middle term—namely 'animal', rational or not rational (in accordance with the opposition or tauto-heterology of the higher genera, which pervade the lower ones). Second, Plato consequently falls into a *petitio principii*, which entails the unsubstantiated, non-mediated, and therefore *gratuitous* and *surreptitious* introduction of the (empirical) species that was to be proved, namely multiplicity. In sum, he resorts to experience, which is not justified by the more general, namely the preconceived tauto-heterology that participates in this and of which it constitutes the essence. Let us put it another way: Plato falls into *petitio principii* because he must presuppose the nature or species of the *definiendum* in order to be able to choose between the purely opposite or tauto-heterological *differentiae* of the participating genus, under one of which this nature must or should re-enter.

dialectical 'opposition' or mutual 'interpenetration' of the higher genera, cannot in itself ground the 'separation', the exclusive-alternative, of the species. The antinomous character of its terms is indissociable from their *interpenetration* and *constitution*, and therefore cannot be directly and simply transformed into the *incompatible* contrariety, or contradictory contrary, required to repulse Aristotle's critique and attain the true mean, the species. As for Heinrich Maier (*Die Syllogistik des Aristoteles*, volume II, 2, pp. 70 ff.), he seems to accept Aristotle's critique, but considers only its formal-logical aspect. Other commentators, from Ross to Robin, scarcely and only superficially touch on this question. Robin, for example (*Aristote*, Paris, 1944, pp. 50-51), concludes that 'it is not certain that Plato's theory of the "communication of genera" might not be otherwise interpreted, more broadly and genuinely originally, than was done on the basis of a *synthetic* and *progressive* method.' This may be compared to the traditional, Hegelian and idealist, interpretation of the 'community of genera', an interpretation constitutionally blind to the deeper bases of Aristotle's critique. Likewise tainted by Hegelianism is the otherwise noteworthy work of Enzo Paci, *Significato del 'Parmenide' nella filosofia di Platone*, Messina-Milan, 1938. See also volume II of Harald Cherniss's *Aristotle's Criticism of Plato and the Academy*, Baltimore, 1944.

Indeed. As we have seen, division, understood in Plato's sense of opposition, implies a process of distinguishing as pure totalization or universalization. But the distinguishing is purely apparent, since the 'opposition' of the 'higher genera' ('sameness' and 'otherness'), being a 'community' of genera synonymous with a 'blending together' of their terms, and consequently a duality-unity, or dialectical antinomy, is in itself incapable of effecting the 'separation' of the species or of differentiating the genera; these differences are said to be 'opposed' because they 'participate' in the community of 'sameness-otherness'. In sum, the 'opposition', since it is a contrariety of compatible contraries, cannot be transformed directly and simply into the incompatible contrariety, the exclusive alternative, of the species, which must emerge from the more general, from the genus. But precisely because of this inability to conclude anything but the more general, or the *pure* form, Plato is compelled, in order to divide—in other words, to distinguish or to think concretely (as he has proposed to do with the problem of the *doxa*)—to resort to a specific matter, to some *content* or multiplicity, which is surreptitious because gratuitous, gratuitous because non-mediated by the form, and non-mediated because *deduced*, i.e. drawn from a preconceived tauto-heterology or dialectic. In sum, Plato is driven to a *petitio principii* that amounts to an outright ontological, and not merely logical-verbal or formalistic, defect.

It is worthwhile to linger on this, the original defect of Platonism, as indeed of any a priori transcendental dialectic, for we have here the ontological *petitio principii* into which the idealist dialectic inevitably dissolves. Indeed, it is the discovery of this defect that prepares the new type of critique of dogmatic rationalism presaged not by Kant, but only by Aristotle's critique of Platonic division and by Marx's critique of the 'mystified' Platonic-Hegelian dialectic: the *materialist critique of pure reason*. Indeed, it was the profound insight of Marx that for Plato—who was 'devoted, in the development of particular questions, to a positive interpretation of the absolute' and for whom the 'Absolute stands on one side, and limited positive reality on the other'—the 'positive', or concrete that 'must all the same be preserved' becomes the 'medium through which absolute light shines'. Hence 'the finite, the positive, points to something other than itself' (*deutet ein Anderes*).[80] We need only add,

---

[80] *Karl Marx, Frederick Engels: Collected Works*, London, 1975, volume 1, p. 497. The full text of this passage will be given below.

bringing the formula up to date, that 'the same procedure has been repeated in more recent times, by virtue of a like law', by Hegel.

This insight into the purely symbolic character with which the finite or multiple is invested by Plato's dialectic is confirmed by any rigorous examination of his diairesis, his classifying, diacritical dialectic. Let us bear the following points in mind.

1. The assumption that distinctions can be made exclusively by opposing or totalizing can be explained only by the typically idealist effort to conceive of not-being or multiplicity, represented by the 'differences' of participating genera, as absolutely non-blunt but purely intelligible. Hence the precondition (*sine qua non*, because of their very ontological composition) of the differences of genera: that they *are pervaded by* the higher genera and their related community, or *tauton-thateron* (sameness-otherness).

2. Through this participation of the *tauton-thateron* in them, the differences must on the one hand be valid (for the heterology or discreteness that is the instance of multiplicity, of the *doxa*, of which account must be taken here) as the contrariety of incompatible contraries, of contradictories, or sameness-otherness in the plural. They must therefore be constituted as such, as differences of the relevant genera. On the other hand, however, they retain no real ontological consistency except that afforded them by the pervasiveness of the *tauton-thateron*, assumed as the sole criterion grounding their being as differences: the ontological consistency of sameness-otherness *in the singular*—one, common, and general—as contrarieties of *compatible* contraries, tauto-heterological and dialectical. In sum, all that remains is their ontological *inconsistency*.

3. Finally, since the higher genera interpenetrate and are dialectical by nature, and since by definition they can *participate in* or *be predicated of* other genera—in other words, since sameness can be predicated of one species only provided it interpenetrates with otherness, which can nevertheless be predicated of a second species—it follows: a) that their compatible contrariety, their dialecticalness, the sole ontological dimension (of unity or universality) that they constitute by nature, lies in and for their functionality as predicates of criteria that unify (and bring into existence) a multiplicity; b) but that, nevertheless, since this multiplicity is inconsistent for the reasons given above (and in fact it is a purely dialectical, formal

multiplicity, in accordance with the descending character of the division), the multiple, the finite, the *doxa*, can really be nothing more than a sign of something other than itself, a *symbol* or *pretext* of the pure or dialectical unity in its production.

Having confirmed the symbolic and 'allegorical' character assumed by the multiple in Plato (and as we shall see, Marx used the term 'allegory' in his critique of Hegel's dialectic), it might seem that the traditional criticist argument against dogmatic rationalism has to be conceded entirely—namely that, since the instance of multiplicity or discreteness is frustrated by the reduction of the 'object' to 'wholly abstract determinations in which it can no longer be recognized', as Feuerbach was to assert against Hegel, it must thus be concluded that the Platonic 'universal' (like the Hegelian) is not objective, concrete, or full, but rather empty (in accordance with Kant's maxim about the 'emptiness' of the 'concept').

But it is just at this point that *the criticist argument against rationalism must be rejected as still external, fundamentally psychologistic, and wholly insufficient.* What must now be done is to demonstrate coherently, on the basis of the actual results achieved, that a process like Plato's can only conclude the 'more general' and must inevitably *take this for the 'middle term'* (as Aristotle pointed out). In other words, Plato inevitably takes *the finite or particular as a symbol of the universal or infinite and, in sum, dissolves the empirical into the speculative* (as Marx pointed out in his anti-Platonic, anti-Hegelian remarks). The ultimate result is a *petitio principii* (as pointed out by the anti-Platonic Aristotle), which is to say a transformation, in turn, of the speculative into the empirical (as pointed out by the anti-Platonic, and therefore, as we shall see, anti-Hegelian, Marx).

In sum, the Platonic, like the Hegelian or any other dogmatic 'universal', *is not at all 'empty'; it is quite full, but vitiated.* It should now be possible to develop Kant's cardinal critique of Leibniz into a materialist critique of the a priori, and thus to draw from it the constructive conclusions of a higher (materialist) criticism that Kant's critique itself was unable to provide, because the dogmatic aspect of the 'thing-in-itself', i.e. the negative conception of the irrational and the consequent phenomenalism and intellectualism, halted the initial anti-dogmatic leap represented by Kant's critique of Leibniz and prevented him from grasping the ontological *petitio principii* which Aristotle, with his spark of materialist genius, had been able to detect to some degree, foreshadowing Marx's insights in this regard. We shall see this more clearly later.

For now, however, let us return to Plato. It is evident that his dialectical division could not take a single step without a tacit, illegitimate recourse to experience, to the (empirical) concepts of genera and species. Strictly speaking, this recourse to experience does not follow, and still less does it precede, the dialectical construction or demonstration of the 'definition' of the essence (up through the indivisible *eidos*) sought by diairesis. Rather, it coincides or is contemporaneous with it; it is conditioned by it and in its turn conditions it, for the process is circular. Just as the tautoheterological, through its preconceived unitary rigour, conditions the empirical genus and, by pervading it rigidifies or unifies it to the point of immobilizing its 'fission' into species and sub-species, so in their turn the particular empirical genera and species intervene in the construction as such, since they alone can constitute the content required by the form (the tauto-heterological) in order to be such. In other words, those subjects needed by the higher genera in order to be predicated of them (in the 'community' of higher and lower genera, or relation, or judgement, which is the constitution of the definition) must *themselves be determined in them*. But if they are to become such subjects, the empirical genera must be *participating* genera, and hence the formalistic, dialectical multiplicity of the definition in which sameness-otherness in the plural, or contrariety of incompatible contraries, is omitted. It is this contrariety of incompatible contraries, however, that expresses the instance of multiplicity or the particular, and is replaced by sameness-otherness in the singular—the contrariety of compatible contraries that expresses the instance of unity or the universal. It is precisely for this reason that the empirical genera become mere pretexts or symbols of things other than themselves, of tauto-heterology. Their presence in the definition is therefore surreptitious and immediate, but nevertheless necessary and inevitable, because of the instance of the content, or of the subject (of the judgement) described above. In sum, the speculative is transformed into the empirical as a consequence and counterpart of the dissolution of the empirical into the speculative. There follows the juxtaposition of universal (= dialectic) and particular (= *doxa*), which completes the vicious circle, which may be termed *the negative ontological circle* of dogmatic, Platonic rationalism.

This sort of circle shows that the 'universal', the dogmatic, rationalist 'concept' in general, is not at all empty, but full—and vitiated. (We shall see this more clearly in our analysis of Hegel's theological interpolation, since the greater complexity of Hegel's logic, more mature than Plato's, which lacked any real theory of judgements,[81] will permit a sharper demonstration of the sophistic game of substantification of the universal, or conversion of the predicate (or universal) into the subject (or particular) and into the predicate of the predicate. This process is merely the inevitable result of a priori reasoning, of the theological interpolation of multiplicity.)

On the other hand, it is undeniable that two instances developed by the problematic of the constitution of the being of not-being, or multiplicity, speak in Plato's favour. These are:

1. Without the dialectic, or unified generic sameness-otherness, the *particular* sameness-otherness in the plural, the contrariety of *contradictories* that grounds the exclusive-alternative of the species is not even possible. Indeed, how can we avoid contradiction (in the particular) without being *conscious* of it, without *thinking it*, i.e. without positing its validity or universality? And how is this possible without a sharpness of intelligibility that reduces the diverse or particular to unity by reducing it to *essential* diversity, which means to supreme essentiality or predicability, which is precisely the *relation* of opposites, or contrariety of compatible contraries?

2. Nevertheless, dialecticization can occur only through division in the concrete, through the sort of functionality of unifying criteria represented by the supreme predicates, which are the compatible contraries in diairesis. This, however, is quite different from Hegel's

---

[81] Stenzel observes: 'Apelt rightly raises the objection that Plato, in his doctrine of "being" and "not-being", has not explained the existence of judgements proper, but only of "formulae of comparison". . . . It is always *the* angler as one of a class, the particular as representative of the universal, that Plato has in mind.' (*Plato's Method of Dialectic*, p. 137.) It is of singular interest to note that the most modern and advanced Plato philology unwittingly confirms Marx's critical intuition of the *theological interpolation of the multiple*, the point of departure of the new (materialist) critique of a priori thought, of which more below. After noting that 'he [Plato] does not consider it possible that sense-perception can ever be a *source* of knowledge' and that 'even here the importance of method prevails over that of the object', Stenzel concludes: 'Plato remained in the most literal sense an Idealist. To him the universal was represented in the particular, while the particular could only be grasped in the Idea; in intuition both elements were united. The problem of the individual *thing* remained unsolved.' (Ibid., pp. 133, 134, 156.)

interpretation, according to which 'what Plato means is that the idea, the universal in and for itself . . . must be taken for themselves', which means 'that there must be no talk of the subject of which these determinations are predicated', and one must 'abstract' from every 'empirical concreteness', such that 'the true dialectic, in its highest form [the 'dialectic of pure thoughts'] is nonetheless contained in *Parmenides*', but not in *The Sophist*, with its classifications!

In other words, the most profound suggestion bequeathed us by Plato arises, despite everything, from the problematic of the 'true *doxa*'. It is this: reason can be conceived as consciousness or thought of contradiction only in relation to *particular contradiction*, which must be averted, which is to say non-contradiction (the a posteriori), and not at all as self-consciousness, 'internal dialogue', or 'anamnesis' (the a priori).

Now, however, let us proceed to the general ontological and gnoseological foundations of Aristotle's critique of diairesis, to the foundation of the possibility of *contradictories*, or contraries *incomposita ex inviciem* (i.e. not composed of one another), the omission of which by the purely dialectical Plato prevented him from attaining the true *doxa*, the specific essence, and thereby from realizing classification.

That Aristotle, on the other hand, did arrive at this conception of contrariety is shown, more clearly than anywhere else, in the following confutation of the Megaric and Heraclitean adversaries of the principle of non-contradiction.[82]

---

[82] What follows should be read in the light of two other essential passages of *Metaphysics*, 1006ab and 1062a, for these exposit the profound problematic inherent in the norm of non-contradiction: the instance of the inevitable *determinateness* of all that is or has a *meaning* (and cf. Aristotle's original and most fundamental instance into which this is converted: the *materialist* instance of the identity of the *necessary*, or rational, and the *non-contradictory*). Here are the relevant passages: 'We can, however, adduce *negative* proof even of this law by refuting our opponent, provided only that he will make some positive statement. For it is quite hopeless to argue with a man who will not produce evidence in support of his own theory; in so far as he declines to reason he is no better than a vegetable. . . . In all such controversies we start by requiring not that our opponent should affirm or deny any particular statement (that might appear to beg the question), but that he should say something which has some meaning for both himself and for others. (This last condition is necessary because, if his statement has no meaning, he is debarred from intelligent intercourse with himself or with anyone else.) If he will do that, then we have some definite starting-point from which to argue; and the onus of proof lies not on ourselves, but on our opponent who, while acquiescing in reason, continues to deny it. . . . First of all, it is obviously true

'If there is to be such a thing as "being essentially man", it will not be the same as "being not-man" (or "not being man").... Our opponent must therefore say that nothing can be defined—that all attributes are accidental; ... Well, if all things are accidental, there can be no original substratum in which the accidents may inhere; yet the accidental [= predicate] always implies predication of something about a subject. This absence of an original substratum involves an infinite regress; but that is impossible, ... One accident can be an accident of another only if both are accidents of the same subject; e.g. the white is musical and vice versa only when both are accidents of man [= second substance]. *But "musical" is an accident of Socrates [= first substance] not in the sense that both are accidents of something else.* There you have the two kinds of accidental proposition. But those which are so in the second sense cannot form an infinite series in the direction of the predicates; e.g. there cannot be another accident of "white Socrates", for such a collection of attributes does not make a single statement. Nor, in the first sense, can "white" have a further accident such as "musical"; for the former is no more an accident of the latter than vice versa. Besides, we have distinguished two senses in which predicates are accidental: whereas in sense (1) one accident is an accident of another, in sense (2) it is not; and therefore not all predications will be of accidents. Even, therefore, if we start with accidental predications, we shall come to something which denotes [first] substance. And if this is so, the law of contradiction is established. If all contradictory statements are true of the same thing at the same time, clearly all things will be one. If we can indifferently either assert or deny a predicate of any subject, the same thing will be a warship, a wall, and a man.... Which lands us in the dictum of Anaxagoras, "all things mixed together", i.e. that nothing really exists. They seem, then, to be speaking of the indeterminate, and while fancying themselves to speak of what

that in any judgement the copulae "is" and "is not" have definite meanings, so that it could not be that everything can be [both] "so and not so".... If a word has an unlimited number of meanings, obviously no account whatever can be given of the thing with reference to which it is used. *Not to mean one definite thing is to mean nothing*; and if words mean nothing there is an end to rational intercourse with others, and indeed with oneself. *For if we do not think of one definite thing we cannot think of anything at all*; ... Let the name, then, as was said originally, signify something and signify one thing.' (1006ab, pp. 125-126.) 'If the word means something and this meaning is truly asserted of a subject, the subject must *necessarily* have this character, and *therefore can never not have it*; so that *opposite statements cannot be true of the same subject.*' (1062a, p. 133.)

exists, they are speaking in fact of what does not; for the indeterminate is that which exists potentially but not actually.'[83]

It seems to me that what remains genuinely vital in this argumentation is Aristotle's idea that the reason it is impossible to predicate contrary accidents of the same subject simultaneously is grounded in the character of the individuality or particularity of that which is 'meant', in this case 'Socrates' (or 'music'). It is this individuality that is the ultimate subject in the attributive judgement of inessential qualities (but not only in such judgements as these), as individual or individuated species; in sum, the subject is a 'first substance'.[84] Indeed, let us examine its fundamental characteristics. They are three.

1. Its *total unpredicability*, since 'that which is called a substance most strictly, primarily, and most of all is that which is neither said of a subject nor in a subject ... [hence] no category is derived from it' and 'things which are not said of an underlying subject I call things in themselves and those which are said of an underlying subject I call incidentals.'[85]

2. Its *numerical*, and not merely specific, *unity*, since 'those things are one ... which are indivisible' and since 'things that are numerically one are also one specifically; but those which are one in species are not necessarily one numerically' (cf. the pure specific essence in the essential predicative forms, which are the foundation of clear demonstration and of science); and finally, since 'one and the same definition, e.g. of man, is applicable to many individuals; but Socrates is one'.[86]

---

[83] *Metaphysics*, 1007a 24ff; pp. 125-127.

[84] See, for example, in *The Works of Aristotle*, translated into English under the editorship of W.D. Ross, Oxford, 1928, the conclusions of Geoffrey Mure to his commentary on the *Posterior Analytics*, 1, I, chapter 22, 83b (cf. 1, I, chapter 19, 81b, 82a). This is a passage in which Aristotle considers the question of the ultimate subject of an accidental predicate in a descending predicative series. Mure comments: 'It is, as so often in Aristotle, difficult to be sure whether he is regarding the infima species or the concrete singular—the first substance of the *Categories*—as the ultimate subject of judgement. I have assumed he means the latter.' Somewhat earlier, Mure concluded in regard to these two passages: 'The ultimate subject of all judgement is an individual substance, a concrete singular.'

[85] *Categories*, 2a 10, 3a 55; *Posterior Analytics*, 1, I, chapter 4, 73b 5-10. The translations from the *Categories*, here and below, are from: *Aristotle's Categories and De Interpretatione*, translated by J.L. Ackrill, Oxford at the Clarendon Press, 1963.

[86] *Categories*, 3b 10; *Metaphysics* 1052a 31-32, 1016b 36, 1074a 33-35 (pp. 305, 15, and 348 respectively).

3. Its *indifference to contrariety*, i.e. to negation or relation in general, since 'what would be contrary to a primary substance? For example, there is nothing contrary to an individual man, nor yet is there anything contrary to man or to animal'. In other words, neither species nor genus, second substance, signifies an 'individual, but rather a class' or 'qualification', because 'it is not one and singular, as is first substance', which is indeed capable of receiving contraries, but while 'remaining identical and numerically one'.[87]

The indispensability of the principle of non-contradiction follows from these characteristics of first substance, Aristotle's fundamental ontological instance. It is a consequence above all of the discrete, numerical unity of the material, or typically multiple, i.e. of the unity, never purely specific, of the individual (or individuated species) and therefore of the correlative vital exigency that it be posited together with and through a sole 'accident', namely one of the contraries (of infinite pairs). It is thus realized as 'something determined', or concrete, exactly because it is discrete and thereby rejects opposition, relation, and the 'indeterminate'. This leads it— in its dynamic aspect—from potential or indeterminate being, within which the contraries stand together, to actual being and the consequent disjunction of the contraries. 'Entelechy separates', as Aristotle himself put it.

All Aristotle's characteristic efforts in his struggle against negation, negativity, and relationality on the terrain of becoming are thus comprehensible (as well as his oscillation, as Calogero put it,[88] between the conception of privation as the immediate reciprocal negativity of contraries and the conception in which the privative contrary and the positive are equated outright). It is likewise evident that Hegel and the Hegelians were wrong to interpret the principle that *actuality separates* as 'the principle of individuation . . . not in the sense of an accidental, merely particular, but rather *pure* subjectivity', for it must be recalled that this principle is linked to the concept that it is the *existing individual*, both numerically and specifically one, *that has no contrary*. Attributive judgement of inessential qualities concurrently leads to the logical-gnoseological conclusion that it is a kind of *intuitive* intelligence, although not of

[87] *Categories*, 3b 24 ff., 4a 10-11; *Physics*, 189a 29-34.
[88] G. Calogero, *I fondamenti della logica aristotelica*, Florence, 1927, pp. 101 ff.

the Platonic type, that enables us to grasp the reality of Socrates (or music) and to confute the opponent of the principle of non-contradiction on this ground as well. Indeed, connected to the logic characteristic of first substance and to its total unpredicability is the fact that individual and essence do not coincide. To assert this even with regard to attributive judgements of accidental qualities requires, of course, that Aristotle extend the distinction between individual and universal from the category of substance to the other categories as well, in this case that of 'quality'.[89] The reason for this non-coincidence must, naturally, be this: 'concrete things involving matter are not the same as their essences, nor are unities of substance with an accidental attribute (e.g. Socrates and musical), because these have only accidental unity'.[90] The deepened elaboration of this reasoning is evident in another passage of *Metaphysics*: 'It may be, however, that where matter is other in a particular way it does make things in a sense other in species. Why, for example, is this horse specifically different from this man, although their matter is included in their definitions? Because there is a contrariety in their definitions.'[91]

This leads back to a distinction made in *Metaphysics* (1054b 16 ff. and 1055a 2): 'Difference [*diafora*] is not the same as otherness [*heteron*]'; that which is different from some thing is 'different in some respect, so that there must be something identical in which the things differ. This identical thing is either genus or species'. For example, contraries are different, since contrariety is a *determinate* difference; whereas what is 'other need not be other in any particular respect'. For example, 'you are other than your neighbour' precisely because 'the matter and the definition are not both one'. Aristotle concludes that ' "other" is not the contradictory of "same". That is why "other" is never predicated of non-existent things, while "not

---

[89] This is documented by Ross (*Aristotle*, London, 1971, pp. 23-24), who points out, following *Categories*, that 'a particular piece of grammatical knowledge' is not 'asserted of a subject'. See also *Metaphysics* 1031b 24 ff. (p. 179): 'As for an accidental term like "the musical" or "the white", since it has two meanings, we cannot say the term itself is identical with its essence. For both the accidental term and the subject to which it belongs are white; so that although in one sense the essence and the term itself are the same, in another they are not, because the essence of "white" is not identical with "the man who is white" or with "the white man", but is identical with the quality "white".'

[90] *Metaphysics* 1037b 4-6, p. 195.

[91] *Metaphysics* 1058b 1 ff., p. 324.

the same" is so predicated. It *is* predicated of all *existing* things', of things that are by 'nature existent and one'.[92]

But the result of the non-coincidence of individual and essence is that the individual concrete thing, whether essential or accidental, is *undefinable*; intuitive knowledge of the 'unity' in which it presents itself is attainable only through the intellect or the senses: 'But when we come to the concrete thing, e.g. this circle, which is a particular individual, sensible or intelligible, there is no definition of it; it is knowable by the aid of intuition or perception.'[93] This may be compared with another passage which treats the dynamic aspect of the problem: 'If no substance can consist of . . . substances actually existing [since in that event two realities would be actual instead of one], all substances will be uncompounded and therefore indefinable', but knowable only through intuition, whether intellectual or sensible. Hence Aristotle's profound insistence that, as we have seen, *the definition of essence is itself undemonstrable.*[94]

The act of non-dianoetic but rather noetic, intuitive knowledge to which Aristotle ultimately resorts in order to legitimate the knowability of the individual or *existing* thing (which does not coincide with but rather eludes the essence,[95] since the latter is merely *diafora*, or abstract difference from something identical, the genus or species) cleaves into a dualism of intelligence and sensation. This dualism, however, tends toward recomposition in the principle that *intellectual activity cannot exist without the activity of imagination:* '. . . unless one perceived things one would not learn or understand anything, and when one contemplates one must simultaneously contemplate an image; for images are like sense-perceptions, except that they are without matter. But imagination is different from assertion and denial; for truth and falsity involve a combination of thoughts. But what distinguishes the first thoughts from images? Surely

[92] Ibid., p. 312.
[93] *Metaphysics* 1036a 1 ff., pp. 191-192.
[94] *Metaphysics* 1039a 1 ff., pp. 197-198.
[95] In *Aristotle* (p. 171), Ross notes that Aristotle never worked out 'a theory of intuitive thought in which this function is correlated with the other functions he assigns to it—the knowledge of the first principles of science and the knowledge of essences and of incomposite substances'. In strictly critical-theoretical terms, I would say that we find in Aristotle only suggestions of some sort of co-presence of the 'cognitive' and the 'practical', of an element of *discreteness* and in that sense intuitive, lyrical, contemplative, or whatever.

neither these nor any other thoughts will be images, but they will not exist without images.'⁹⁶

Now, the character of this sensation and 'image' (with which the intellect cannot dispense if it is to be concrete, *intuitive* intelligence in the most profoundly Aristotelian sense of the word) plays a cardinal role in Aristotle's further arguments against those who reject the principle of non-contradiction.

'No sense', Aristotle writes, 'contradicts itself at the same moment about the same object, nor at different moments with regard to that object's quality, but only with regard to the object itself. Take a wine: you may, in consequence of its own change, or of some change in your own physical condition, find it at one time sweet and not so at another; but sweetness itself is always the same definite and unmistakable quality which everything must necessarily have in order to be sweet. Yet all these theories of our opponents [the Protagoreans] . . . destroy necessity inasmuch as they destroy substance. For the "necessary" cannot be in one way and in another; so that if anything is of necessity, it cannot be "both so and not so".'⁹⁷

For our purposes, two points about this argumentation must be noted in particular. First, Aristotle, unlike Plato, presses his polemic against Protagoras onto the terrain of the adversary himself: sense-perception proper, free, as Ross points out in his *Aristotle* (p. 162), 'from any admixture of association and interpretation'. The cardinal result of this is that Aristotle defines the nature of sense-perception as a sort of *immutability* or staticness that can only signify a non-dialectical identity or sameness (i.e. not properly *eidetic* or ideal in the Platonic sense), if only because the *actuality* of sense-perception considered here signifies the *disjunction* of contrary qualities, since actuality has its ultimate foundation, as we have seen, in the concept that the *individual* has no contrary. (Aristotle explicitly appeals to his doctrine of becoming and actuality in this regard, in *De sensu et sensibili*, 447b 10-20, and elsewhere.) In sum, Aristotle dissolves every Heraclitean, descriptive, or psychologistic conception of the senses as a 'flux' and implicitly posits the instance of the senses, or of feeling in general, as a pure discreteness, or un-dialectical sameness, capable of grounding, as staticness-

---

⁹⁶ *De Anima* 432a 7-14 (*Aristotle's De Anima Books II, III*, translated by D.W. Hamlyn, Oxford, 1968); cf. *De Memoria et Reminiscentia* 449b 31: 'Without imagination there is no intellect.'
⁹⁷ *Metaphysics* 1010b 21 ff., pp. 137-138.

ecstaticness, so-called artistic contemplativeness as described in the first chapter of the present work—'aesthetic disinterestedness' in the Kantian sense of the term. Second, the argument in support of the being and truth of 'every substance' and of 'that which exists of necessity' (in short, the argument in defence of the supreme logical and ontological principle) draws particular force from what Ross calls the characteristic 'infallibility' of sense-perception. From this it can be concluded that *logos*, like being, 'cannot be "both so and not so"', exactly because, since its specifically gnoseological foundation is the noema-image, just as its ontological foundation is first substance or individuated species, this (dianoetic) logos can only be conceived as endowed with the staticness—which is to say, un-dialecticalness—characteristic of the noema-image or aesthetically-founded noema, in other words, in the discreteness typical of the senses. It therefore cannot be conceived otherwise than as a *'yes' that excludes 'no'*, an alternative of truth or falsehood.

(It should be added that three of Aristotle's concepts imply a deeper, and certainly more productive and vital, meaning than is usually suspected by interpreters. These are: a) The concept of the general relationship between truth and the senses, namely that what is sensed is always true and never false.[98] b) The concept of the specific relationship between the logical principle and the senses, in regard to which Ross, who is, incidentally, the most astute critic on this subject, observed in his *Aristotle* (p. 162): 'Sense does not contradict itself about the sensum. Thus as regards sensa, there is no reason to doubt the law of [non-] contradiction.' c) The concept of the relation between the principles of non-contradiction and the excluded middle on the one hand and the principle, never explicitly formulated, of determination, the noetic principle, on the other. In this regard, Calogero's attempt to accentuate the distinction between dianoetic and noetic logic and to establish the hierarchical 'superiority' of the latter over the former is quite misguided, for he has failed to note not only the deeper meaning of Aristotle's polemic against Protagoras, but also the nature of the aesthetic foundation of the noema, and therewith the full import of this foundation in relation to discursive, *dianoetic* logic, Aristotle's specific contribution to which was his discovery of the senses.)

---

[98] On this point, see Maier, *Die Syllogistik des Aristoteles*, volume I, pp. 5 ff.

Aristotle's critique of Platonic diairesis is thus motivated, at bottom, by the demand for a new ontological (and logical) dimension, a sort of contrariety (i.e. relation) of incompatible contraries, or *contradictories* in the Aristotelian sense, through which division of the *more general* can be attained, and thus the specific essence unattainable by Plato's purely dialectical division. This requisite, if considered carefully, would seem to express a profound instance which can only be that of the material, the multiple, the discrete, or whatever one may call it. Indeed, without this, it is difficult to find any meaning or justification either for the ontological figures of first substance and dividing actuality (incompatible contrariety) or for the corresponding logical and gnoseological figures, the principle of non-contradiction and the dianoetic logos and noema-image. On the other hand, if these latter figures were devoid of meaning, we would lose the very considerable assistance they afford us in the resolution of our problem, namely: how to establish the falsity of Plato's a priori method of 'dividing', of *making distinctions*?

In other words, we cannot afford to dispense with the 'determinateness' or concreteness without which there is no thought, not even for Plato himself. Of course, the *other* hypothetical Platonic instance, of unity or dialectic, which we are criticizing here, examining its limitations and import, can be of no use to us here. It is therefore necessary to repeat the hypothesis of a different instance— that of multiplicity, materiality, or discreteness, and corresponding positivity. Of this there can be no doubt. What must be done is to continue, with Aristotelian (and Marxist) instruments, the examination we began earlier with Kantian instruments.

This will enable us to establish the following conclusion, the full import of which we shall grasp only later: the question of the concreteness or determinateness of thought, on which the dispute between Plato and Aristotle over diairesis turns, can move towards resolution if we bear three points in mind. First, the particular 'determinateness' of thought in the Aristotelian sense is due to the absolute and non-relative character of the noema, or, as we would put it, the *conceptus*, whereas Platonic determinateness depends on the dialectical character, unity, or relationality of every genus that is pervaded by the higher genera; it is therefore determinable only in and through its interpenetration with its 'opposite'. Second, the noema is not relative, for it is specifically noema-image, which means that the noema is grounded in the discreteness, which is to say immutability and staticness-ecstaticness (contemplativeness) of the senses (*nihil in intellectu quod non prius in sensu!*). Third, only such a *conceptus* or conception constitutes division, determination, or specification of the 'more general', of the universal, since it is from the discrete, which is the positivity of its aesthetic or intuitive foundation, that this conception borrows the specification of the universal that it actuates. Thus, since it is genuine *doxa*, determinateness, or concreteness, it avoids the particular deficiency of descending a priori division: its *surreptitious specificity* (the ontological *petitio principii* described above).

Whence arises, however, the *veracity* of this doxa, which must nevertheless be conception or thought (logos)? How can this veracity, which is synonymous with validity, universality, or unity, be derived from the non-relativity or multiplicity of the noema, in which alone the positivity characteristic of the instance of the discrete, Aristotle's anti-Parmenidean instance, is expressed? Aristotle affords us no answer to this decisive question. Even he, then, did not genuinely resolve the problem of the 'true *doxa*', the problem of determinate, concrete, and real thought, although he did take the first steps towards its solution.

This critical excursus through Platonic and Aristotelian logic thus leads us to the following comparative conclusions.

1. The logic of Plato offers us two, not at all unimportant suggestions. First, without 'opposition', or dialecticism, there can be no justification for the relationality, unity, or universality that incompatible contrariety (or non-contradiction) requires for its own validity or universality (or particular consistency, as we shall see). Second, dialecticization can occur only through division, in the concrete. The higher genera therefore have meaning only inasmuch as they can be predicated of appropriate subjects, or empirical participating genera. In other words, they have meaning only as *functional* criteria that unify a multiplicity. On the other hand, this logic is unequal to its most profound instances, because of its dialectical-deductive methodological criterion, as a result of which it never manages to go beyond the 'more general', or undifferentiated universal, in which it is maintained by pure tauto-heterology, because of the presupposition of species, of multiplicity. This constitutes a genuine ontological (and not merely formal-verbal) *petitio*

principii, for it gratuitously postulates a something—multiplicity, discreteness, matter, or whatever it may be called—which, because of the inevitable sophistry and defectiveness of the a priori mode of thought itself, of which it takes no account, is actually indispensable for the understanding of being in general.

2. The logic of Aristotle, unlike Plato's, does succeed in suggesting a means of overcoming the indeterminateness or absolute unity to which the Parmenidean opposition of being and not-being leads. The reason for this relative success is that Aristotle's logic, which, on the basis of the supposition of first substance, grounds the determinateness of the concept in undialectical immutability or sameness of sensation, and thereby in the singularity (and contingency) of the aesthetic or intuitive, attains the principle of non-contradiction, which establishes, against the indeterminateness and consequent formal ambiguity of the Eleatic-Platonic logos, formal dianoetic determinateness as specifically discursive. Nevertheless, Aristotle achieves this through the sacrifice of negative predication and therefore of negativity and relationality in general. (This is connected—through the formula that allows not the 'simple being' of not-being, but rather its 'qualitatively determined being', whence the equalization of the privative contrary and the positive—to the general anti-Eleatic principle of the multiple sense of being.) His logic therefore loses sight not only of the dialectical character or unity of being, but also of the validity (universality) without which the principle of non-contradiction itself cannot stand.

3. The ultimate reason for the failure of Plato's solution of the problem of the true *doxa* must be sought in his conception of truth as *internal dialogue* or *self-consciousness*. (See, for example, *Theaetetus* 190 c: 'forming opinion [*doxazein*] is talking to oneself'. See also *Theaetetus* 187a and 190a, and *The Sophist* 263e: thought 'is a silent inner conversation of the soul with itself'.) This conception, founded on the theory of reminiscence, contaminates concrete thought, which is intended to be the true *doxa*, with a priorism, with abstract rationalism. If to this we add the reduction of division to a descending or deductive rather than immanent dialectical process and the failure to characterize the judgement as a specific nexus of subject (the particular) and predicate (the universal), then we may also grasp the consequent reduction of the knowledge (and the being) of the *individual* Theaetetus, for

example, to the pure and simple intellectual intuition of the *eidos* 'man'.[99]

In turn, the ultimate reason for Aristotle's failure to resolve this same problem lies, conversely, in the large dose of still abstract and uncritical a posteriorism that informs his theory of the concrete individual. This, leaving aside the naive realistic ontologism and the consequent naturalistic and metaphysical finalism, is apparent (in gnoseology and logic) in the empirical and immediate assumption of the noema-image, for which the union in this noema-image of essence and existence is so extrinsic that it can give rise only to a dianoetic logic of formalistic-verbal persuasion within which the fundamental logical element is the *isolated word*,[100] which ultimately and abstractly reflects (through second substance) the individual *thing*, which is undialectical first substance. It is this that mars Aristotle's contribution to the discovery of discursive or concrete reason, of the intellect or dianoia; but the contribution is inseparable from his more fundamental contribution to the philosophical discovery of the *senses* and *matter*.

If we now compare Hegel's logical principle with Plato's and Aristotle's, we may observe as follows.

1. Hegel's solution of the fundamental problem of the dialectic proves one-sided, less comprehensive and productive than Plato's as

---

[99] In Plato, then, we already find the tendency, subsequently developed by Hegel, to hold that the universal, the predicate, is the concept of the particular, the subject, and *exhausts its nature* (Hegel), since it is the *substance*, the essence, of *what is being spoken of* (Hegel). It therefore *annuls* the subject as the *basis* of the judgement, thereby annulling the judgement itself. Finally, let us note that we have here the first instance of the *substantification* of the predicate or universal, its transmutation into the subject, the ultimate consequences of which we shall examine later. Marx uncovered this same procedure in Hegel, calling it the (theological) interpolation of the content or multiple.

[100] In *Die Syllogistik des Aristoteles* (volume II, 2, pp. 150, 180, 184), Maier expounds the law of the syllogism as follows: 'The law of the syllogistic function must be understood thus: a concept must be led to a second if it is to serve to determine others, but cannot determine those from which it is derived. The former is the case for the general and the particular.' He then observes: 'The *word* that embodies what is general in *house* is the root of the validity of the syllogism and of the syllogistic principle. Indeed, the logical principle flows immediately from language. It is the logical-ontological meaning of the word. But we must add immediately: of the *isolated word*. And this limitation is characteristic.' The only way he can account for this, however, seems to be to cite Aristotle's usual general presupposition: 'the word, concept, and thing coincide' (p. 235).

presented in *The Sophist* and *The Statesman*. Hegel, who disregards the problem of the true *doxa*, to which Plato the theorist of diairesis did direct his attention, never goes beyond the concept of a dialectic of *pure thoughts*, a monotriad of reasoning, which he identifies with the *turning into self*—or instantaneous reconstruction of an original, dogmatic unity—called pure or essential self-consciousness.

2. Hegel's formulation of the logical principle as a pure, synthetic principle fails, *a fortiori*, to satisfy the exigencies inherent in Aristotle's logical principle, since the latter represents not only a general instance contrary to Parmenides's and Plato's identity or unity of being, but also a particular integrative instance of Platonic diairesis, intended as it is to ground the concept of contradictories as incompatible contraries, which evaded Plato but without which the precondition of diairesis or classification itself disappears.

3. Hegel's logical principle is therefore insufficient on two counts, not only in comparison with Aristotle's anti-Eleatic and anti-Platonic instance, but also, in a certain sense, in comparison with the anti-Eleatic and self-critical instance of Plato himself.

The comparison between Hegel and Plato is therefore detrimental to the former. Hegel's concept of the dialectic as subject excludes from the 'tarrying with the negative' (which is the subject) that positive that 'closes its eyes to the negative'—of which the self-critical Plato vaguely felt he had to take account, since he was also interested in experience and the related problem of the *separation* of genera-beings. Having done this, Hegel inevitably turned out to be a more dogmatic Platonist than Plato himself, since he so rigidly accepted the concept of *the genus that is mediated in and with itself rather than in and with the species* (mediation and self-mediation) which Aristotle imputed to Plato even when the latter was embroiled in the self-critical effort to pose the problem of the diairetic, or diacritic dialectic, reproaching him for taking the genus (the more general) instead of the species, for the mediator.

In sum, it must be acknowledged that Hegel's conception of the dialectic as subject effectively bound his thought to the most typical Platonic dogma: the concept of truth, and of validity in general, as a dialogue of the soul within itself (as reminiscence). This concept, which he integrated with Kant's *cogito* or *I think* as transcendental

apperception, has become the modern, Hegelian *know thyself*[101]—
the mythical turning into self that is pure self-consciousness, the
dogmatic self-reconstitution of a dogmatic unity. The parallel with
Plato's innate—and therefore *merely* obscured or forgotten—ideas
is evident.[102]

Here we may also grasp the ultimate significance of the encounter
of Hegel and Kant through Plato. Because he was dominated by
Platonic apriorism—the apriorism of the theory of anamnesis,
which prevented Plato from *realizing* the dialectic, despite his profound conception of the indissolubility of dialectic and diairesis—

[101] If we are to grasp the real relationship between Socrates and Hegel, we cannot
disregard the sort of scepticism that lies at the root of the ancient, Socratic 'know
thyself': it is a constructive scepticism, like Plato's, whose compass (unlike Plato's) is
not conceptual-intellectual knowledge and the corresponding antinomies, but rather
the sensible subjective irrational, to the deprecation of which intrepid faith in
thought, i.e. the *intellect* (Socratic 'reason'), leads. Here, however, Socraticism coincides, in a certain sense, with the scepticism of a Sextus, who in his own way renders
such homage to thought as to seriously consider it alone, philosophically and scepti-
cally, by recognizing that it is 'a trickster' and that, on the other hand, sensible representation, as 'involuntary' emotion, is not the object of 'investigation', nor is it the
'criterion' of the existence of a thing. In sum, it is unrelated to the problem of truth
and falsity but has to do with 'conduct', 'life', and therefore is not 'overthrown' but
'assented to' by scepticism, since, 'we cannot live and do nothing at all'. (*Outlines of
Pyrrhonism*, I, 19-24.) It therefore appears legitimate to conclude that Socraticism
and scepticism share a substantial interest (positive for the former, negative for the
latter) in 'reasoning', and that this comes into play in ancient, pre-critical scepticism,
since it ignores the positive aspect of the philosophical problem of the senses as such.
On 'irony' see, for example, Stenzel, *Die Metaphysik des Altertums*, Munich-Berlin,
1931, p. 92; and p. 93 on the negative, almost mystical significance of 'know thyself'.
These elements—anti-aesthetic irony, demon of reason, self-consciousness—were the
germinal elements of a rationalistic mysticism which, transmitted through Plato, were
later developed in the Hegelian system, where 'know thyself' becomes 'essential self-
consciousness'.

[102] It is no accident that in the preface to the *Phenomenology of Spirit* (pp. 27-28),
the *totalization* and *preservation* of the positive, or determinate being, is formulated
as a *recollection*, 'something that *recollects* itself [*sich erinnert*]'. It should be noted
that only a singular historic blindness can prevent certain critics (Alexandre Kojève,
among others), who attempt directly to rally Hegel to the cause of existentialism, from
taking notice of Hegel's constitutional Platonism. It should, for example, be superfluous to observe that in the introduction to the *Phenomenology* (pp. 51-52) the
human inquietude described by Hegel is merely—and cannot be anything but—
romantic inquietude rationalistically systematized into a metaphysical dogma.
('Consciousness, however', Hegel tells us, 'is explicitly the Concept of itself. Hence it
is something that goes beyond limits, and since these limits are its own, it is something
that goes beyond itself.... Thus consciousness suffers this violence at its own hands.'
It is a violence suffered 'at the hands of Reason' against the 'unthinking inertia' of the
'anxiety' of 'the truth'.) In short, Hegel's philosophy of the anxiety of the truth
cannot be coherently married to an *existential* analytic of anxiety of death and of
'finite freedom'.

Hegel was led to view Kant's theory that the transcendental unity of apperception was a priori as meaning that it held priority over the multiplicity of its content. He therefore interpreted Kant's notion of self-consciousness, his *I think*, as pure or essential self-consciousness. In so doing, however, Hegel lost sight of the fundamental *critical* instance: that of category-*function*, which, since it is essentially connected to the instance of a heterogeneity (in the synthesis) of the intuition and the concept (which is the outcome of the cardinal critique of Leibniz), can be satisfied only by the conception of a synthesis which, far from being understood as the priority of the synthesis over its elements, must be understood as the result of the reciprocal priority or transcendence of the elements. In short, it is a synthesis that is properly a *syn-thesis of heterogeneities*, similar to the sort of Aristotelian-type *synolos* adumbrated by the critical Kant in his gnoseological concept of *original acquisition*.

It is this above all that must be kept in mind in explaining the 'uncontrollability' or 'absence of critical counter-instances' that mars Hegel's dialectic, his lack of critical discernment.[103]

And it is this question of the uncontrollability of Hegel's dialectic which—by means of a deeper examination through further research into the ultimate implications and consequences of a dialectic of pure thoughts, a dialectic which is, in this sense, one-sided—can lead us to a genuinely critical conclusion about this dialectic.

Now, if we replace the diadic rhythm of Plato's tauto-heterology (dichotomic diairesis) with the triadic rhythm of Hegel's dialectic, the substitution not only does not efface but indeed makes clearer our verdict on Platonic tauto-heterology: it contains a tacit and illegitimate recourse to the empirical. The difficulty persists.

We find the same problem in Hegel. Tauto-heterology—i.e. conceptual unity, or the speculative proposition—comes into play by

---

[103] Thus, for example, Nicolai Hartmann, *Die Philosophie des deutschen Idealismus*, II, *Hegel*, Berlin, 1929, p. 185; cf. p. 186: 'For Hegel the dialectical procedure is characteristically one-sided. But this is not at all characteristic of the *essence* of the dialectic. . . . Undialectical thoughts are occasionally comprehended in the dialectic. . . . As with Kant and the problem of the antinomies, . . . as with Aristotle and the paradoxes of energy and of *eidos*, . . . so for Hegel, such occasional dialectics are a striking illustration that in the genuine dialectic antinomies *exist* and are *not* "resolved".' Hartmann's critique may be compared to the apology of Kroner, who (in *Von Kant bis Hegel*, II, p. 343) supports his claim that Hegel's dialectic is concrete by arguing that 'Hegel is quite well aware that "pure" thought is no thought, that thought is simultaneously intuition. Intuition, Being, thinks of itself.'

conditioning the empirical (the dualistic or discursive proposition) through its preconceived unitary rigour. This is true in the sense that since this unity is the substance or exhaustive essence of what is being spoken about—in other words, the form which is itself 'the intrinsic becoming of the concrete content'—it follows, for example, that in the discursive proposition regarding the death of Aristotle on such and such a date, we would have a judgement, or truth, only if some circumstance had been challenged and the given figures were affirmed for some reason, for in that case these figures would be taken as something universal, as subsisting even without the *determinate* content of the death of Aristotle. In sum, the 'positive that closes its eyes to the negative' is excluded from the dialectic, or 'tarrying with the negative', and the merely synthetic nature of the principle of non-contradiction is affirmed.

The empirical in turn comes into the dialectical construction in that it is the inevitable *subject* of the predicate (which is the universal, i.e. the unity of the concept). In short, it is what is being spoken about, that whose motive is being sought—for example, the determinate content that is the death of Aristotle, of which the concept is the substance or essence. However, as we have seen, precisely since the unity of the concept is the form that is itself 'the intrinsic becoming of the concrete content', it therefore *excludes* the 'positive that closes its eyes to the negative', inherent in the empirical or subject, and replaces it with, or interpolates, the intrinsic becoming of the content or multiplicity, deemed by Hegel concrete since it is purely formal, i.e. formalistic. The determinate content of the death of Aristotle, then, exists only in order to occasion the affirmation of these figures-factors, which subsist, indeed, as something universal, even without this determinate content. Precisely for this reason, the empirical becomes an occasion or pretext that represents something else,[104] an allegory or symbol of (triadic) tauto-heterology. Its

---

[104] See notes 80 and 81 above. Here is the text of Marx's criticism of Plato (and Hegel): 'Where the Absolute stands on one side, and limited positive reality on the other, and the positive must all the same be preserved, there this positive becomes the medium through which absolute light shines, the absolute light breaks up into a fabulous play of colours, and the finite, the positive, *points to something other than itself.*' (*Karl Marx, Frederick Engels: Collected Works*, volume 1, London, 1975, p. 497, emphasis added.) To demonstrate that Marx's criticism is philologically accurate in relation to Hegel as well as Plato, we may advance the following important passage of the *Science of Logic* (p. 532): 'The illusory being is not *nothing*, but is a reflection, a *relation* to the absolute; or, it *is* illusory being in so far as *in it the absolute is reflected*. This positive exposition thus arrests the finite before it vanishes and

presence in the dialectical construction is *gratuitous* and *surreptitious*—but nonetheless inevitable and necessary for the instance of the subject. Here, then, as before, there is a transformation of the speculative into the empirical, as a consequence of and counterpart to the dissolution of the empirical into the speculative effected by the constructive-deductive process of the dialectic as dialectic of pure thoughts.

This is the ontological *petitio principii* that impugns the constitution of the *concrete* content understood in the Hegelian sense, namely the formalistic or dialectical multiple: the *postulation* of the determinate, empirical content through the constitution of the concept (concrete in the sense that its intrinsic becoming is the form itself). It is the unforeseen consequence of an uncontrollable dialectic, the *retribution*, unsuspected by most critics, suffered by the abstract-rationalist and dogmatic dialectic as *hypostatized* universal. The dogmatic concept is not at all 'empty' but full with vitiated content, and the negative ontological circle is sterile.

We must therefore attentively examine the process of substantification, or hypostatization, of the predicate or universal in which Hegel's, like any aprioristic, dialectic characteristically consists. It is through this process that the illicit recourse to the empirical will unfold in its entirety.

Let us note immediately that we have already encountered this process of hypostatization—the transformation of the predicate, universal, or abstraction, into the subject, substrate, or concrete, and the consequent transformation of the real subject into the predicate. It is evident in these formulations of Plato and Hegel: a) the explanation-substitution of the *eidos* 'human' for the individual 'Theaetetus'; b) the concept or *predicate* which, as the substance or essence of the particular or subject, not only exhausts its nature as subject and thereby annuls it as subject (thus also annulling the dualistic, discursive, real proposition), but also replaces it.

Let us now note that the time-honoured illusion of metaphysics that fuels every aprioristic conviction—namely the illusion that the substrate-matter, Aristotle's *upokeimenon* (the first non-mythical

---

contemplates it as an expression and image of the absolute. But the transparency of the finite, which only lets the absolute be glimpsed through it, ends by completely vanishing; for there is nothing in the finite which could preserve for it a distinction against the absolute; it is a medium which is absorbed by that which is reflected through it.'

formulation of substrate), can be exhausted in the substrate-essence—is expressed quite openly in Hegel's claim that there is a predicate, an essence, that can exhaust, annul, and replace the subject or substrate by exhausting its *nature*.

To hypostatize, then (in the exact historical and technical sense of the word), is to fall into erroneous realism, the (absolute) realism of metaphysicians and apriorists. In other words, to apriorize *is* to hypostatize. Let us put it another way. Whoever hypostatizes loses sight of the profound and original critical admonition inherent in Aristotle's distinction between first substance, or ultimate subject, and second substance, or essence. Indeed, whoever does this presumes functionally to replace the former with the latter, with essence (which is substantified, i.e. intended also as the substance *par excellence* that is the former).

At this point, in this historic-critical framework, we may now examine the entire vitiated structure of Hegel's hypostatization (including the conversion of the subject into the predicate and vice versa). We shall do so primarily by drawing on one of Marx's analyses (the first of its kind) of the 'mystified' dialectic of Hegel's *Philosophy of Right*. In this manner we shall be able to grasp the full significance and import of the absence of any critical counter-instance in Hegel's dialectic and will thus genuinely conclude our assessment of it.

4

Let us begin with Marx's analysis of Hegel's deduction of the transition from the family and civil society to the state, as presented in paragraphs 261-266 of the *Philosophy of Right*.[105]

In his 'Critique of Hegel's Doctrine of the State', Marx observes:

'The family and civil society are conceived as conceptual spheres of the state, indeed as the spheres of its *finite phase*, as its *finite phase*. It is the state that is sundered into them and *presupposes*

---

[105] The following quotations from Marx's 'Critique of Hegel's Doctrine of the State' (1843) and his 'Economic and Philosophical Manuscripts' (1844) are taken from Karl Marx: *Early Writings*, translated by Rodney Livingstone and Gregor Benton, Penguin in association with NLR, Harmondsworth, 1975. Quotations from Hegel's *Philosophy of Right*, both within the *Early Writings* and in Della Volpe's text, are from the translation by T.M. Knox, Oxford University Press, 1967.—*Translator's note.*

them. It does so "in order to rise above its ideality and become explicit as *infinite real mind*".... It "*therefore assigns* to these ideal spheres the material of its reality *in such a way that* this assignment etc. is *visibly* mediated"....

'The logical, pantheistic mysticism emerges very clearly at this point.

'The *real* relationship is "that the assignment of the material of the state to any given individual is mediated by circumstances, his caprice and his personal choice of his station in life". This fact, this *real relationship* is described by speculative philosophy as *appearance*, as *phenomenon*. These circumstances, this caprice, and this personal choice of a station in life, this *real mediation*, are merely the *appearance of a mediation* which the real Idea performs on itself and which takes place behind the scenes. Reality is not deemed to be itself but another reality instead. The ordinary empirical world is not governed by its own mind but by a mind alien to it; by contrast, the existence corresponding to the real Idea is not a reality generated out of itself, but is just the ordinary empirical world.

'The Idea [the predicate] is subjectivized [that is, hypostatized] and the *real* relationship of the family and civil society to the state is conceived as their *inner, imaginary* activity. The family and civil society are the preconditions of the state; they are the true agents [because, as 'real subjects' they are 'real beings']; but in speculative philosophy it is the reverse. When the Idea [the predicate] is subjectivized, the real subjects—civil society, the family, "circumstances, caprice, etc."—are all transformed into *unreal*, objective moments of the Idea [that is, they become predicates] referring to different things [that is, they become 'allegories' or 'symbols'].

'...the assignment of the material of the state "to a given individual is mediated by circumstances, his caprice, and his personal choice of a station in life". However, the latter are not regarded as true, necessary and intrinsically self-justified; they are not *as such* deemed to be rational. If they are held to be rational it is only in the sense that, while they are regarded as furnishing an *illusory* mediation, and while they are left just as they were, they nevertheless acquire the meaning of a determination of the Idea, of its result or product.... It is a history with two aspects, one esoteric, the other exoteric. The content is relegated to the exoteric side [i.e. to the 'ordinary empirical world']. The interest of the esoteric [that is, the 'arcane realm' of 'speculative philosophy'] is always directed towards the rediscovery of the history of the logical [or pure] concept in the state. However, the actual development [and the fact that there really is a content] takes place in the exoteric sphere.

'...In other words the political state cannot exist without the natural basis of the family and the artificial basis of civil society. These are its *sine qua non*; and yet the condition is posited as the conditioned, the determinator as the determined, the producer as the product [i.e. the state]; the real Idea only condescends to become the "finite phase" of the family and civil society in order that by their transcendence [*Aufhebung*] it may bring about its own infinity and enjoy it. It *"therefore* assigns" (i.e. in order to achieve its goal) "to these ideal spheres the material of this its finite reality" (this? which?: these spheres *are* its "finite reality", its "material").... Thus empirical reality is accepted as it is; it is even declared to be rational. However, it is not rational by virtue of its own reason, but because the empirical fact in its empirical existence has a meaning other than itself [i.e. it is 'allegorical']. The fact which serves as a starting-point is not seen as such but as a mystical result. The real becomes a mere phenomenon [of the Idea], but the Idea has no content over and above this phenomenon.... In this paragraph [§262 of the *Philosophy of Right*] we find set out the whole mystery of the *Philosophy of Right* and of Hegel's philosophy in general....

'The transition from the family and civil society to the political state takes the following form [in Hegel's §266]: the spirit of those spheres, which is *implicitly* the spirit of the state, now behaves as such to itself and becomes *real* to itself as their inner truth. Thus the transformation does not result from the *particular* nature of the family, etc., and the *particular* nature of the state, but from the *universal* relationship of *freedom* and *necessity*. We find exactly the same process at work in the *Logic* in the transition from the sphere of Essence to that of the Concept. In the *Philosophy of Nature*, the same transition can be observed from Inorganic nature to Life. It is always the same categories which are made to supply now one sphere and now another with a soul. The problem [for Hegel] is merely to discover the appropriate abstract determinants to fit the individual concrete ones....

'... He does not develop his thought from the object, but instead the object is constructed according to a system of thought perfected in the abstract [a priori] sphere of logic.'[106]

Let us take another example, Marx's analysis of Hegel's deduction of the political constitution (in paragraphs 269-276 of the *Philosophy of Right*). Marx observes:

'How then can he justify his conclusion [in §269]: "This organism is the political constitution"? Why not: "This organism is the solar system"? Because he has defined the "different members of the state" as "the various powers of the state". The statement that "these different members of the state are its various powers" is an empirical proposition and cannot be passed off as a philosophical discovery; nor is it in any sense the result of a logical argument. By defining the organism as the "differentiation of *the* Idea", by speaking of the various [dialectical!] elements of *the* Idea and then interpolating the concrete fact of "the various powers of the state", the illusion arises that a *definite* content has been elucidated. . . . At any rate, what he says applies to any organism and there is no predicate to be found which might justify the subject "this". The goal he hopes to reach is to define the *organism* as the *political constitution*. But he has failed to construct a bridge *leading from the general idea of the organism to the particular idea of the organism of the state or the political constitution*. Moreover, even if we wait to the end of time it will never become possible to construct such a bridge. . . .

'The truth is that Hegel . . . has converted into a product, a predicate of the Idea, what was properly its subject [i.e. the various powers; in other words, he 'makes of them a predicate of their own predicate']. He does not develop his thought from the object [the political constitution, in this case], but instead the object is constructed according to a system of thought perfected in the abstract sphere of logic. His task is not to elaborate the definite idea of the political constitution, but to provide the political constitution with a relationship to the abstract Idea and to establish it as a link in the [triadic dialectical] life-history of the Idea—an obvious mystification.

[106] *Early Writings*, pp. 61-65, 69. The general tone of Marx's critique of Hegel in these passages may be compared to Galileo's comments about the Jesuit Christopher Scheiner, a scholastic astronomer: 'This fellow goes about thinking up, one by one, things that would be required to serve his purposes, instead of adjusting his purposes step by step to things as they are.' (Galileo Galilei, *Dialogue Concerning the Two Chief World Systems*, translated by Stillman Drake, University of California Press, second revised edition, 1967, p. 94.)

'Another claim is that the "various powers of the state" are "fixed by the nature of the concept" and that therefore by means of them the universal "engenders itself in a *necessary* way" [by producing itself]. Thus the various powers are not determined by "their own nature" but by something alien to them. Similarly, their *necessity* is not to be found in their own essence, much less has it been critically established. Rather, their fate is predestined by the "nature of the concept", it lies sealed in the holy archives of the Santa Casa (of the Logic).[107] . . . "Idea" and "concept" are here autonomous abstractions [as 'idea made subject', or hypostatized].'[108]

And yet again, in the course of the same argumentation, Marx quotes §272 of Hegel's *Philosophy of Right*: 'The constitution is rational in so far as the state outwardly differentiates and determines its activity *in accordance with the nature of the concept*. The result is that *each* of these *powers* is itself the *totality* of the constitution, because each contains the other moments and has them effective within itself, and because the moments, being expressions of the differentiation of the concept, simply abide in their ideality and constitute nothing but a *single individual* whole.' Marx then comments:

'Thus the constitution is rational in so far as its moments can be resolved into the categories of abstract logic. The state must not differentiate its activity in accordance with its own specific nature, but in accordance with the nature of the concept which is the mystified movement of abstract thought. The rationality of the constitution is therefore abstract logic and not the concept of the state.'[109]

The preceding argumentation means that:

1. The 'universal is made autonomous' (i.e. it is substantified, hypostatized) or 'reduced to the subject' of the judgement and thereby 'directly compounded with empirical existence' (which is the 'real subject') and 'this limited existence [the real subject] is at once uncritically judged to be the expression of the Idea', in other words, the expression of its own 'product' or 'predicate'. The result is that Hegel 'denies to the thing [the real subject] that which is particular to it and attributes [*unterschiebt*] to it in its limited guise, a meaning opposite to this limitation'. Hence, 'the meaning [of the particular

---

[107] The Santa Casa was the Inquisition prison in Madrid.
[108] *Early Writings*, pp. 68-70.
[109] Ibid., pp. 74-75.

118

thing] is not in that of self-determination, but of an allegory foisted on to it', i.e. 'interpolated' (*untergeschobene*).[110]

2. As a result of this exchange, inversion [*Umkehrung*], or 'transformation [*Umschlag*] of the empirical into the speculative', there is also an exchange, inversion, or transformation of 'the speculative into the empirical'. In other words, 'the actual development takes place in the exoteric sphere' (i.e. in the empirical world), such that the 'development, however, always takes place on the side of the predicate', or mystified predicate, the empirical 'real subject' transformed into predicate. This 'does not represent any gain in meaning, but only a change in *form* of the old meaning'. And indeed, the 'detail of the argument is based on wholly empirical foundations, and very abstract and very unsound empirical foundations at that'.[111]

Now, in regard to the first point, it must be kept in mind that:

1. Precisely because there has been a hypostatization (of the universal, of course), the universal (the dialectic), which is the predicate, is *immediately confounded* with empirical existence, the particular or real substrate or subject, in the sense that the universal, a substrate-essence, replaces the substrate-matter, which is the particular or real subject, exchanging the reality-immediacy of this with its own reality-mediation, and positing the erroneous premise of *absolute realism*, the dogmatic postulate of metaphysics in general, of *aprioristic* rationalism.

2. The character of *mere allegory of the universal* acquired by the real substrate, or subject, is therefore due to the nature of this theological interpolation through hypostatization, since the latter claims to exhaust the *material* in the essence of form, in such a way that, given the denial and substitution of the *thing*, or real subject,

[110] Ibid., p. 102. This may be compared with the following general characteristic of Hegel's idealist method as allegorizing theological interpolation: 'Real man and real nature [the 'real subjects'] become mere predicates, symbols of this hidden, unreal man and this unreal nature [i.e. they become predicates of the substantified idea, predicates of their own natural predicate]. Subject [or the particular] and predicate [or universal] therefore stand in a relation of absolute inversion [*Verkehrung*] to one another; a *mystical subject-object* or *subjectivity* [i.e. universality] *encroaching [übergreifende] upon the object* [i.e. particularity or nature], the *absolute subject* and a *process*, as a *subject* which *alienates* itself....' ('Economic and Philosophical Manuscripts', in *Early Writings*, p. 396.)

[111] *Early Writings*, pp. 102, 190, 149, 98, 62, 65, 99, 95.

all that remains of matter is its value as *symbolic expression* or manifestation of the form, idea, or universal. In other words, the real subject becomes the mystified predicate.

In regard to the second point, however, it must be kept in mind that:

1. As a result of the transformation of the empirical into the speculative—hypostatization in the strict sense, since 'the empirical is *philosophically* dissolved'—there is another, simultaneous transformation, this time of the speculative into the empirical. This, in turn, constitutes a 'philosophical restoration of the empirical'.

2. This *restoration*—which consists in the fact that the development, progress, or articulation of the universal proceeds by virtue of the *mystified predicate*, the real, empirical substrate or subject transformed into predicate—is at once defective and inevitable: *defective* because it is the restoration of an empirical which, having been presupposed a priori, is *gratuitous* (for example, the fact or determinate content of the 'death of Aristotle', which the speculative, metaphysical universal *does without*, as we have seen) and therefore tacitly and *surreptitiously* presumed; *inevitable* since this empirical element is nevertheless the indispensable substrate-subject of the *judgement*, in other words, that of which the reason is sought in the judgement (the date of the death of Aristotle, for example). In sum, it is the restoration of an empirical that is abstract and unsound because it is not mediated and is therefore gratuitous and surreptitious, for it has been *transcended* in hypostatization or apriorization.

3. This restoration-subreption, which is none other than Hegel's ontological *petitio principii* and *negative ontological circle*, ultimately emerges, with all its characteristic sterility, as the *result-retribution* of the philosophical dissolution of the empirical in which Hegelian hypostatization consists, of the *dialectic of pure thoughts*, the triadic dialectic or tauto-heterology.

It can be shown with increasing ease that this result-retribution of hypostatization raises its ugly head not only in the *Science of Logic* (as we have seen in the examples of the 'judgements': 'Aristotle died on such and such a date' and 'a carriage is passing'), but throughout the work of Hegel, both in particular and in general.

Let us look first at a particular case. What is the ultimate, *real* conclusion of the *Philosophy of Right*? 'At every point', Marx writes, 'Hegel's political spiritualism can be seen to degenerate into the crassest *materialism*. . . . Nature [i.e. matter, the empirical] takes revenge on Hegel for the contempt he has shown her. If matter is to be shorn of its reality in favour of [rational] human will then here human will is left with no reality but that of matter.' And: 'The political constitution at its highest point [the 'High Chamber' of 'equals', etc.] is thus the *constitution of private property*.' (This is a reference to Hegel's theory that the High Chamber was the 'supreme synthesis' of the contradictions of the modern state, since he conceived it as a legislative power that was 'representative' but composed of 'born' legislators, not subject to the 'accidentality of popular election', but members of the 'substantial class' of land-owners and majorat gentlemen!) And finally: '*The "inalienability" of private property* [under primogeniture] *implies the "inalienabi-lity" of the universal freedom of the will and of ethical life*',[112] or ethical morality (*Sittlichkeit*) towards the re-evaluation of which Hegel strove with his theory of the state (the 'universal') as the *precondition* of civil society (the 'particular'), in order to overcome both Kant's *Moralität*—his 'abstract' individualistic morality of 'law' as personal 'maxim' and of 'duty' as pure 'intention'—and the contractual-political atomism of Rousseau and the theorists of natural law in general. How futile is the a priori dialectical 'trans-cendence' [*Aufhebung*] of one ideology by another!

The same argument may be expressed in different terms: 'Hegel should not be blamed for describing the essence of the modern state as it is [the 'constitutional monarchy of contemporary Europe' with its corresponding civil society] but for identifying what is with the *essence of the state*.' (And: 'Hegel's logic is cogent if we accept the presuppositions of a constitutional state [the product of its time]. But the fact that Hegel has *analysed* the fundamental idea of these presuppositions does not mean that he has demonstrated their validity.'[113]) What this means is that since Hegel winds up passing off the Prussian (and European) constitutional monarchy of 1820 and the *class-divided* civil society that was organically linked to it as the *essence* of the universal state, he thus bears witness—against his own a priori approach—that it is actually civil society in general, namely the world of the 'particular', of *material* needs and relations of existence, that *determines* the state, the idea, the 'universal'. In

---

[112] Ibid., pp. 174, 166, 169.
[113] Ibid., pp. 127, 96.

sum, then, Hegel's uncritical, idealistic, and spiritualistic premises *themselves justify* the crass materialism of a class-divided civil society and its corresponding state.[114] It is a *surreptitious* crass materialism which, as a typical example of an abstract, unsound, non-mediated empirical, emerges precisely as the *result* of the hypostatizations in which such premises consist. In short, it is the result-retribution cited above, the transformation of the speculative into the empirical as the counterpart of the dissolution of the empirical into the speculative. In sum, it is the result-retribution of hypostatization, the clearly futile, scientifically and practically sterile result of the aprioristic (moral) dialectic, the 'mystified mobility' of 'abstract thought'.

More generally, we may note with Marx that Hegel 'implies that self-conscious man, in so far as he has acknowledged and superseded the spiritual world, . . . goes on to reaffirm it in this alienated form and presents it as his true existence, restores it and claims to be *at home in his other-being as such*. Thus, for example, having superseded religion . . . he still finds himself confirmed in *religion* as *religion*. Here is the root of Hegel's *false* positivism or of his merely *apparent* criticism. . . . Therefore there can no longer be any question about a compromise on Hegel's part with religion, the state, etc. [Hegel's 'conservatism'!], since this untruth is the untruth

---

[114] Even recent and well-informed Hegel critics have failed to grasp this point; for example, Henri Niel, *De la méditation dans la philosophie de Hegel*, Paris, 1945, pp. 293 ff.: 'Indeed, although on the one hand it [Hegel's morality] presents society not as a fact imposed on us from without but as an ideal end that we must realize, on the other *it subjects us absolutely to presently existing social forms*, for it is through them alone that we can realize this ideal. . . . The trouble is that the spiritual grandeur Hegel attributes to the state is ambiguous in essence . . . , it is only in a *purely ideal fashion* that the citizen participates in political life, while his concrete real life unfolds in civil society, where externality, alienation, reigns. *In fact, nothing is changed* in the restrictions civil society imposes on our freedom; *it is in the idea alone* that we are free. Moreover, alienation itself is consolidated, for it appears as a precondition of political society' (emphasis added). What is lacking here is any perception of the connection—of premise and consequence—between the 'in the idea alone' and the 'nothing is changed'. In short, Niel is unaware of the materialist critique of a priori thought, and therefore of the materialist *consciousness of method* without which even Marx's exhortation to 'change the world' instead of only 'interpreting it' remains too vague, and even subject to the ideological errors of traditional pragmatism, as is particularly evident in the writings of those who, like Niel, are ignorant not only of the Marx of the *Early Writings* but also of Marxism-Leninism. Below we will discuss the ideological foundations of Hegel's conservatism, which lie in his philosophical method. On Marx's critique of Hegel's philosophy of right, see my study *Marx e lo Stato moderno rappresentativo* (1947), reprinted in *Per la teoria di un umanismo positivo*, Bologna, 1949.

of his principle.'[115] Hegel's so-called *conservatism* is therefore much deeper and more organic than might seem, for it has its ideological reflection in his fundamental concept of progress or development itself, with its defect of the mystified mobility of abstract or aprioristic dialectical thought. It is here that lies the defect of Hegel's 'positivism', which is actually 'false' and 'uncritical'. Marx concludes: 'In the *Phenomenology*, therefore, despite its thoroughly negative and critical appearance and despite the fact that its criticism is genuine and often well ahead of its time, the uncritical positivism and equally uncritical idealism of Hegel's later works, the philosophical dissolution and restoration of the empirical world, is already to be found in latent form, in embryo, as a potentiality and a secret.'[116] This uncritical positivism, then, is characteristic not only of Hegel's baroque philosophies 'of nature' and 'of history', with their manifestly sterile concatenations of speculative dissolutions and restorations-subreptions of natural scientific and historiographic *facts*, but also of his philosophy 'of spirit' and of the entire metaphysical *Encyclopaedia* of the 'philosophical sciences'.

Now, this discovery[117] by Marx of dialectical 'mystification' as the

[115] *Early Writings*, pp. 392-393.

[116] 'Economic and Philosophical Manuscripts', in *Early Writings*, pp. 384-385, emphasis added.

[117] I say 'discovery' advisedly. Although it is true that Feuerbach had already remarked against Hegel that speculative philosophy 'is a path that leads never to true objective reality, but always and only to the realization of its own abstractions', it is likewise true that Feuerbach concluded only that 'the object is reduced to wholly abstract determinations, in which it is no longer recognizable'. In other words, Hegel's 'universal' is *empty*. Feuerbach failed to realize the actual consequence of the substantification of the universal (or hypostatization): the inevitable *surreptitious* content or multiple, in accordance with the reciprocal *transformation* discussed above. For further discussion of Feuerbach's superficial (Kantian) critique of spiritualism and abstract rationalism, or idealism, see my *Per la teoria di un umanismo positivo*, p. 47. Finally, it is remarkable, though evident, that Marx's analysis of the *structure* of the process of hypostatization in Hegel is either ignored or regarded as a dead letter by those critics of idealism who, like John Dewey, have noted most clearly that the fundamental error of idealism in general is the 'hypostatization of a logical function into a supra-empirical entity' (*Logic—The Theory of Inquiry*, New York, 1938, p. 132), but who nevertheless do not go much beyond the Feuerbachian critique, since they are unaware of the real consequences of hypostatization, which can be uncovered only by a structural analysis of the procedure. This remains true despite the frequently penetrating observations of someone like Dewey. For example: 'The essential error of the "rationalistic" tradition in logical theory consists in taking the consistency of the constituents of the *conceptual* contents (which form the *predicate)* as a final criterion of truth or assertibility. Subject-matter which, in its *logical* form, is a means for performing experimental activities to modify prior existences is mistaken to be final and complete in itself. *Thereby an inherent ontological status is imputed to it.*' (Ibid., p. 131, emphasis added, and cf. p. 198.) Or the following scattered

real 'secret' of Hegel is of the same order as Aristotle's discovery of the illegitimacy of Plato's dialectical diairesis. Hegel's hypostatization—the surreptitious restoration of the empirical world subsequent to its *philosophical* dissolution—corresponds in substance to Plato's *postulation* of the (empirical) 'species' or *definiendum*, a consequence of his effort to divide or classify the genera on a *purely* rational or philosophic basis (on the basis of the higher genera, or compatibles, or tauto-heterology). Marx's discovery therefore falls within the purview of critical anti-Platonic and anti-idealist instances. This in itself constitutes confirmation of its general import and fitness to stand as a critique of a priori reasoning in general, generated by the radical materialist critique of Hegel's dialectic.

As we shall now see, however, it also coincides with Galileo's critique of the aprioristic foundations of peripatetic physics and therefore forms part of the sequence of critical instances from which modern experimental natural science arose, and not part of the sequence to which Kant's critique of the 'transcendental dialectic' belongs. The latter, in fact, is a merely apparent critique of the

---

observations of Joseph Ratner, a follower of the Dewey school: 'To satisfy the constant and natural craving of the mind for natural food, Hegel tried, by an act of unnatural violence, to force the mind to swallow the natural world whole! Instead of permanently satisfying the hunger of the mind, this grotesque act of intellectual outrage gave it convulsive indigestion. And the spasmic regurgitations of Absolute Idealism are splattered over all the pages of subsequent cultural history.... In its solitary confinement, in its ideal isolation, the formula, if we may trust Aristotle, becomes either a god or a brute. For living experience, there is no genuine difference between the alternatives. The inevitable consequence of deification is the brutalization of human life.... This method of substituting derived, refined objects of reflection for the gross and macroscopic subject-matter in primary experience . . . is the refined philosophical or logical equivalent of personification, namely the depersonalized personification that is technically known by the not too unambiguous term "hypostatization".... The high rationalist tradition in modern and contemporary philosophy, working with the Greek formula up its sleeve, substitutes the Third Law [the typical Newtonian 'object of reflection'] for the horse, stone and rope [= 'subject-matter in primary experience'] and claims that the substituted article is the ultimate reality. Whitehead and Russell both follow this tradition. The inflexible rationality of scholastic thought was, precisely, an inflexible idolatry of the "logical" instrument then available to their hand. The most popular idolatry of the instrument now current is that exhibited in the logical positivism movement.' ('Introduction to John Dewey's Philosophy', in *Intelligence in the Modern World: John Dewey's Philosophy*, New York, 1939, pp. 37, 200, 210, 223, 238.) For another example, this time negative, see the abject Hegelianism (indeed, the reverence for Leibniz's *demonstratio seu identitas*) of the epistemologist Emile Meyerson, who even endorses a Hegelian proposition that states: 'the other, the negative, contradiction, dispute, form part of the nature of the spirit.' (*De l'explication dans les sciences*, Paris, 1927, p. 141.)

process of hypostatization, for in the end it simply replaces the *metaphysics of being* (for example, the hypostasis 'soul', i.e. the substantification of the soul) with a *metaphysics of knowledge*, in particular with a new hypostasis: the 'I think' as the *absolute* formal precondition of 'experience'. The significance of all this is momentous: by implicitly demonstrating that not only Hegel the aprioristic philosopher of nature, but also Hegel the aprioristic moralist and logician, was a sort of new peripatetic Simplicio, Marx's critique demonstrated *a fortiori* that apriorism, Hegelian or otherwise, is sterile and illegitimate in philosophy *in general*, and therefore also in the so-called moral sciences. The prospect of a *new science* was thereby opened: philosophy as a historical, experimental science of humanity and all its problems.

Let us examine a typical example of this coincidence: the passage of the *Dialogue Concerning the Two Chief World Systems* in which Galileo rejects the Aristotelian-scholastic thesis of the geocentric universe precisely on the basis of a critique of the *method* of 'a priori discourse' employed by his adversary, Simplicio. Galileo concludes by charging Simplicio with 'paralogism', or 'begging the question'; in other words, Simplicio 'presupposes what is in question' or 'what we doubt'. The critical premise concerns the aprioristic, metaphysical theory of motion.

'With Aristotle', Sagredo says to Simplicio, 'you began by removing me somewhat from the sensible world, to show me the architecture [or 'ideal world' = mathematical-metaphysical models of the heavens and the earth] with which it must have been built. . . . [Next,] as to the explanation of what Aristotle means by simple motions, and how he determines them from properties of space, calling those simple which are made along simple lines, these being the straight and the circular only, I accept this willingly. . . . But I resent rather strongly finding myself restricted to calling the latter [circular motion] "motion about the centre" [*the* centre, the empirical centre of the earth] (while it seems that he wants to repeat the same definition in other words) and the former [straight motion] *sursum* and *deorsum*—that is, "upward" and "downward". For such terms are applicable only to the actual world [i.e., the 'sensible world'], and imply it to be not only constructed, but already inhabited by us. Now, if straight motion is simple with the simplicity of the straight line, and if simple motion is natural, then it remains so when made in any direction whatever; to wit, upward, downward, backward, forward, to the right, to the left; . . . provided only that it is straight, it will be suitable for any simple natural body. Or, if not, then Aristotle's supposition is defective.

'Moreover, it appears that Aristotle implies that only one circular motion exists in the world, and consequently only one centre [the earth] to which the motions of upward and downward exclusively refer. All of which seems to indicate that he was pulling cards out of his sleeve, and trying [tacitly] to accommodate the architecture to the building instead of modeling the building after the precepts of architecture. For if I should say that in the real universe there are thousands of circular motions, and consequently thousands of centres, there would also be thousands of motions upward and downward.'[118]

It is thus clear that Galileo's critique—which exposes the qualitative surreptitious residues, the abstract empirical or non-mediated elements of the geocentric theory (such as the terrestrial 'upward', 'downward', and 'centre')—has uncovered what may be called, in Marx's terminology, a *restoration* of the empirical, which had been philosophically dissolved in the hypostasis represented by the finalistic-valutative concept of the universe as a world of mathematical perfection. Galileo's ultimate verdict on the (not merely formal) defectiveness and organic sterility of any subsequent inference or deduction similarly based on a priori discourse is implicit in his exposure of this hypostasis.

Galileo then recalls the general scholastic argumentation in support of the 'structure of the Aristotelian universe', characterizing Aristotle's procedure thus:

'Having very well and methodically begun his discourse, at this point—being more intent upon arriving at a goal previously established in his mind than upon going wherever his steps directly lead him—he cuts right across the path of his discourse and assumes it as a known and manifest thing that the motions directly upward and downward correspond to fire and earth. Therefore it is necessary that beyond these bodies . . . there must be some other body in nature [the heavens] to which circular motion must be suitable. This must, in turn, be as much more excellent as circular motion is more perfect than straight. Just how much more perfect the former is than the latter, he determines from the perfection of the circular line over the straight line.'[119]

[118] *Dialogue Concerning the Two Chief World Systems*, pp. 15-16.
[119] Ibid., p. 18.

Galileo then concludes, against the peripatetic thesis of a geocentric universe: 'I say that all Aristotle sees of the motion of light bodies is that fire leaves any part of the surface of the terrestrial globe and goes directly away from it, rising upward; this indeed is to move toward a circumference greater than that of the earth.... But he cannot affirm that this is the circumference of the universe, or is concentric with that, so that to move toward it is to move toward the circumference of the universe. To do so he must suppose that the centre of the earth, from which we see these ascending light bodies depart, is the same as the centre of the universe. Now that is just what we were questioning, and what Aristotle intended to prove. You say that this is not an obvious fallacy?'[120]

With regard to Galileo's genuinely modern discourse on method, then, we may observe as follows.

1. Against the abstract metaphysical rationalism of the peripatetic scholastics, Galileo renews and deepens the critique of Aristotle at his most Aristotelian of the abstract dialectical rationalism of Platonic classification. This renewed critique demonstrates that the conceptual system of scholastic physics is sterile and cannot generate progress, because it aprioristically ignores and transcends experience, to which the fact 'in question' belongs. It *therefore* 'supposes', or rather presupposes and illegitimately postulates, what needs to be investigated. Subsequently, the 'more common symptoms' upheld by Simplicio against 'mathematical curiosities' are compared with the 'more general' with which Aristotle reproached Plato.

2. Galileo's rejection of the metaphysics and (final) causes of the scholastics, of their misguided absolute realism, of their 'Reality', acquires its full foundation and revolutionary philosophical significance in the light of this discovery of the real, and not merely formal or verbal, 'paralogism' into which the aprioristic logic of the scholastics falls. This rejection, as well as the consequent methodological imperative of 'saving appearances', or paying strict attention solely to phenomena or to the *how* of the facts, was expressed as follows in a letter Galileo wrote to Roberto Bellarmine in 1615: 'It is true that to show that the mobility of the earth and stability of the sun conform to appearances is not the same as to demonstrate that such hypotheses about nature are *really* true. But it is equally and

[120] Ibid., pp. 35-36.

even more true that if the other commonly accepted system cannot be squared with such appearances, then it is indubitably false, since it is clear that the former system, which does accord perfectly with the facts, can be true; no greater truth can or should be sought in a position than that it corresponds to all the particular appearances.'

3. The *spirit* of Galileo's method of research lies in its analysis of the empirical world—of physical appearances and phenomena—into a rational array of quantitative mathematical functional relations, in its formulation of syntheses that can be verified experimentally. This spirit of the search for truth, which stands opposed to the spirit of dogmatic exposition characteristic of the scholastics, was extended into the field of moral philosophical problems, and the historical, social, and human phenomena related to them, by Marx's (dialectical) analysis of *presuppositions of facts*. This analysis, as the 'specific logic of a specific object', which is 'philosophy as science' (for 'the pure ideality of a real sphere could exist only as science'), must replace the procedure according to which 'one contents oneself with recognizing the presupposed determinations of the pure concept', or 'synthesis' a priori, which is in any case too generic not to result in a pseudo-, and consequently sterile, synthesis. In short, the moral Galileanism of a *sociology* of the state must replace the *metaphysics* of the state.

(This is the *positive* general conclusion implied in Marx's 'Critique of Hegel's Doctrine of the State'. It is evident that a critique of the internal contradictions of a metaphysics of society, law, and the state, i.e. an analysis that reveals the *historical* difficulties presumed to have been resolved a priori, must inevitably lead to a *functional* scientific-experimental conception of a new society and a new system of law, thus satisfying the real, historically developed instances, separate from and in contrast to the metaphysical preconceived solutions. This was the profound, positive, and constructive result towards which Marx was striving when he burst Hegel's generic syntheses, laden with their undigested empirical elements, with the prick of his analysis of Hegel's specific presuppositions of fact—for example, the historical-comparative, or sociological, analysis of the medieval and modern representative system. In the following chapter we will discuss the general methodological conclusions that may be drawn from this.)

In order further to clarify this cardinal point about the generic, sterile synthesis, let us apply Marx's critique of Hegel to Rousseau's and Kant's 'natural law' and to Kant's ethics. In this manner we can complete the *generalization* of this critique.

To start with, let us note this: if, as is evident, so-called natural or (pure) rational rights are but rights attributed to an eternal and unchanging human nature, and are therefore mystified predicates of a mystified subject (hypostatized 'human nature'), then they must inevitably be exposed—in the course of time, which the 'eternal' of the hypostasis strives vainly to transcend—as *mystified rights*; in other words, as instances of privilege.

Indeed, because of the process of hypostatization—by which the subject or substrate-matter (in this case Rousseau's 'physical inequality' or individual-empirical differences in talent, strength, etc.) assumes the value of attribute or predicate of the mystified subject, which is the substrate-essence (in this case the hypostasis of generic, eternally immutable human nature), thus becoming a mystified predicate, for it is the predicate of its own predicate—its universality is merely that of the general generic it represents. At the same time, such universality, since it is not mediation, will coincide with the pure particularity of this material subject, the individual empirical inequalities. The latter are *thereby* established as values, i.e. (natural) rights. Now, since it is obvious that without subject, particular, or matter there can be no predicate, universal, or form (and vice versa), if the function of the former, the real subject, is usurped by the latter, the predicate, as occurs in any hypostatization, the predicate itself nevertheless cannot be eliminated; it must therefore be replaced in turn. Since there is no third element, the only candidate for replacement is the real subject, which becomes contorted into the predicate of its own natural predicate. But it can do this only by *borrowing* its character as predicate from the substantified predicate or universal, i.e. from the general generic (or 'more general', to put it in Aristotelian terms) and therefore by *maintaining* an ambiguous positivity of its own as a real or material subject which is *unmediated* (except dogmatically) precisely because it is transcended, through hypostasis, by the more general. It is this 'unsound empirical', composed of the instances of *natural* rights as a priori ('innate') rights, that provides the materialist explanation of their decay into sterile or unjust rights—in other words, into privileges.

I say materialist explanation because this unsound, abstract, and non-mediated empirical points to the revenge of materialism in history, vainly disregarded in the hypostasis that is the a priori. In other words, the instances of liberty, property, etc. asserted a priori by these rights, attributed to an abstract, never changing humanity, prove capable (exactly like the substantial schemata of the 'most common symptoms' of physics rejected by Galileo) of bearing only un-mediated, or arbitrary, content. In sum, they lack historical, experimental, or functional universality and therefore lack that specific, efficacious normativity through which alone right, and indeed any value in general, can be established and maintained as such.

The aprioristic formulation therefore renders the universality of these instances fictitious, for by rendering them historically and therefore materialistically incapable of defence against lack of liberty and injustice, it brings about their decay into unjust and sterile instances. By way of example, we need only consider how absolute, abstract, and inhuman traditional bourgeois 'property rights' have turned out—in time—to be; and they were justified precisely as 'natural' rights, as *attributes* of the hypostatized substance-person called 'natural man', the a priori man endowed with metaphysical 'human nature'. In place of real people we have the instance of the substance-person, the a priori person, which turns out, under the blows of the *facts* of the economy, etc., to be the instance of an opposite *privileged person*: a person, or individual-value, which is privileged, i.e. a negation of value.

As for Kant's 'categorical imperative' or 'absolute ethics', we may observe as follows. If man is moral only as 'noumenal' or purely rational man (i.e. excluding the phenomenological, individual empirical man, with his economic interests), then man, the individual human, since he is unable—given the assumption of 'duty for duty', or universal for universal, which is the assumption of a purely rational being—to rely in his actions on the 'pathological' or empirical suggestions that arise from the real historical human world in which he lives, with its particular specific problems of living together, is compelled to act in accordance with a norm—of idealization or absolute universalization of his own 'maxims' of action—the inherent, ineliminable content of which (and a norm without content is meaningless, like a predicate without a subject) can only be, in truth, the phenomenological, empirical individual *in his immediacy*. In other words, we are back to the particular, phenomenal man who, precisely because he must be sacrificed to the noumenal or purely rational man in order to obtain the moral man, not only persists (because of the ineliminable instance that the form or norm must have a content), but persists as content or particular un-mediated with the form or universal. He is not genuinely invested or regulated by the norm, since the latter, as categorical norm of absolute and dogmatic universalization, has transcended him. This content or particular thereby remains *immediate* content, the unsound abstract empirical. In sum, we are left with phenomenal, abstract, abnormal, and asocial, inhuman man.

This would account for Kant's well-known 'utilitarianism'—the 'inopined', 'surreptitious' utilitarianism into which Kant's 'rigourism' dissolves, for it is a *theological* utilitarianism (already present in the Analytic of the *Critique of Practical Reason*, much more subtle and profound than in the Dialectic, the 'postulates'). His utilitarianism arises from a foundation of moral value that is actually still transcendentalist and a priori. One has only to think of his utilitarian, economic appreciation of the 'consequences' of the violation of this so rigid moral law in the famous example of the 'committed deposit'. One has only to think not only of the falsity and immorality of Kant's categorical request for 'restitution of the deposit' (if the holder was insane or a public enemy, it would be imperative *not* to restitute it, and so on), but also of the not-at-all-accidental foundation of the intrinsic reason for such falsity and immorality. Kant's very concept of moral law, under which the law, with its own absoluteness, 'immediacy', and abstractness, gives rise to the immediacy and abstractness of the particular content, which, since it is thus transcended by the law, remains precisely unaffected by it and *therefore* surreptitiously and defectively present: in this case as the universal anarchic and asocial instinct of 'property' characteristic of *bourgeois* property. Similarly for the 'false promise' and the 'lie', or for the reduction of (material) 'labour' to its 'market price' *without* the 'dignity' due 'virtue'—and so on for all the aspects of this 'absolute' ethic of the *petty bourgeoisie*.[121]

To complete this critique of the *generic synthesis* all that remains is to integrate Lenin's restatement of the scientific method of *Capital*

---

[121] On the historical positivity of Rousseau's natural law and Kant's categorical imperative, see *Per la teoria di un umanismo positivo*, especially pp. 143-148, 167-183, 192, 203-205. See also *Rousseau and Marx*, translated by John Fraser, Lawrence and Wishart, London, 1978, pp. 49-70.

in contrast to traditional sociology, which proceeds through the a priori schema of a fixed and eternal generic 'human nature' and 'society in general'. 'In the same way, of course', Lenin remarks ironically, arguing against the sociologist Mikhailovsky 'neither is *Capital* the appropriate work for a metaphysician-sociologist who does not realize the sterility of a priori arguments about the nature of society and does not understand that such methods, instead of contributing to a study and elucidation of the problem, only serve to insinuate into the concept of "society" either the bourgeois ideas of the British shopkeeper or the petty-bourgeois socialist ideas of the Russian democrat—and nothing more. That is why all these theories of the philosophy of history arose and burst like soap bubbles, being at best a symptom of the social ideas and relations of their time, and not advancing one hair's breadth man's *understanding* of even a few, but real social relations (and not such as "harmonize with human nature"). The gigantic step forward taken by Marx in this respect consisted precisely in that he discarded all these arguments about society and progress in general and produced a *scientific* analysis of *one* society and of *one* progress—capitalist.'[122]

This restatement, incidentally, was reinforced by Lenin's contemporaneous reiteration of Engels's polemic (strictly inspired by Marx's critique of Hegel's mystified dialectic) against Eugen Dühring's charges, repeated by Mikhailovsky, that historical materialism was marred by remnants of 'triadism' and an abstract dialectic. 'And so', retorted Lenin sharply in an unfortunately little remembered protest, 'the materialists rest their case on the "incontrovertibility" of the dialectical process! In other words, they base their sociological theories on Hegelian triads!' Lenin then warns that in the writings of materialists, 'the insistence on dialectics, the selection of examples to demonstrate the correctness of the triad, is nothing but a relic of the Hegelianism out of which scientific socialism has grown, a relic of its manner of expression', and recalls that 'the theory should not be blamed for its origin'. (In any case, Lenin adds, did not Marx himself warn in the postface to the second edition of *Capital* that he 'coquetted with the mode of expression peculiar to' Hegel?)

Lenin then correctly appeals to the well-known insistence of Engels on the historic-economic and scientific character of, for

[122] 'What the "Friends of the People" Are and How They Fight the Social Democrats', in *Collected Works*, volume 1, London, 1977, p. 145.

example, Marx's analysis of the phenomenon of primitive accumulation. He concludes by quoting Engels's *Anti-Dühring*, as follows: 'where are the dialectical frills and mazes and conceptual arabesques; where the mixed and misconceived ideas according to which everything is all one and the same thing in the end; ... It is only at this point, after Marx has completed his proof on the basis of historical and economic facts, that he proceeds: "The capitalist mode of appropriation, the result of the capitalist mode of production, produces capitalist private property. This is the first negation of individual private property, as founded on the labour of the proprietor. But capitalist production begets, with the inexorability of a law of nature, its own negation. It is the negation of the negation". .... Thus, by characterizing the process as the negation of the negation, Marx does not intend to prove that the process was historically necessary. On the contrary: only after he has proved from history that in fact the process has partially already occurred and partially must occur in the future, he in addition characterizes it as a process which develops in accordance with a definite dialectical law. That is all.' In sum, Lenin concludes, with decisive clarity: 'Marx never dreamed of "proving" anything by means of Hegelian triads.'[123]

Let us, then, regather the threads of our argument. We may summarize as follows. Plato's higher genera; the substantial schemata of the peripatetic and scholastic physicists; the innate principles of 'natural law'; Kant's practical moral laws; Hegel's pure concepts; the schemata of aprioristic sociology—all these are marred by the sterility, both theoretical and practical, that condemns all *generic syntheses*, not at all because they are 'empty', but rather because they are *pseudo-syntheses*. Any procedure that entails a priori reasoning, hypostasis, or metaphysics—in other words, any criterion based on an 'absolute' or 'eternal'—is condemned to just this sterility.

The generalization of Marx's critique of the mystified dialectic of Hegel enables us to conclude our negative assessment of Hegel's dialectic with two further observations.

[123] Ibid., pp. 163 ff. For the quotations from Engels within Lenin's article, see also *Anti-Dühring*, Moscow, 1962, chapter XIII, especially pp. 178-185. On this whole question, see *Per la teoria di un umanismo positivo*, pp. 9-18, 197-200.

First, the concept that there is an *original*, given unity (in other words, that oneness, the universal, lies at the absolute origin of things), a concept characteristic of Platonism, both ancient and modern, is the fundamental dogmatic criterion of Hegel's dialectic, for it amounts to the concept of a *pure* and therefore formalistic or abstract unity from which can arise only an equally formalistic multiplicity, a gratuitous multiplicity of pure concepts, with its characteristic wholly illusory and apparent negation-preservation in the negation of the negation (of the original unity).

Second, the immobile unity or theological-mystical exhaustive truth into which this dogmatic conception of unity dissolves is none other than a hypostasis, or philosophical (theological) dissolution of the empirical world which—since it consists in the substantification of an abstraction, which means, as far as logic is concerned, the transformation of the natural predicate (the universal) into the subject—has its result-retribution in the restoration-subreption of the empirical, manifested in the false mobility of this hypostasis of the original or given unity that formed the starting-point.

On the other hand, the systematization of this generalization of the critique requires that the following instances be deepened.

1. The result-retribution of the hypostatization, the substantial and not merely formal *petitio principii*, is the crucial evidence that reveals the presence, in the process of cognition (and practice), of a positive element that cannot be neglected without erecting an obstacle to this process and throwing it into disorder: the element, or rather co-element, that we call 'empirical' or 'material', an extra-formal or *extra-rational* element. The real (formal) efficacy of the 'form', in this case the 'predicate' (or the 'norm', etc.), therefore lies not at all in absolute mediation (self-mediation or mediation of the genus within itself), as presumed by the hypostases of metaphysical realism or formal ontologism, but rather in the *functionality* of the 'form' itself, which cannot exist unless the 'form' is subject to 'control' by the 'material' or 'empirical'. In hypostasis, however, the 'material' is transcended or neglected by this 'form', and the substrate-matter, or the empirical, is replaced by substance-essence.

2. This crucial evidence ultimately reveals the necessity for a radical change in the method of philosophy, through the consistent trans-valutation of the meaning of the traditional concepts and criteria most laden with critical-rational possibilities. In this case, Aristotle's

concepts of 'matter' and 'material substratum' (Marx used Aristotle's *upokeimenon* in this sense) must be shorn of their meta-physical and acquire a *functional* significance and character. The subject, or (material) substratum, must thereby be transformed from a formal-ontological into a logical-experimental, or ontological-material, value. In short, it must become the *subject* of the judgement, and every judgement, indeed every (concrete) value, must be experimental and historical.

But we shall postpone fuller consideration of these points to our dis-cussion of the historical-scientific theory of logic delineated in chapter IV.

Finally, the establishment of the defectiveness and sterility of the metaphysical dialectic of Hegel (and of any aprioristic logic), although it implies recognition of the radical insufficiency of Hegel's reduction of *reason* (or consciousness of contradiction) to self-consciousness (= mediation of itself with itself, the self-mediation of an *original unity*), nevertheless leaves an important problem unresolved: what is the possible meaning, if any, of the instance of consciousness of contradiction, once we discard the Hegelian, and generally idealist and spiritualist, response?

It cannot be denied that such an instance does have meaning; as we have seen, it may be deduced primarily from the self-critical Plato, who developed the dialectic as an instrument for the division and ordering of empirical classes.

Now, the undeniable merit of Hegel, and his implicit *positive* con-tribution to the development of philosophy as an experimental human science, is that he proposed this instance to modern con-sciousness precisely as the genuine, synthetic instance of reason against the instance of the false, analytic reason of traditional meta-physics (from Parmenides to the scholastics to modern pre-critical rationalism), the common denominator of which was the claim to erect as *principium rationis* the principle of identity and non-contradiction that Aristotle the philosopher-metaphysician of matter had discovered as *principium intellectus*, or principle of dis-cursive logic, with a consequent anti-Parmenidean, anti-monist, and anti-idealist function. In other words, Hegel pointed out that it was the peculiar role of the rational element *to sharpen*—to render *intelligible*—the blunt or non-intelligible differentiation of the diverse or empirical through an *essential* difference as the relation of *compatible* contraries (opposition).

The first part of our inquiry concluded with the transformation of the criticist solution of the historically fundamental aporias of the Eleatics into the *problem*-hypothesis of the 'being of not-being' as the problem of the contingency or existentiality of judgements and therewith the problem of the logical principle of identity and non-contradiction. The second part now concludes with the transformation of Hegel's solution of these fundamental aporias into the *problem*-hypothesis of the 'being of not-being' as simultaneously the problem of the *necessity* and *validity* of judgements, as the historical problem characteristic of the dialectical principle, the logical principle of contradiction—in other words, the problem of the peculiar *rational* element, or rather co-element, of the process of cognition (and practice, etc.).

The particular task of the final part of our inquiry will be to embrace both aspects of the problem of the 'being of not-being' in its entirety, the complex and concrete problem of the 'logical principle' as the principle not merely of the *thinkable* or *necessary*, but also of the simultaneously thinkable and *sensible* or *contingent*; in sum, the philosophical principle of cognition. The solution will arise from the complete historical verification of the hypothesis in which this problem takes shape: tauto-heterological identity. The method employed will be exhibited and substantiated, particularly since it will likewise be shown that these same methodological criteria must be applied in the resolution of the other outstanding problems facing experimental human science.

III

From the Ancient Critique of Platonism to the Modern Critique of Pure Reason

III

We have seen that the problem of the logical principle, as the problem of both the thinkable and the sensible, can be reduced to the problem of judgements, or concrete cognitive discourse. Moreover, the method we have adopted consists of a historical-scientific inquiry through which we replace the supposed eternal truths and 'principles' of an everlasting philosophy (or Reason) postulated by a dialecticized history of philosophic systems with a sense of the temporal, historic continuity of the problems of philosophy, ascertained through a critical, philological examination of the various systems, the goal being to identify the particular contributions of these systems to the common problematic. It thus becomes possible to formulate, on the basis of a sort of mean of all these contributions, resolutive hypotheses whose functional truth is afforded them by their congruence with the problematic instances developed during the inquiry itself (a logical inquiry, in this case). To conclude our investigation, then, it remains only to bring our fundamental gnoseological problem (of judgements) into sharper focus by synthesizing the positive and productive results of the history of philosophic logic considered in its two characteristic *classical* moments: tauto-heterology and non-contradiction. Before going into our own theory of judgements, then, we must draw the conclusive balance-sheet of Plato's dialectical division and Aristotle's original principle of non-contradiction, as well as of the basic problems connected to both.

Let us begin with Plato. On the one hand, it is evident that tauto-heterology, with its preconceived unitary rigour, conditions the empirical genera that participate in it and unifies them in such a way as to remove all justification for its division into parts-species and sub-species. On the other hand, the genera and the particular empirical species do come into play as such in the dialectical, or tauto-heterological, construction of the definition, since these alone can constitute the participating genera and therefore the subjects required for the sort of judgement represented by diairesis, by the higher genera that participate as predicable and are thereby, in a certain sense, functional and dialectical. (It is not in the process of participation of the former in the latter, to which classifying discourse is to be reduced, that the dialectical spark is struck, the 'singular community', as Stenzel puts it, of being and not-being, or sameness and otherness, through which the genus 'ruler' can be appropriately classified, since it is its own sameness inasmuch as it 'interpenetrates' with its otherness, which is the 'remainder' with which we 'do not bother'.) The problem is that precisely in order to be these subjects, the empirical genera become participating genera, and therefore a multiplicity that is merely apparent, since formalistic. In other words, it is a multiplicity that is not at all dialectical, but rather *dialecticized*; it is preconceived as tauto-heterological, or deduced. Exactly for this reason, the empirical genera become mere occasions or symbols of the (preconceived) tauto-heterology. *Their* presence in the definition is immediate and gratuitous, but nevertheless inevitable, because of the instance of the subject of the judgement (an instance that Plato, unlike Hegel, did not at all disregard). In sum, the result obtained is sterile, since vitiated.

Finally, we may note that:

1. The logic of Platonic division affords us two fruitful suggestions. First, in the concrete, in discourse, it is impossible *to avoid* contradiction unless one is conscious of it, that is, without tauto-heterologizing, since it is the character of opposition of the differences that, by making them equal sections of the genera, is posited as the criterion of their *assimilation* or *unity* without which these differences would not be parts-species; in sum, non-contradiction as *rational* partition or discrimination would otherwise remain inexplicable. Second, it follows that classification can occur only through dialecticization; hence: dialectic as tauto-heterology, diadic dialectic, concrete and discursive, but not the Hegelian triadic dialectic, or pure, self-sufficient, abstract dialectic.

2. Nevertheless, this logic is ultimately unequal to its most profound instances, for an unshakable apriorism persists in its rationalistic conception of not-being as pure *eidos* and its consequent conception

of the dialectic as a descending-deductive process. Indeed, this logic dissolves into the gratuitous postulation of a something—whether it be called *doxa*, multiplicity, matter, or whatever—that is proven, by the very defectiveness and sterility of aprioristic thought, which takes no account of it, to be a positive and indispensable element of knowledge in general. We may therefore proclaim the following general formula of the materialist critique of (a priori) pure reason: the positivity and indispensability of matter itself as an element of knowledge follows from the very defectiveness and sterility of any (aprioristic) reasoning that takes no account of the material, of the extra-rational. This may be termed the non-dogmatic, gnoseological, and methodological axiom of matter and therefore of the matter-reason relationship as a relation of heterogeneities.

As for Aristotle, we have established above all that:

1. The prime root of the non-contradictory character of truth lies in the act of perception, i.e. in actualized sensation, which is itself knowledge, since its actuality expresses the disjunctive nature of every actuality through the immutability of the sensed quality, which, since it is due to the numerical unity or discreteness *par excellence* of anything that 'has matter' or is derived from it, removes the sensed quality from the presumed Heraclitean-Protagoran 'flux' of contraries and thereby removes it from the indeterminate.

2. The axiom *nihil in intellectu quod non prius fuerit in sensu* assumes a quite radical significance in this respect, if it is enmeshed in the genesis of the logical principle itself. This is shown by the 'infallibility' bestowed upon sensation precisely because of the numerical unity, oneness, singularity, or punctuality of the material quality that is sensed. The 'determinateness' that makes thought real and actual must be regarded as derived from this axiom, which thereby implies that 'every word means something, or rather, something unique'.

In sum, then, Aristotle's defence of the principle of non-contradiction rests substantially on two lines of argumentation, one ontological, proceeding from first substance, the other gnoseological, proceeding from sensation. The ontological argument, of course, is the principal one, and it reappears at the conclusion of the gnoseological: 'And it is in this manner that they negate the reality of every substance, since for them there is nothing necessary in the world'. In this context, 'every substance' must mean above all first substance, since, as we have seen, this is 'substance in the most fundamental and primary sense of the word' and since *the cardinal mediation of 'necessity' and 'non-contradiction' is consigned to the concept of substance*: 'since that which is necessary cannot be both "so and not so"'. But what better than first substance can mediate the *necessary* (or rational) with the *non-contradictory*, from which Aristotelian 'necessity', or determinate form, or disjunctive entelechy, is obtained?

Moreover, since it is matter that makes first substance what it is, and since the feature that best expresses the materiality of matter is numerical unity, we must conclude that the driving force of the entire 'confutation' of the opponents of the principle of non-contradiction, the criterion that unites the ontological and gnoseological arguments, is the concept of matter as numerical unity or discreteness *par excellence* (radically different from 'specific' or formal unity). This concept, of course, is linked to the concept of actuality, on which it is strictly dependent, since it is an actuality that *divides* contraries. Hence, just as the ontological confutation hinges on the 'numerical indivisibility' of the individual, which provides the justification for the fact that the individual, first substance, receives contraries while remaining identically and numerically one and therefore becomes actual through a single contrary, so the gnoseological confutation hinges on the numerical unity, oneness, or singularity of the sensed *material* quality, which justifies the immutability that removes this quality from the indeterminate and makes it *actual* and *true*. In sum, it is Aristotle the metaphysician of matter, in this sense an empiricist and anti-rationalist, who confutes the Heraclitean and more generally the Eleatic opponents of the principle of non-contradiction, precisely in the name of the anti-Eleatic instance that 'being has a plurality of meanings'.

In conclusion, if we compare this quintessentially Aristotelian theory of '[non-]contradiction', or contrariety of *contraria incomposita ex inviciem*, with the more traditional theory, we find two, quite different gnoseological and logical meanings of non-contradiction: 1) the anti-Eleatic meaning, which ultimately makes non-contradiction an indubitable principle *of the senses* and of discursive or intellectual cognition founded on the knowledge already provided by the senses (in the form, one may say, of a positively *intuitive* act); 2) the traditional theory, which regards this principle as the *actus rationis par excellence* (the view of the scholastics) and the *summum veritatis criterium in abstractis scilicet neque ab experimento pendentibus* (the view of Leibniz, to whom we owe the rationalist axiom *nihil in intellectu quod prius non fuerit in sensu nisi ipse intellectus*). The traditional interpretation thereby makes non-contradiction, beyond its role in formal logic, the principle of *logical possibility* and of cognition through pure 'essences'—in other words, the principle of metaphysics. In sum, this traditional interpretation transforms the principle of non-contradiction into a principle of an Eleatic type, the principle of an *analytic reason* (or intellect straining towards reason), which simply re-states Parmenides's so-called principle of identity (being is and not-being is not) in a new form, usually something like this: *essence, form, or truth is, while non-essence, non-truth, or matter is not.* The ancient Parmenidean principle is thereby transmuted to the modern plane of a rationalist logic of the infinite.

Four points may be adduced against this traditional interpretation, all of them more or less consciously related to and in support of Aristotle's original theory: 1) Galileo's instance of a 'discourse' in which 'the conclusion necessarily follows in this manner alone'; the positive instance contained in his critique of scholastic 'a priori discourse'; 2) Marx's instance of non-contradiction, implicit in the materialist critique of a priori thought and in the consequent thesis of philosophy-science as the *'specific logic of a specific object'*; 3) Kant's attempt to turn the principle of non-contradiction into a principle of experience; 4) recent epistemological analyses, which we will examine shortly, of the role of *elimination* or *negative exclusion* in scientific-experimental research—the analyses, for example, of John Dewey and his philosophical school, partially inspired by Galileo.[1]

---

[1] Karl Jaspers's *Philosophische Logik* (I, *Von der Wahrheit*, Munich, 1947), of course, is miles from these positions, given the author's existentialist-mystical point of view. In regard to the principle of non-contradiction, he concludes, quite coherently, as follows (pp. 286-301): 'Knowledge comes about through judgements in the concept, in accordance with the principle of non-contradiction. But this is also the form in which knowledge is apprehended.' We find the same conclusion in the work of Nicholas of Cusa (of whom Jaspers is naturally a great admirer, as he is of Plato and Eckhart). Indeed, Jaspers says nothing more about the principle of non-contradiction than was already said, for example, by Christoph Sigwart (compare Sigwart's *Logik*, 1925, I, pp. 188-193, with Jaspers, pp. 286-296): 'The principle [of identity] states: A *concept* is identical with itself. It is a logical necessity of the fact of the concept. Only where there is identity is there *concept*; where there is not, there is

only fluid, thoughtless, constantly changing Intuition.' Hence it is clear that the pre-Kantian metaphysician Jaspers, like any formal logician, is not interested in the *formation* of the concept (or judgement), but begins with the concept *already made*, which is not adequate for 'philosophical' logic these days. Quite a more extensive capacity in this respect is evinced by P.S. Popov in his essay 'The Logic of Aristotle and Formal Logic', in *Philosophy and Phenomenological Research*, September 1947, pp. 1-22. Popov, who begins by developing some of the points of Friedrich A. Trendelenburg's *Logische Untersuchungen*, has acutely emphasized that the principle of non-contradiction 'has, in his [Aristotle's] eyes, primarily an existential, ontological connotation'. Moreover, he has understood that 'Aristotle's doctrine of essence contains an extremely fruitful idea in the recognition of the living, objective, concrete, sensually perceptible reality as "*first essence*"' and that the conception of first substance is itself a 'materialist statement'. This position of Popov's appears particularly important in view of the persistent misunderstanding of Aristotle (by Marxists no less than Hegelians and mystics), particularly since he agrees with Marx, who was well aware that there was another Aristotle besides the one adored by the Thomists, Leibniz, and the formal logicians. A comparison, particularly from the logical-verbal point of view, between the Aristotelian and Parmenidean principles of non-contradiction may be found in Svend Ranulf, *Der eleatische Satz vom Widerspruch*, Copenhagen, 1924, pp. 160-169n. On Aristotle's critique of Parmenidean *being*, see Harald Cherniss, *Aristotle's Criticism of Pre-Socratic Philosophy*, Baltimore, 1935, especially pp. 72 ff. Among Italian studies of Aristotle, see: the edition of *Metaphysics* edited by Armando Carlini; Emilio Oggioni's introduction to *Metaphysics* (Padua, 1950), a philologically cogent and interesting study, though inspired by metaphysical premises; C.A. Viano, *Logica di Aristotele*, Turin, 1955; and Giorgio Colli's annotated translation of the *Organon*, Turin, 1955.

IV

Tauto-Heterological
Identity
and the
Scientific Dialectic

IV

Let us attempt to hew out a materialist theory of judgements.

We may begin where Hegel begins in his *Phenomenology of Spirit*, with the problem of the This, or of 'sense-certainty'. We have already seen that Hegel's aesthetic *Aufhebung* cannot be considered a proper solution. In order to see our way more clearly to the materialist solution of this and related problems, however, let us recapitulate his illusory solution.

Sense-certainty, Hegel maintains, must face the question: What is the This? If we take it in the twofold aspect of its being, as the Now and the Here, the dialectic that the This contains within itself will acquire a form just as intelligible as the This itself.

To the question, What is the Now? we respond, for example, that Now is Night. At noon, however, this sense-certainty has vanished, has become stale. The Now that is Night is preserved, that is, it is treated as what it professes to be, as something that *is*, but it proves rather to be something that *is not*. The Now, then, is preserved, but as something negative. The self-preserving Now is therefore not immediate, something 'meant', but rather something mediated. Indeed, 'the Now is determined as a permanent and self-preserving Now *through* the fact [*dadurch*] that something else, namely Day and Night, *is not*'. So determined, however, the Now is still 'just as simply Now as before, and in this simplicity is indifferent to what happens in it [*bei ihm herspielt*]'. Just as little as Night and Day are its being, just as much also is it Day and Night. It is 'not in the least affected' by this its other-being, through which it is what it is. 'A simple thing of this kind, which *is* through negation, which is neither This nor That, a *not-This*, and is with equal indifference This as well as That—such a thing we call a *universal*.' In fact, then, it is the universal that is the truth of sense-certainty. And perception, the

Wahr-nehmung, undermines the 'immediate' certainty or 'sensation' that is 'meant'. It is evident, moreover, that if the universal is the truth of sense-certainty, and if language, the 'work of thought', expresses only this truth, then it is impossible for us even to express in words any sensuous existence which we 'mean'. Indeed, 'the sensuous This that is meant *cannot be reached* by language, which belongs to consciousness, i.e. to that which is inherently universal. In the actual attempt to say it, it would therefore crumble away'.[1]

Continuing, however, we find that the same will be the case when we consider the Here, which is the other form of the This. Here is, for example, the tree. If I turn around, this 'truth has vanished and is converted into its opposite: "No tree is here, but a house instead". "Here" itself does not vanish; on the contrary, it abides constant in the vanishing of the house, the tree, etc., and is indifferently house or tree. Again, therefore, the This shows itself to be a *mediated simplicity*, or a *universality*.' In conclusion, the This has been posited as a not-This, as 'annulled and superseded' (*aufgehoben*), and since 'supersession [*Aufheben*] presents its true, twofold meaning of negation: it is a negating, and simultaneously a preserving', the nothing, as the Nothing of This, 'preserves immediacy and is itself sensuous, but it is a *universal immediacy*'. 'Thus the singular being of the senses does indeed vanish in the dialectical movement of immediate certainty and becomes universality, but it is only a *sensuous universality*. My "meaning" has vanished, and perception takes the object as it is *in itself*, or as a universal as such' (*Allgemeines überhaupt*).[2]

We are now in a position to ask ourselves: Is it true that the This, the universal as such, is *indifferent* to being house or tree? In other words, is it true that sense-certainty is merely 'universal as such', indifferent and indeterminate universality, as Hegel claims, in an assertion reminiscent of Leibniz's notion of sensation as 'confused idea', the conception rejected so vigorously by the critical Kant? Must we renounce the cardinal critical instance according to which 'sensibility is something very positive, an *indispensable addition* to

---

[1] *Phenomenology of Spirit*, pp. 59-60, 66. Cf. *The Science of Logic*, p. 117: 'even the expression "this" contains no distinction; each and every something is just as well a "this" as it is also an other. By "this" we *mean* to express something completely determined; it is overlooked that speech, as a work of the intellect, gives expression only to universals.'

[2] *Phenomenology of Spirit*, pp. 62-63, 77.

intellect in affording us knowledge'? In other words, must we now abandon the instance that 'intuition and concept are representations wholly distinct in kind', i.e. that they differ 'in nature' and not merely 'in degree', like Leibniz's difference between 'confused' and 'distinct' *cognitio*?

This is precisely the alternative any investigation of sense-certainty confronts, any investigation of the *contribution of the senses to real knowledge*: either regression to dogmatic rationalism or rejection of and liberation from it once and for all. The point, when all is said and done, is to decide, for example, whether 'tree', by which we mean the most common notion of 'tree', can indeed be constituted through a universal which, in its simplicity, is wholly indifferent to the 'individual' tree, to the 'sensible' or *material* aspect of tree.

To start with, in what does the universal of tree consist? What is the This, etc. *that we say* of tree? Let us assume the everyday, commonplace notion—say, a 'certain kind of plant with a straight wooden trunk dividing into branches', and so on. Next let us analyse this *tauton*, or conceptual sameness, in the light of the deepest and most typical Platonic and Aristotelian instances.

Provided we steer clear of his preconceived, aprioristic tauto-heterology, Plato does afford us a positive criterion in this profound instance: *part and species are not the same thing*. Hence, although it is true that every species, every conceptual sameness or complex of features, is something partial, not everything that is partial is necessarily species or conceptual sameness. From this we conclude that without some degree of *equivalence* of parts—without some assimilation or unification of them—these parts would never be parts-species; in sum, they would never be species or concepts. No *rational* partition or distinction would then be possible. In the end, then, the opposition-relation of the parts is indispensable: tauto-heterology, or dialectic, is indispensable.

This instance is repeated in the most modern methodology of scientific knowledge. John Dewey, for example, perhaps without suspecting its Platonic origin and nature or the particular problem (of the dialectic) that it expresses, has written: 'For example, there are persons who have the quality of being cross-eyed, of being bald and of being shoemakers. Why not form a kind on the basis of these qualities? [Compare this with Plato's negative examples of classification in *The Statesman* 262a-263d: 'animals and men or animals and cranes'; these are negative examples inasmuch as they represent division of a genus into 'unequal', or logically non-equivalent, parts.] The answer is that such a set of conjoined traits is practically worthless for the *purpose of inference*. This set of traits has no evidential value in respect to inferring other traits that are also conjoined but not observable at the time . . . the traits which descriptively determine kinds are selected and ordered with reference to their *function* in promoting and controlling extensive inference. In other words, while every characteristic trait is a quality, not every quality is a trait [cf.: part and species are not the same thing]. No quality is a trait in and of itself. . . . For a quality to be a trait it must be used as an evidential sign or diagnostic mark.'[3]

Here, then, we have the instance of rationality, unity, or the universal, which is the instance of the dialectic. But it should be noted carefully that we are now able to grasp this instance with some degree of clarity and cogency precisely because we have hit upon the problem of the species of empirical concepts in general—in other words, the problem of conceptual multiplicity, which leads in turn to the instance of matter no less than to that of reason. The explicit discovery of this instance is associated with the name of Aristotle, although the first to grapple with it was the self-critical Plato, who, as we know, never came so close to comprehending the nature and instance of reason—i.e. the dialecticity or unity of things—as when he plumbed the empirical classifications, presaging and anticipating the particular task and contribution of Aristotle, the genius of distinction. The real import of the work of Plato could not be fully elucidated until Aristotle, in his turn, had set himself to his specific task. So we, in our own investigation, are compelled to travel a like path. It has become increasingly clear that the elucidation of the Platonic instance of reason impels us to the Aristotelian instance of matter—and vice versa. We find ourselves directed, then, to a circle. As we shall soon see, that circle may be regarded, historically and theoretically, as the circularity of idea-hypothesis and fact, of deduction and induction.

But let us return to the particular case at hand. It is evident that if we want to avoid the difficulties of aprioristic tauto-heterology and its *petitio principii*, all we can retain of Plato's approach is his instance of the equivalency or unity of the parts in every rational,

---

[3] John Dewey, *Logic—The Theory of Inquiry*, London, 1939, pp. 268, 270.

conceptual *distinction*—in other words, in every determinate conception. In this case, the explanation for the validity and therefore universality or corresponding predication of the conceptual sameness 'tree'—or more precisely, the judgement 'this is a tree'—must be sought in a unity that, while it is indeed dialectic, cannot signify a dialectic of tree and not-tree, like Plato's species (which are *united* only because they are tauto-heterologically preconceived).

The dialectic we are seeking must be free of all non-mediated, undigested particular or empirical elements (which are consequences of preconceived tauto-heterology), but *not at all free of*, or abstracted from, the particular or empirical (although by nature distinct from it). In other words, this dialectic is not at all free in the Hegelian sense, for this, as we know, would afford us merely Hegel's undigested empirical, false positivism, and ontological *petitio principii*. Now, such a dialectic must avoid the Platonic and Hegelian *petitio principii* but at the same time must not lose sight of the twofold lesson of Plato and Hegel: just as it is true that dialecticization can occur only through division—i.e. in the concrete, or with positive reference to the empirical—so it is equally true that the peculiarity of reason is that it sharpens or renders intelligible the blunt or unintelligible difference as the relation of compatible contraries, or 'dialectic'. Such a dialectic is meaningless unless it can be constituted while respecting the empirical, i.e. while fully respecting the positivity of content-multiplicity, matter, or whatever term one uses.

Thus, the genuine synthetic instance of reason, the instance of unity, barely is it discovered, directs us, for its own elucidation, to the instance of matter, or multiplicity. We thus confront the general problem of a dialectic that has to take due account of the positivity of matter at the very moment that it dialecticizes matter—in other words, a unity that draws that which unifies it, or makes it part-species, from the very resistance or 'rigidity' of its parts (a transvalued Hegelian expression to which we will return). In our case, then, we must examine what it is that constitutes the positive particularity or partiality in the part-species, i.e. in the notion-judgement of tree. Only then—and not before—will we be able to clarify its being as part-species, rational partition, conceptual determination, or formal difference.

What is it, then, that constitutes the positive, irremediable particularity of this part-species and distinguishes it from any other?

What, in sum, establishes it as *part*? Certainly not conceptuality, which would force us back to Hegel's position that 'the concept, since it is a synthesis, contains determination and difference *within itself*' (and in truth, if the concept is assumed to be 'essential self-consciousness', then its self-division does follow). This solution, however, leads directly to the ontological *petitio principii* we have already rejected, for it posits a futile universal 'indifferent' to the positivity of the singular or sensible (and contrary to the illegitimacy and sterility of a priori thought, which takes no account of this positivity, it proves to be an element that is not at all negligible, but is rather indispensable, for cognition).

If the specific foundation of difference in general cannot be found in the concept, then it must be sought elsewhere, in that indispensable element, or co-element, of part-species: the sensible or material element. To begin with, then, it seems clear that—whether it be common sense, which characterizes 'feeling' and the senses in general by saying 'that which I feel you do not feel' (and, vice versa, says 'Let's come to agreement, *let us reason*'); or whether it be Aristotle, who discovers that the immutability of the actualized pure sensation of 'sweet' is due to the 'numerical' or discrete unity, the oneness, of the sensed material quality and who thereby confutes the opponents of the law of non-contradiction on the evidence of the immutability of pure sensation; or whether it be Kant when he relates the singularity and 'existence' of a thing to actualized sensation, on which basis it is said, 'I *have seen it*'—any consciousness without preconceptions or apriorism must grant the *sensible* and *material* the positive characteristic proper to *singularity* or *oneness* as a synonym of *discreteness*. Second, it seems equally clear, as a consequence of this, that only the peculiar, positive instance of the senses and of matter, i.e. the instance of *discreteness*, can justify the difference or determinateness that *is part* of the part-species. Indeed, in the case of the sameness-tree, how do we distinguish the characteristic feature 'straight trunk', etc., rather than 'animal' or 'mammal', etc., if not through that variation and diversity afforded us by experience in its *genuine* 'wealth of sensation', recognizable only from its source, which is matter?

Moreover, if this is the case, then it is clear not only that the sensible (the sensible tree in this case) cannot be degraded to the status of something marginal to the universal, or something 'associated with it', but also that it is so positive in its particularity as to require precisely the universal in its positivity: a 'name' or concept, if it does not signify a *determinate* thing, may as well signify nothing (as Aristotle said). Thus, the analysis of what makes the 'determinate thing' part or determinate—since it is a question of part-species, or a determinate thing that 'has meaning', or a concept—directs us to a further analysis of what makes the part part-*species* or the determinate thing something *having meaning*, or a *conceived* concept. We are thus inevitably driven to a fresh examination of the instance of unity, or of the universal, as the instance of relationality or the dialectic. In other words, the elucidation of the instance of matter in turn directs us to the instance of reason. We will see this more clearly as we proceed.

In our case, however, we must now ask how 'straight trunk', etc. can be a characteristic feature, or complex of features—in sum, how it contains the universal that specifically contributes to the constitution of the *meaning* or *predicate* of a thing. We know that the instance of the universal or of reason is the instance of relationality or the dialectic, as the instance of the equivalence, or unity of value, of the parts. But we also know that such equivalence, the dialectic, cannot be abstracted from the parts it assimilates or unifies—in other words, that if it is abstracted it is inevitably mystified, through the characteristic mystification effected by the theological interpolation of the parts, or multiplicity, and the consequent ontological *petitio principii* into which it dissolves. Now, a careful examination of how to render the dialectic free of this apparent paradox will tell us what we want to know—provided we bear in mind the complex, twofold, simultaneously negative and positive meaning of the impossibility of making the dialectic abstract. We shall then find that:

1. The meaning, significance, validity, or truth of 'straight trunk', etc. is established by the fact that it belongs to a universe in which everything stands or is assimilated (as in Parmenidean being), in which *every* individual—i.e. every instance of discreteness (and *not merely* every sensible tree or sensible, material aspect of 'tree')—is equivalent to every other individual.

2. Nevertheless, such equivalence, or unity of parts—in sum, universality—far from having to be interpreted as *preconceived* tauto-heterology or a *formalistic* synthesis of the antinomies of reason (in sum, as self-sufficient or mystified dialectic), must rather

be understood as *functional* tauto-heterology or dialectic, in the sense that negativity, or the relationality synonymous with dialectic, takes shape only because it is discrete—i.e. in reference to the positive instance of discreteness or matter. Hence, the uni-verse, like Parmenidean being, is indeed one and continuous being that 'is not separated . . . from its connection with being'. But this is so because, contrary to Parmenides, it is simultaneously that not-being, or multiplicity, which, as well as being such that 'it [being] is prevented from conjugating with its analogue', conjugates it precisely to its analogue, i.e. to being itself. In short, the universe is a universe because it is a pluri-verse. In other words, unity is either multiple unity or it cannot be.

Even more decisively, we shall discover that:

1. Universality, validity, or truth dissolves into such articulations of the discrete that the emergence of any one of them—in our example the articulation that is the category of *quality* (the This, the Property, etc.)—is *ipso facto* the emergence of every other in an instantaneous *coincidence*. It is therefore evident that, if it is divorced from being and not-being, etc., *quality* has no meaning or *predicative value* (and therefore can have no meaning except a defective ontological and hypostatized one). It is thus ever more evident that it is the predicative *function* alone that establishes the categorial continuum without which it is meaningless to talk about universality or validity.

2. Nevertheless, *predicative function*, or the function of the predicate, is also a meaningless expression (which collapses back into abstract predicability) unless the *function of the subject* is simultaneously acknowledged and respected—in other words, unless the gratuitousness of the subject, with all its weighty consequences, is avoided.

3. If what we have called the emergence of an articulation or category is *ipso facto* the emergence of every other, this is possible just because the predicative function, which establishes such a continuum, is resolved into a negativity or *diacritic* relationality, and therefore into a diadic dialectic (but not at all a triadic dialectic, as a preconceived and self-sufficient dialectic of 'pure thoughts' or rational antinomies, with the corresponding 'artificially constructed' dialectical passages, as Engels put it, i.e. marred by the

dogmatism characteristic of the return to an original unity). This dialectic is diadic precisely because it *reflects and translates*—in the reduplication and equalization in which its own positive instance of relationality is expressed—*discrete* or numerical unity, which is the positive instance of *matter*.

4. Consequently, the logical and gnoseological structure of the part-species, notion, discursive proposition, or judgement ('tree' = 'this is a tree') consists in a generic instance of identity, or non-contradiction ('so and not so', or in this case, tree and not not-tree). But this instance unquestionably demonstrates that it is the expression not only of a profound, radical instance of discreteness (because of its disjunctive character), but also of an instance of assimilation or unification of the discrete (subject) through the categorial or relational continuum evinced in the predicative-qualifying formula itself: 'so and not so', or 'such, not such'. It therefore directs us to yet another radical instance, that of negativity or dialecticity (so-not so); but this, in its turn, re-directs us to the first radical instance of discreteness, the positive instance of numerical unity or matter, precisely in order to explain the disjunctive, diacritic character which, as we shall see more clearly later, constitutes the negativity or dialecticity of which it is the instance. We therefore have a circularity of the radical instances of discreteness and dialecticity, which is expressed in the logical-gnoseological structural principle of *tauto-heterological identity*.

5. Finally, it is, so to speak, the confluence of these two radical instances—of reason, unity, or dialecticity on the one hand, and of matter, multiplicity, or discreteness on the other—that is manifested in the logical-gnoseological form of a diadic dialecticism, the structure of every 'species' and 'genus', of every concept or concrete conception (so-called empirical, i.e. experimental and real, concept), or of every concrete, cognitive discourse (or judgement). This structure corresponds, in every one of its articulations, to the historical and objective instances that typically underlie it. Indeed, it is quite evident that:

a. This structure responds, through its diadic dialecticity, to the Hegelian (and Platonic) instances of essential difference as relation of (compatible) contraries, understood as the sharpening, or rendering intelligible, of the blunt or unintelligible differences of the diverse or empirical. It does so because it maintains the vital nucleus of this instance, namely the concept of predicativity or categoriality as a relational continuum, which is to say, as negativity. On the other hand, it is able thus to respond because it has wholly discarded the aprioristic character of self-sufficient or abstract dialectic typical of Hegel's 'triadic dialectic of pure thoughts', his dialectic of 'essential self-consciousness'.

b. This response to the Platonic-Hegelian instance is wholly comprehensible and justified, provided that we recall that it also implies the response to another (typical) Hegelian instance implicit in the first: that it is only at the apex of the rigidification and sharpening of intellectual determinations that their transformation into their opposite occurs, i.e. that the dialectic as negativity emerges. This second response is conditioned by our rejection of Hegel's defective and merely apparent defence of the intellect, wherein the intellect, as we have seen, is dogmatically assumed for purposes of a *total* intelligibility in which it is inevitably lost. It is therefore conditioned by taking due account of the 'qualitative sphere' of the ordinary empirical world, which was neglected by Hegel the aprioristic defender of the intellect: the Aristotelian realm of matter, whose positive characteristic is that of numerical or discrete unity, on which alone the constitution of a pure relationality-negativity as discrete depends. In other words, it is a diadic (and not intellectually triadic) dialecticism, but it is dialecticism nonetheless; it establishes a relational continuum, a continuum *par excellence*, precisely because it is not a 'pure', but a *functional* dialecticism, a dialecticism of matter.

c. Finally, the response or comprehensive correspondence to this single and double Hegelian instance is possible because the structure described above responds *at once* to the fundamental Aristotelian instance of the inevitable determinateness of everything that is or has meaning, from which it follows that there can be no thought (or dialecticizing) without thought of a *determinate* thing: the materialist instance that the necessary or rational is non-contradictory. It is this instance that justifies rejection of Hegel's merely apparent and false apology for the intellect. The justification rests on the ineradicable positivity of matter and the senses as 'discrete unity' (the basis of the 'specific unity' of the form). Similarly, Hegel's classical instance of predicativity as negativity justifies rejection by this structure of Aristotle's substance-attributes or rigid species-essences, in sum, of all the Aristotelian and scholastic dross of metaphysical form and matter and the corresponding syllogistic or ontological logic, which increasingly borders on formalism-verbalism. (But Hegel's mistake, too infrequently pointed out, was to have rejected not only Aristotle's metaphysical and therefore rigid and static defining forms, but also the profound empirical instance of the problematic of the *discrete*, i.e. of matter and the senses, which is the problem of a discursive logic, or logic of the intellect.)

Let us, however, examine the concrete logical-gnoseological shape of the diadic dialectic we have just postulated so generically. Exactly how is the species 'tree', 'horse', or whatever constituted on this basis? Or, to put it another way: how can the judgement in which the species, or empirical concept, consists be constituted? To say, as John Dewey does, that 'the predicates, when formally generalized as descriptive terms, are represented as "such and such"' and that 'the singular [or sensible] is described (discriminated and identified) as one of a kind [species] by means of a conjunction of traits which make it *like* certain other things already determined'[4] is to content oneself with an excessively simple and extrinsic response, one that leaves the most important point unexplained: how does one get from the *such-and-such*, i.e. from *category* (quality, the This, and so on), to the *empirical* features of the *species*. In other words, how is the whole which is species as empirical genus and empirical objectivity constituted from these elements, the categorial and the empirical?

Now, it is clear from the preceding argumentation that on the one hand if the species requires the category of *quality* in order to be constituted as species, that is to say objectivity or predicate, this means that it actually requires *all* the categories, i.e. a categorial continuum (since quality has no functional-predicative meaning and therefore no meaning whatever unless it implies being, and so on). On the other hand, it is equally clear that if a categorial continuum that is not synonymous with a relational and therefore diacritic continuum has no predicative function, then the species, precisely to be constituted as species or predicate, nevertheless also must be *part*-species or *subject*-predicate, that is, a discrete point within the categorial continuum. In sum, it requires the positivity of the empirical sensible, or material element, for otherwise we are again plunged into the Hegelian and Platonic difficulties examined above:

4 Ibid., pp. 247-248.

the underestimation and falsification of the dualistic proposition, or genuine judgement, consequent to the substantification of the idea, the act of making the idea itself the subject of the judgement, which is what the theological or metaphysical interpolation of multiplicity amounts to.

Continuing the analysis, however, it is equally clear that the subject-predicate relation—namely the judgement—which is what we are dealing with now, is so constructed that its structure (the essential structure of every judgement or conception) exhibits the reciprocity or circularity of two radical and positive instances: a) the constitution of the predicate as a dialectical categorial continuum that is diacritic-relational, i.e. negativity; b) the discreteness that renders the categorial continuum relational and therefore genuinely functional or predicative, is nevertheless linked to the positive instance of the subject, discrete, or material.

It follows that the predicate owes its dialecticism or relationality not only to the positive instance of reason, or the instance of the equivalence of parts, but also and no less to the positive instance of matter, or the discrete, which makes relationality diacritic and therefore relationality as such. We therefore have a dialecticism which, in the case at hand (the This that is tree), presents itself indeed as an assimilation—in quality—of individual or discrete elements; but this assimilation of elements (plant, straight trunk, and so on) is possible because its foundation actually rests on the one hand on the positivity of matter—that is, the discrete (without a *why* there is the subject 'animal' instead of 'plant')—and on the other hand on the categorial-predicative continuum, which is constituted as such, immersed in the universe, and renders objective the positive discrete or subject because it received from it (as discrete) the function of its own relationality-negativity or dialecticity; it is dialecticized as quality. Quality thus passes over into the categorial remainder, establishing it as continuum. It is diadic dialecticism because it is disjunctive, and disjunctive because it is a functional dialecticism of the material (or discrete). The disjunction, then, is not ascribed to reason itself, since there is no question of the self-division of reason à la Hegel.

We may therefore summarize as follows. Tree is tree *for everyone* because it is 'plant, straight trunk, etc.'—in other words, it is a This, it is property, etc. But it is just this because the sensible, empirical, or subjective elements, as the discrete element, condition that opposition, or dialectical (negative-relational) emergence of the quality or This, which creates the objectivity of 'plant, straight trunk, etc.'. (It is here that we begin to see the reason for what was said earlier about the concept of horse: precisely *because* they are empirical, which means subjective and diverse, the elements that combine in the concept of horse do so in a particular way, all in the same way, in the *unity sui generis* that is horse. We shall return to this point later.)

But all this means that it is only in a *tauto-heterological identity* that we can find the answer to the fundamental problem of the participation of the principle of non-contradiction in the conditioning of the object, the *Gegenstand*. The answer is that this participation is none other than the inescapable participation of the senses as such, of matter in its purity and positivity. It is the participation of discreteness (cf. Aristotle's intuitivity or indiscriminability) without which, it may now be seen, the negativity characteristic of the contradictory character, or dialecticity-functionality, of thought is not possible (cf. Kant, the category-function and the heterogeneity of the intuition and the concept). It is here that lies the constituent, concrete non-contradictory character of knowledge as unitary-coherent, or determinate, discourse (inescapable even for Hegel, despite himself).

Now, this concrete non-contradictory character is expressed with precision in the formula of tauto-heterological identity. It is from this standpoint that it is legitimate to transform Hume's (and Kant's) non-contradictoriness and non-absurdity of the negation of the 'fact' into the contradictoriness and absurdity of the negation of this fact. The reason for this is that Hume and Kant still intend the principle of (non-)contradiction as the Parmenidean, scholastic, and rationalistic reformulation of Aristotle's original anti-Parmenidean instance—a reformulation that concerns the 'truths of reason' (and not the truths of fact), which is precisely the reduction of (non-)contradiction purely to *principium rationis* or to the principle of an abstract *analytic reason* (a deformative process initiated, of course, by Aristotle himself, or rather by the Platonistic and *Greek* Aristotle whose intellectual forms are rigid, static, and discrete as species-essences, i.e. ontological or metaphysical forms). We, on the other hand, mean by non-contradiction the concrete non-contradictory character of which sensation is part as the positive instance of the discrete (matter), an instance that stands in functional reciprocity with the instance of unity or reason. We thus retain Aristotle's original and fruitful instance of the discrete, i.e. of matter, the instance that lies at the root of the problematic of dianoetic logic, the logic of the intellect. We have, however, discarded the Aristotelian-scholastic absolutization, metaphysicization, and consequent ossification of formal-intellectual discreteness (whence the metaphysical forms of an immediately, dogmatically, or abstractly analytic reason, in other words, an intellect *dogmatically* elevated to the status of reason).

Our standpoint, then, is that of a non-contradictoriness that is a rational principle because it is mediated as a principle of the intellect; in other words, the principle of non-contradiction as we see it is at the same time consciousness of contradiction, since the latter is, for us, a functional dialecticism, a dialecticism of matter and not a self-sufficient mystified dialecticism, synonymous with essential self-consciousness. From this standpoint, it is legitimate to correct the conclusion associated most closely with Hume, in order to draw all the critical consequences of Hume's reassessment of *feeling* within the problematic of 'existence' and 'things in fact'. Ultimately, it is the modern lesson, which nevertheless may be traced back to Aristotle's original identification of necessary and non-contradictory, that interests us in this new meaning of non-contradiction: the lesson of the contradictory character, or absurdity, of the negation of what is real. Not only because every judgement or reasoning may be reduced to judgements of experience; not only because these judgements are thus founded not in any mythical a priori 'schema' or 'general procedure of the imagination', or anything of that kind, but rather in the discreteness of matter; and not only because this means, as we now know, that the rational unfolds as (diacritic) relational-negative and, in sum, functional (otherwise it is the defective and sterile rationality of any hypostasis, a priori reasoning, or metaphysics); but also because it means that, since this rational is rational only in its function as predicate of the subject, which is the *discrete* (matter), the necessary, with which it is synonymous, it will possess not only the punctuality, unity, or virtuality of non-contradiction, but also the *contingency* that is synonymous with this discrete. In short, it is the necessity of the fact as contingent necessity that now interests us as the solution of the problem of the contingency or existentiality of the judgement.

This *necessity of the fact* will become increasingly clear in our analysis of scientific method. For the moment, it is sufficient to indicate its logico-structural significance in the *non-contradictory character of the fact itself*—in other words, in the concrete non-contradictory character of tauto-heterological identity, a type of non-contradictoriness with which we replace Hume's (and Kant's) still dogmatic non-contradictory character of the negation of the fact. Our purpose is to salvage, by materialistically transvaluing, the lesson of the positivity of the discrete, which is inherent in particular in Hume's (still phenomenalist) concept of feeling as the foundation of belief or 'assent to existence'. This substitution is rendered inevitable above all by the cogency lent this new type of non-contradictoriness by Aristotle's deepest materialist conclusion: that the necessary is non-contradictory.

The following general conclusions may be drawn from this materialist analysis of the most common sorts of judgements.

1. In the complex totality of subject and predicate of which the most common judgements consist (judgements in which we find the solution of the problem of a synthesis of heterogeneities, from which we began with the anti-Leibnizian Kant), the predicate (the universal) is neither ex-tracted nor in-ducted from the subject (the particular), contrary to the dogmatic empiricist claims of the positivist theory of 'abstraction', which holds that we proceed from 'some' to 'all' trees and thence to the concept of tree. In fact, 'all' trees again poses the same essential problem, that of the predicative function of the universal, which is already posed by 'some' and indeed even by 'a single' empirical tree, since even at this stage the essential problem of the functionality of the subject has already arisen, thereby implying the problem of the functionality of the predicate. Nor is the subject de-duced from or 'exhausted by' the predicate, allegedly the 'substance', 'essence', or 'concept' of 'what is being talked about', as is claimed by modern dogmatic rationalism—for example, by Hegel, who, updating the mistaken conceptual realism of the metaphysicians (for such is the real meaning of his axiom: 'that which is rational is real, and that which is real is rational'), hypostatizes the predicate, falls into the consequent ontological *petitio principii*, and thus pays the price of his disregard of the reciprocal functionality of predicate and subject.

2. The subject-predicate complex likewise enables us to jettison: a) the traditional, pre-Kantian rationalist theory of the attributive-

analytic judgement a priori, which regards the subject as a concept-*essence*; b) Kant's own theory of synthetic judgements a priori, founded on the gnoseological hypostasis of the 'I think', with all its dogmatic phenomenalist consequences and the related thing-in-itself; c) Hegel's rival dialectical theory of synthetic judgements a priori as *speculative propositions*, i.e. that *unity of the concept* according to which the form is itself the 'intrinsic becoming of the concrete content', and the equally false synthetic judgement whose subject is allegedly 'exhausted' in the predicate.

3. The judgement, just because it is a subject-predicate complex, proves to be at once *analytic and synthetic*: analytic because of the specific contribution of the subject or discrete-matter (sensation, feeling, raw fact or given, etc.) and its corresponding functionality; synthetic because of the specific contribution of the predicate or universal-category and its functionality. As such—by virtue of the reciprocal functionality of its elements, which is the key to everything—the judgement overcomes the dogmatic and effete modern problematic of the a priori and the a posteriori. At the same time, two centuries-old problematics are also drawn to a close: a) that of the ancient rational or formal intellect (= intellect as form *par excellence*) that usurps the prerogatives of reason (a typical symbol is the *finite sphere* of Parmenidean being, into which Plato himself fell when he discovered the dialectic, but as division, and in which Aristotle the anti-Parmenidean but also anti-dialectical metaphysician of matter remained imprisoned); b) that of so-called modern or formal reason (= reason as form *par excellence*) usurping the prerogatives of the intellect on the grounds that it contains and 'goes beyond' it (a typical symbol is the *infinite sphere* of the mystical-dialectical Nicholas of Cusa, to whom the pan-theistic and dialectical Hegel appeals, defender of the positivizing intellect, but for purposes of a *total* intelligibility).

But this approach rings down the curtain on these problematics because it incorporates what remains philosophically *functional* and therefore valid both in Plato's and Hegel's theories of reason as diacritic tauto-heterology (in which Parmenides's sphere already looks to be losing its finitude) and consciousness of contradiction (in which Nicholas of Cusa's sphere to some extent grants the instance of the intellectual, or finite) and in Aristotle's theory of non-contradiction, which inherently poses the instance of an *anti-*

Parmenidean and therefore materialist principle of identity. (The metaphysical logic of the scholastics and of the pre-Kantian rationalists, like Leibniz for example, does not figure in this framework, given the historic position of compromise quite patent in their common formulation of the logical principle of [non-]contradiction as a Parmenidean-Aristotelian principle proclaimed the principle of *Christian Reason*—that is, of the 'mind of God'. This was a sort of mélange of the Greek principle of the finite and the Christian principle of the infinite, of the principle of the *eidos* and the principle of the *spirit*. In this respect, Nicholas of Cusa's mystical critique of Aristotle's principle represented the Christian revolution in logic, which reached both its apogee and its decline in Hegel.)

Let us now examine this outline of the structure of the most common judgement; we shall see that it is the same as that of scientific judgement and reasoning.

The task now before us is to seek confirmation, in the methodology of the natural sciences, of the structural principle of tauto-heterological identity in which the functional reciprocity, or circularity, of reason and matter (sensation) is expressed. In other words, we must now show that this reciprocity or circularity is the same as the reciprocity or circularity of *deduction* and *induction* (in the strict sense), that is, of idea-hypothesis and fact, law and phenomenon, cause and effect.

Let us begin at the beginning, with Galileo's truly modern discourse on method, whose ultimate consequences and overall schematic import may be summarized as follows.

1. Against Aristotelian-scholastic *deductive* science, which is formally syllogistic since its content consists in the hypostases of the conceptual realism of species-essences and the corresponding finalism, Galileo upholds a *deduction*, and more properly a reasoning, that on the one hand effects a quantitative or mathematical 'resolution' and 'composition' of the qualitative or empirical elements (for example, the fact of the acceleration of the motion of a falling body), by which the *idea* of the 'proportionality of the space traversed with respect to the time the body has been falling' is formulated as a *true hypothesis* of the cause of the fall of bodies. On the other hand, he does not at all seek *proof* of the *truth* of his hypothesis, which thereby becomes a causal *law*, in its own strength—

that is, by substituting the mathematical concept of function for the physical-metaphysical concept of cause-*essence*, a substitution through which the antecedents of any consequence would simply be dissolved in the axiom of the quantitative *relations* of the latter, in which case we would face the fundamental difficulty of diverse antecedents or causes of the same effect (*plurality* of causes)—through the self-evident *unity* of the hypothesis.[5]

Instead, he seeks confirmation of the truth of his hypothesis in

[5] This is the interpretation of Ernst Cassirer and Antonio Banfi; it seems to me guilty of excessive rationalism. In his excellent Galileo *Antologia* (Florence, 1941, p. 83n), Banfi comments as follows on the 'recognition of the difficulty of determining the value of a phenomenon and of the principle that the same effect can be produced by diverse causes': 'This implies that the observed necessary connection of A as antecedent with B as consequent does not suffice to establish that A is the cause; for there can be other phenomena, A', A'', A''', etc., which have B as consequent. In that case we must proceed to decompose the phenomena of the series A into their elements, a, b, c, d, etc., in order to discover among them the element a, common to all, that constitutes the *real* causal antecedent of B. The value of the quantitative analysis of the phenomenon and its expression in mathematical formulae lies in the process of this decomposition and the establishment of these relations. . . . But this also leads to overcoming the causal point of view, to a point of view that *determines* a phenomenon not with respect to another assumed to be its cause, but with respect to the *entire set* of its relations. The concept of cause, mathematically transposed into the new science, thus dissolves into the concept of *function*' (emphasis added). It is quite true that both here and in his fundamental *Galileo Galilei* (Milan, 1949), Banfi insists that 'the new science is a continuous medley of experience and reason' and that 'all scientific knowledge is the resolution of an empirical *discontinuity*—the fact—into a rational continuum of relations . . . [that] are *concretely* thinkable only on a basis of *discontinuity*' (emphasis added). But it is also true that he fails clearly to bring out the *functionality of the fact*, given, or experiment, and therefore underplays its specific gnoseological and *logical* import in scientific reasoning. In other words, he fails to bring out the moment of negation-exclusion, or the *validating* instance it represents (only one fact disproves another). Without this moment it is impossible to resolve the fundamental difficulty of diverse antecedents of a single consequence, a difficulty that cannot be resolved purely by a mathematical function, or functionality of reason, as the first citation from Banfi would seem to suggest. The same one-sided tendency seems apparent in Giulio Preti's quite interesting study 'Il problema logico dell'induzione sperimentale nella fisica', in *Studi filosofici*, 1944, no. 5, an essay influenced by the symbolic logic of Russell-Whitehead and Carnap. Preti quite rightly points out that 'to perform an experiment "well" means genuinely to eliminate as far as possible the elements that render the phenomenon singular, so as to arrive at the production of a phenomenon-type, i.e. a phenomenon that best embodies the ideal of abstraction, of indiscernibility'. This, however, can be achieved only if it is genuinely not forgotten that the 'phenomenon-type', 'typical' as it may be, is nonetheless a 'phenomenon', or *given*, with all this implies in a rigorous and complete gnoseological and logical problematic. (As for logical positivism in general, see Appendix 3.) For Cassirer, see: *Das Erkenntnisproblem in der Philosophie und Wissenschaft der neueren Zeit*, Berlin, 1922-1923, volume I, pp. 305-306 and 411n. He attempts to assimilate Galileo not only to Kant, but even to Leibniz.

experiment with the 'model' which, since it affords the *disproof* or *elimination*—on the basis of a *model fact*—of other rival facts which, as antecedents of the same consequence, compete as hypothetical explanations of this consequence. This disproof enables reason genuinely to surmount this fundamental difficulty; in other words, it averts the *fallacy of affirming the consequent*: the belief that since if the hypothesis is true, certain (connected) events should occur, then the hypothesis is indeed true simply because these events (consequences of the hypothetical antecedents) have indeed occurred.[6] The conclusion, then, is that Galileo posits the instance that *reason is either functional or it is not reason*—in other words, it is not productive of truth (and recall that the general materialist critique of a priori reasoning was based on the methodological critique of scholastic a priori discourse by the physicist-epistemologist Galileo). In

---

[6] Horace W.B. Joseph, *An Introduction to Logic*, Oxford, 1925, p. 393: 'Where a hundred instances will not *prove* a universal connection, one will *disprove* it. This is the cornerstone of his [Bacon's] method: *maior est vis instantiae negativae*. . . . But the fundamental principle of the method by which Bacon proposed "to interpret nature", the principle on account of which he called it *exclusiva*, is correct; it is that where you cannot (as in mathematics) see that a proposition *must* universally be true, but have to rely for the *proof* of it on the *facts* of your experience, there is *no other way* of establishing it than by showing that *facts disprove its rivals*'. 'Facts . . . cannot *prove* an hypothesis by their agreement with it, except so far as at the same time they disprove its rivals by their disagreement' (p. 465n). ' . . . to show that the facts agree with the consequences of our hypothesis is not to prove it true. To show that is often called "verification"; and to mistake verification for *proof* is to commit the *fallacy of [affirming] the consequent*, the fallacy of thinking that, because if the hypothesis were true, certain facts would follow, therefore, since those facts are found, the hypothesis is true. It is the same mistake as that of incomplete elimination, in the establishment of a simple causal relation: the same as the result of overlooking what is called the plurality of causes' (p. 532). (On Bacon and Galileo and the experimental method, see Susan Stebbing, *A Modern Introduction to Logic*, London, 1933, pp. 489 ff., 319 ff.) In *Logic—The Theory of Inquiry*, John Dewey comments: ' . . . agreement is a necessary but not sufficient test. For an affirmation of the antecedent merely because the consequent is affirmable is fallacious. Eliminations or negations have to be effected which determine that *only* if the antecedent is affirmed does the consequent follow' (p. 264). 'Even so, while the inference was plausible that dew is of the kind that accorded with the hypothesis entertained, what was "proved" was that dew *might* be formed in this way. It was not shown to be the *only* way in which it could be formed. The conditions of agreement, constituted by multiple satisfaction of the function of affirmation, were strongly confirmative of the hypothesis. But until the conditions of negation (exclusion) were conjunctively satisfied, there existed the fallacy of affirming the antecedent because the consequent was affirmed. . . . Operations of variation and elimination of conditions were undertaken so that the inferred conclusion would have a high order of probability. These *limiting* conditions were experimentally produced' (p. 431). See also the 'contradictory facts' and 'counterproof' of Claude Bernard, cited below.

positing this instance Galileo implicitly recognized a new, non-formalistic meaning of the principle of non-contradiction, as is already apparent in the profound conclusion inherent in the experimental instance itself: that the typical model-facts prove (that is, verify reason) *by disproving*, by negating, other, rival facts: hence the positivity of elimination, i.e. of negation, or logical privation, of the *'positive that closes its eyes to the negative'*. This is a lesson of Galileo, and of Bacon before him, of which only a materialist conception of experiment can truly make us conscious, as we shall now see.

2. Against the *inductive* science of Bacon, and empiricist and positivistic science in general—which is distrustful of *hypotheses* (which are considered 'premature anticipations' of nature) and incapable of regarding them as guides to experimental observation, to the point of concluding, as Comte did, that 'truly philosophical hypotheses must constantly display the character of *simple anticipations* of what experience and reasoning could have *immediately laid bare* had the circumstances of the problem been more favourable'[7]—

---

[7] *Cours de philosophie positive*, Paris, 1864, volume I, lesson 28 (and cf. Edmund Koenig, *Entwicklung des Kausalproblems in der neueren Philosophie*, volume II, p. 222). But against Comte and positivism Claude Bernard observes in his classic *An Introduction to the Study of Experimental Medicine* (translated from the French edition (1865) by Henry C. Greene, New York, 1927): 'Of course I admit that facts are the only realities that can give form to the experimental idea and at the same time serve as its control; but this is *on condition* that *reason accepts* them. I think that *blind belief in fact*, which dares to silence reason, is *as dangerous* to the experimental sciences as the *beliefs* of *feeling* or of *faith* which also force silence on reason.... A *fact is nothing in itself*, it has value only through the idea connected with it or through the proof it supplies' (p. 53, emphasis added). ' "Experience", says Goethe, "disciplines man every day". But this is because man reasons accurately and experimentally about what he observes; ... The insane, who have lost their reason, no longer learn from experience; they no longer reason experimentally. *Experience, then, is the privilege of reason*' (p. 12, emphasis added). 'Indeed, I was not the first experimenter to cut this part of the cervical sympathetic nerve in living animals. Pourfour du Petit performed the experiment at the beginning of the last century.... But none of them noticed the local temperature phenomenon, of which I speak, or connected it with the severing of the cervical sympathetic nerve, though this phenomenon must necessarily have occurred under the very eyes of all who, before me, had cut this part of the sympathetic nerve. *The hypothesis*, as we see, *had prepared my mind for seeing things in a certain direction, given the hypothesis itself*; and this is proved by the fact that, like the other experimenters, I myself had often divided the cervical sympathetic nerve ... without perceiving the fact of heat production which I later discovered when an hypothesis led me to make investigations in this direction. Here, therefore, the influence of the hypothesis could hardly be more evident; we had the fact under our eyes and did not see it because it conveyed nothing to our mind.... To sum up, even

Galileo upholds an *induction* which, although it rests on an experience that consists not at all in the Baconian search for empirical constants disclosing the presence or lack of certain abstract *'forms'* or principles of corpuscular structure regarded as the causes of particular sensible properties, but rather in 'very frequent and palpable accidental observations' (for example, the empirical fact of the acceleration of falling bodies), concludes in that 'more precise experience', the typically *functional* experience, that consists in the *experiment*, always regarded as the test of an idea-hypothesis, namely the *disproof* or *negation* (or contradiction) by one fact (-type) of other more or less hypothesized facts.

Negation, discreteness, or analysis is therefore a function of affirmation, unity, or synthesis (hypothesis). Hence the affirmation-negation, exclusive affirmativeness, or identity-non-contradiction which is the characteristic aspect of Galilean law, i.e. of the hypothesis that is true (and is therefore form) only inasmuch as it is experimentally verifiable. In sum, it is no longer Bacon's preconceived or abstract form, and therefore juxtaposed to experience and non-mediated (a pseudo-form!), but is instead mediated with experience, since it stands in reciprocal functionality with it, for it has just been demonstrated that the empirical fact or datum either is *functional*, i.e. a fact-type, or *it is not a fact*, i.e. it is not productive of effectuality or reality.[8] We therefore have a reciprocal functionality of reason and experience, which is to say, of predicate (category) and subject (matter), of synthesis and analysis.

3. Consequently, the *'necessary* demonstrations' of Galilean science constitute a *non-contradictory rational of a new type*, and a new dimension of knowledge. There are two reasons for this.

First, the reciprocal functionality of hypothesis and empirical

---

mistaken hypotheses and theories are of use in leading to discoveries. *This remark is true in all the sciences*' (pp. 169-170, emphasis added). See also the next note.

[8] The *functionality of the fact* or, as Claude Bernard said: 'Experience is the privilege of reason.' Bernard observes as follows on the reciprocal *functionality of reason*: 'Yes, the experimenter doubtless forces nature to unveil herself by attacking her with all manner of questions; *but he must never answer for her nor listen partially to her answers by taking, from the results of an experiment, only those which support or confirm his hypothesis*' (p. 23, emphasis added). 'Our ideas are only intellectual instruments which we use to break into phenomena; we must change them when they have served their purpose' (p. 41). As for 'listening partially', note below Bernard's comments on the necessity of 'counterproof' and the decisive instance of 'contradictory facts'.

datum establishes a rationality or necessity that is, indeed, non-contradictory; but it is non-contradictory not by virtue of the Parmenidean absoluteness of Aristotelian-scholastic species-essences, but rather by virtue of the instance of the discreteness and contingency of the empirical datum, since it is from the experiment (the testing of the hypothesis) that the necessity of the *fact* arises. (See Galileo's 'conclusion [that] is inescapable [since] no worthwhile argument can be produced against it'; or: 'true [things], i.e. necessary, or those that cannot possibly be otherwise'.[9]) Second, the law, or *species*, in which the necessity, or necessity-contingency, of the fact is expressed therefore constitutes a variety of knowledge—embodied in a 'true hypothesis'—that is infinitely superior not only to the systematic-apodictic knowledge of Aristotelian-scholastic metaphysical science and the no less apodictic knowledge of Bacon's metaphysical 'forms' of 'experience', but also to Kant's principles of the pure intellect, the constituents of '*pure* natural science'. The latter, as presumed 'tarrying with the negative' or relational, is intended (but in vain) to confute—through the condemnation, correct in itself, of the separation of the positive from the negative characteristic of Aristotelian-scholastic and rationalist species-essences—Galileo's *scientific* positive that closes its eyes to the negative (the 'conclusion' that is 'in this manner alone' and therefore 'cannot be any other way'), in other words, Galileo's (genuinely critical) non-contradictory or necessary character *of the fact* (cf. the contradictory character, or absurdity, of the negation of the fact). This necessity of the fact, however, is nonetheless contained *in nuce* in Aristotle's most genuine and productive gnoseological instance of the determinateness of everything that has a meaning: in other words, in Aristotle's original, materialist instance of the identity of the rational and the non-contradictory as the instance of the positive that closes its eyes to the negative, which Aristotle held to be founded ontologically on 'first substance' and which we, eschewing any metaphysics, hold to be founded on, or inherent in, the numerical unity or positive discreteness of the empirical, of the material, understood not as ontological substratum but as purely logical and functional *subject* of the judgement. (Implicit in this assertion is that we understand philosophy as a scientific, since material, ontology

---

[9] *Dialogue Concerning the Two Chief World Systems*, p. 185; *Dialogues Concerning Two New Sciences*, second day.

and no longer as a formal or metaphysical ontology of the traditional sort, from Plato to Aristotle, Hegel, and others.[10]

4. The superiority of the new knowledge, of the 'new sciences', may be positively and appropriately expressed in the words of Galileo himself, which need only be shorn of their dogmatic-theological residues and mythological foliage. Then we may say: a) 'Taking man's understanding *intensively*, in so far as this term denotes understanding some proposition perfectly, . . . the human intellect [which 'makes logical advances laboriously and step by step' and is therefore 'time-consuming reason'] does understand some of them [the propositions of mathematical sciences] perfectly, and thus in these it has as much absolute certainty as Nature itself has. . . . But with regard to those few which the human intellect does understand, . . . its knowledge equals the Divine in objective certainty, for here it succeeds in understanding necessity, beyond which there can be no greater sureness.'[11] b) Once the theological and metaphysical remnants are expunged (not only Galileo's but any others as well), in accordance with the conclusions of the general materialist critique of a priori reasoning, it remains only to recognize the universality of the *method* of the new knowledge, of the new sciences—in other words, the method of scientific-experimental knowledge, which is determinate, delimited, and contingent knowledge, but of perfect necessity and truth because of its perfectible and open form. We may then conclude that the 'objective certainty' inherent in the necessity of the fact itself also applies in the so-called 'moral' or 'strictly philosophical' sciences, hitherto the nearly uncontested domain either of the conceptual realism of the most explicit theology and metaphysics, or of the outright naive realism, metaphysical in its own way, of positivism and vulgar materialism.

Before dwelling on this latter point in detail, and thereby concluding our inquiry, however, we must further specify the sort of dialecticism—functional or discursive-concrete—eminently implied in the

---

[10] Banfi's correct thesis of a Galilean 'scientific ontology' (*Galileo Galilei*, pp. 334, 356) thus acquires its full validity—but only provided it is systematized in the more general concept of *material ontology*, which can be deduced from a materialist methodological critique of a priori reasoning. Hence *any* form of knowledge worthy of the name is *experimental science*, and in this sense is discourse on being, i.e. ontology, but *material and not formal*. Otherwise one falls back into metaphysics, with its apriorisms, whether 'dialectical', 'existential', or whatever; in other words: *hypostasis*.

[11] *Dialogue Concerning the Two Chief World Systems*, p. 103.

necessity of the fact, that is, in the *law* produced by Galileo's discovery of the experimental method and the corresponding reciprocal functionality of reason and experience. We have seen that the necessity of the fact, the law of (scientific) species, arises from the experiment. Now, however; we must also realize that in general the experiment represents the test *of a hypothesis*, and the hypothesis constitutes a *unification*, in the form of a complex of relations (mathematical or otherwise) of empirical antecedents and consequences. In addition, and more specifically, we must note that:

1. The hypothesis, as a statement of relationality, is the expression of the dialectical instance, the instance of reason.

2. Nevertheless, the hypothesis can satisfy this instance—in other words, it can itself constitute a rational, non-premature, non-fantastic anticipation of nature—only if it is not an abstract or self-sufficient relation, i.e. a pseudo-synthesis, but is rather genuine negativity, and therefore a diacritic relation, a dialecticism not pure but functional, which means a dialecticism of the discrete or material.

3. This dialectic (Galileo's 'demonstration') must therefore also be identity and non-contradiction ('in this manner alone'). In sum, it must inevitably be an effective, i.e. genuinely relational, instance: the *true* hypothesis, but true because experimental (avoiding the fallacy of affirming the consequent). Thus it is that this dialecticism must be diadic and therefore must simultaneously be a disjunction. The disjunction is grounded in the instance of positive discreteness, or punctuality, which is the instance characteristic of the (verificatory) experiment. Here we have the *function*, or discursive-concrete and therefore diadic (disjunctive) dialecticism that is the *law*, typically and eminently *temporal* (provisional) or *historical* discourse: the sole non-mythical *intellect*.

This would afford us an explanation for something that has been made increasingly evident by the most modern scientific methodology, from Claude Bernard to Engels to Dewey and his school—in support, whether consciously or not, of Galileo's demonstration 'in this manner alone' and in partial, but nevertheless significant, confirmation of Bacon's empiricist principle of the 'greater power of negative demonstration': the fundamental role of *negative*, in conjunction with affirmative, propositions of science (whence the 'fallacy of affirming the consequent' is averted and 'counter-proof' established). At issue here is the role of *negation-exclusion* or *elimination*, and therefore of the 'positive that closes its eyes to the negative' in the general process of the formulation of *laws*.[12] Claude Bernard implicitly acknowledged the instance of discreteness and therefore of negation and contradiction inherent in the *fact* as such when he observed in his *Introduction to the Study of Experimental Medicine*: 'Counter-proof, then, is a necessary and essential characteristic of the conclusion of experimental reasoning'. And he concluded: 'Some physicians fear and avoid counter-proof; as soon as they make observations in the direction of their ideas, they refuse to look for contradictory facts, for fear of seeing their hypotheses vanish' (pp. 55-56).

We have, then, a typically contradictory character of the fact as such, which, grasped concretely, as the functionality of the fact with respect to reason, emerges as a (specific) condition of the affirmation-*negation* or non-contradictory rational that constitutes the *necessity of the fact* (that is, the absurdity or irrationality of the negation of the fact)—in other words, Galilean law. (The other condition, as we know, is functional dialecticism—that is, tauto-heterology, or consciousness of the contradictory character of the fact.) This tells us, for example, that everything that does not result from the specific intervention of the thyroid gland is excluded in and through the experimental verification of the hypothesis that the thyroid is the cause of the metamorphosis of the tadpole into the frog.[13] Here we may also recall

[12] 'The form of development of natural sciences, in so far as it thinks, is the *hypothesis*. A new fact is observed which makes impossible the previous mode of explanation of the facts belonging to the same group. From this moment onwards new modes of explanation are required—at first based on only a limited number of facts and observations. Further observational material weeds out these hypotheses, doing away with some and correcting others, until finally the law is established in a pure form. If one should wait until the material for a law was *in a pure form*, it would mean suspending the process of thought until then and, if only for this reason, the law would never come into being.' (F. Engels, *Dialectics of Nature*, translated by Clemens Dutt, New York, 1963, pp. 158-159.) For Claude Bernard, see above. For Dewey, see note 6 above, and also *Logic—The Theory of Inquiry*, pp. 181, 189 ff., 337 ff., 436, 464.

[13] See, in my *Per la teoria di un umanismo positivo*, p. 198, the delightful tadpole-frog 'dialectic' of the 'materialist' Teissier, a typical case of Hegelianism well and truly 'stood on its head'. In truth, it is but a new teleology parading under the label 'dialectical materialist'. In this case Teissier, who is a good biologist, fortunately corrects himself in scientific (which is to say, experimental) practice, with all this implies from the standpoint of method and materialist logic. Not without reason did Lenin say that the scientist engages in dialectics without knowing it. Finally, let us not forget that Gerolamo Fracastoro and the other scholastic physicists swept away by

the process by which Galileo advanced from the definition of uniformly accelerated motion (and from the hypothetical identification, on an empirical basis, of the motion of falling bodies with it) to the verification of this hypothesis and thereby to the final elimination of the previous formula that speeds were proportional to the times of accelerated motion, and its *reduction* to the formula that spaces were proportional to quadrants of time. The elimination and reduction were effected through experimental testing on the model of the inclined plane; hence the formulation of the last hypothetical 'proportionality' as a law of motion of falling bodies. In other words, the conclusion follows necessarily in a particular manner alone, and no other valid reason can be adduced.

It therefore follows from this renewed examination of the structural genesis of physical laws:

First, that the idea, the scientific or 'working' hypothesis (the only kind of idea that can avoid the danger of becoming hypostasis) is verified as such, as idea or concept, if it is genuinely *necessary*; on the other hand, it is genuinely necessary only if it is exclusive of every other rival. It must, however, derive this exclusivity, or determinateness, not from itself in an illusory manner, in other words (and here is the source of error) from its unitary character of non-numerical unity or ideality (as the absolutized Aristotelian-rationalist species, or any ontological species or hypostasis whatever), but rather from that eminent testability embodied in the technical experiment (of the hypothesis). It is the experiment that satisfies the positive instance of numerical unity, namely the discreteness of the material.

Second, that the Galilean method, the method of this genuinely new and modern science, continues and develops by confirming, and in turn being confirmed by, the following cardinal logical and historical instances: a) Aristotle's instance—understood in its

---

Galileo constantly played the formal game of 'opposites'. (In relation to Fracastoro's *De sympathia et antipathia*, Cassirer noted in his *Das Erkenntnisproblem in der Philosophie und Wissenschaft der neueren Zeit* (volume I, p. 400): 'All elements strive towards reciprocal contact, for in it alone can they maintain and safeguard their permanence; for the vacuum, as the distinct logical opposition to the concept of body, is a constant threat to their *physical* existence.') That the scholastic physicists were dealing with (Aristotelian) incompatible opposites rather than (Platonic or Hegelian) compatible opposites does not alter the substance of the question as far as today's imperturbable 'dialecticians' like Teissier are concerned, since they also are playing with mere (sterile) concepts. We may also recall Antonio Tari, the Hegelian who 'dialecticized' zoology—in his own lively imagination at least.

original, materialist sense (later negated by the Eleatization and mystification of the dianoetic)—that lies at the root of the anti-Parmenidean norm of non-contradiction: the instance that whoso-ever does not think of a determinate thing does not think at all; in sum, the instance of concrete thought, which is cognitive discourse; b) Bacon's most profound inductivist and empiricist instance, embodied in the fundamental principle of the 'exclusive instantia' or 'negative instantia' *par excellence*. It was by virtue of this principle that Bacon held that the most enduring sort of proof was the dis-proof or confutation by one fact of rival facts purporting to account for the same consequence. He thus intuitively saw that the gnoseo-logical value of experiment lies in the *nullifying* character conse-quent to its positive discreteness, the synonym of the material.

Let us now bring all this to bear on our previous observations about 'horse' (or 'tree'), or the most common concepts and species. We have noted that the elements that we combine in the concept of horse are combined in the same manner by everyone precisely *because* they are empirical, or discrete. In other words, they form an exclusive unity, and therefore a (diadic) dialectical synthesis, which is the genuinely concrete concept of horse, tree, man, and so on. It therefore follows that whether we are dealing with the most vulgar or the scientific Darwinian notion of species, or with Galilean or Einsteinian laws of cause and effect, their necessity or rationality is (albeit to varying degrees) the necessity of the fact as illustrated above: namely the non-contradictory rationality characteristic of a predicate (the category) that stands in reciprocal functionality with the subject (the empirical datum). In sum, it is precisely a functional, or material, dialecticism.

Now, however, let us examine this reciprocal functionality just once more, this time from the standpoint of the reciprocal func-tionality or circularity of deduction and induction. In so doing we shall demonstrate definitively that concrete determinate thought is eminently embodied in scientific knowledge, contrary to what is still believed by both intuitionists and rationalists, equally dogmatic since they are equally spiritualist and therefore metaphysical.[14]

---

[14] Typical among the intuitionists is Henri Bergson, with his Plotinism, adapted for terrestrial use. Consistent with himself, he deprecates both scientific thought and the materiality and objectivity of things. It is sufficient to recall his cardinal concept of 'continuity', i.e. the pure *unity* of *duration*, which is designed to account for the qualitative heterogeneity of the 'facts' of consciousness. This is why Bergson main-tains the supra-rational ('super-essential') of Proclus and the mystics, but nonetheless

This time let us examine the law of the evolution of species and the methodological consciousness it aroused in Engels. Here it is instructive to note that at first this law was of interest to Engels as an opponent of the 'pan-inductivists', the *Induktionsesel* (asses reeling under the burden of amassed inductions); in other words, the correctly anti-empiricist and anti-positivist Engels.[15] He noted that it was impossible to prove the evolution of species through induction alone and that the concepts of species, genus, and class had been rendered *fluid* by the theory of evolution, since this theory was based on the *deduction* of one species from another through the

exchanges it for an actual *ir-rational*. Hence Georg Simmel and all contemporary *metaphysical* 'irrationalism', which amounts to a renovated neo-Platonism (up to and including Jaspers), despite its quite illusory anti-Platonic function. It should also be added—in the interests of further clarifying the theological, since metaphysical, character of this 'irrationalism'—that at its root lies none other than the transformation (of theological origin) of the concept of *life* into the concept of *spirit*, which transformation was handed down from the Gospel of Saint John to mystics like Nicholas of Cusa, to Hegel the romantic, and finally to contemporary 'intuitionists'. 'If *vitalism* is sterile today', Bergson tells us, 'this is due to our science of the spirit, which is still in its infancy.' (This concept is expounded and exalted in the volume *La philosophie réligieuse de Bergson*, by Lydie Adolphe, preface by Emile Bréhier, Paris, 1946, p. 100. See also Le Roy, et al., Jankélowitch, *Bergson*, Paris, 1931, which Bergson himself called 'correct and exact', especially pp. 168 ff., 214 ff., for the approbation of Bergson's mysticism and his return to Plotinist 'ecstasy'.) All contemporary 'intuitionism' and 'irrationalism', with its belated mysticism and romanticism, thus marks a typically decadent phase of modern thought: its consistently anti-scientific (anti-Galilean) position signifies precisely an attempt at a sophisticated neo-obscurantism in logic and epistemology, with the corresponding (bourgeois) individualist morals typical of Bergson's 'privileged souls'—or 'beautiful souls', as the German romantics said. This is the true—negative and worse—meaning of the spiritualist and idealist 'reaction' against science in which the glory of contemporary intuitionism is said to consist. In conclusion, the following remarks of Dewey about the typically concrete, *determinate* thought that is *scientific* knowledge merit some attention: 'Dogmatic restriction of science to generalization compels denial of scientific traits and value to every form of practice . . . , it involves logical suicide of the sciences with respect even to generalizations . . . , ignores the outstanding fact of scientific inductive reference: namely, controlled reconstitution of the singulars which are the ground of generalization.' (*Logic—The Theory of Inquiry*, pp. 439-440.) ' . . . if the generic character of the propositions of physical and biological sciences were ultimate, such propositions would be entirely useless from a practical point of view; they would be quite incapable of practical application because they would be isolated from intellectual continuity with the particular cases to which application is sought'. (Dewey, *Problems of Men*, New York, 1946, p. 218.) Here Dewey is criticizing only the rationalists, 'traditional (formally rationalistic) theory', and not the intuitionists, who—with their *mystical* search for the singular and their consequent deprecation of the intellectual concept (reduced to convenient 'convention', to 'label'), a deprecation they share with 'dialectical' rationalists (cf. Hegel's and Croce's 'pseudo-concepts')—are certainly no less metaphysical and dogmatic.

[15] *Dialectics of Nature*, p. 155, 204-205.

hypothesis of 'heredity'. In sum, he argued, species, genus, and class have thereby become *relative* or *dialectical* concepts, of no use at all in pure induction.[16]

It is equally instructive to note, however, that Engels later became interested in this same law from another methodological angle, that of the accidental or inductive element, and that he recognized that it was precisely the infinite *accidental differences* among the individuals of a species, accentuated to the point of sundering the character of every species (the force of 'contradictory facts'), that compelled Darwin to question the traditional concept of species, with its *metaphysical* rigidity and immutability. The accidental thereby vanquished traditional *necessity*[17] and posed the instance of a new necessity, that of the *hypothesis*. Finally, it should also be noted that Engels felt compelled to conclude both that Darwinian theory was a practical realization and satisfaction of the Hegelian instance of the intimate link between necessity and contingency (or accidentalness) and that *deduction* and *induction* functioned cooperatively and were reciprocally *interlinked*.[18]

Now, Engels's not at all one-sided conclusion is particularly significant in that it reconfirms that it is in scientific knowledge, precisely as *determinate thought* par excellence, that we find the eminent manifestation of the principle that satisfaction of the instance of unity or necessity requires satisfaction of the instance of discreteness, here represented by the *accidental differences* of the natural individuals, to which we owe the rupture of the unity—rigid because metaphysical—of the traditional, Aristotelian-rationalist concept of species. In other words, the instance of a genuinely dialectical thought, of non-rigid categories and relations, is not the metaphysical *self-instance* of *thought itself* (as essential self-consciousness), as Hegel maintained, but is rather the scientific instance of the reciprocal functionality of thought and matter, or nature.

[16] 'The concepts with which induction operates: species, genus, class, have been rendered fluid by the theory of evolution and so have become *relative*: but one cannot use relative concepts for induction.' Ibid., p. 226.

[17] 'Precisely the infinite, accidental differences between individuals within a single species, differences which become accentuated until they break through the character of the species, . . . compelled him to question the previous basis of all regularity in biology, viz. the concept of species in its previous metaphysical rigidity and unchangeability. . . . Chance overthrows necessity, as conceived hitherto . . .' (*Dialectics of Nature*, p. 234.) In the margin of the manuscript Engels had written: 'The material chance occurrences which had accumulated in the meantime smothered and shattered the old idea of necessity.'

[18] Ibid., pp. 226; 230-234.

'An example', Engels writes, 'of the necessity of dialectical thought and of non-rigid categories and relations in nature: the law of falling, which already in the case of a period of fall of some minutes becomes incorrect, since then the radius of the earth can no longer without error be put $= \infty$, and the attraction of the earth increases instead of remaining constant as Galileo's law of falling assumes. Nevertheless, this law is still continually taught, but the reservation omitted!'[19] Well said, as far as it goes; but in our view it has three important implications.

1. The non-rigidity, or dialectical character, of thought either signifies the rigorous extirpation of every *hypostasis*, in which case the dialectical character of thought *is* its functionality, and the concept (or category) recovers its *normal* value as predicate *of a subject distinct from this concept*; or else we inevitably fall back into hypostasis, into the *substantified* predicate, in which case it is difficult to see any possible anti-metaphysical and anti-dogmatic significance of the instance of the non-rigidity or dialectical character of thought.

2. Non-rigid categories are therefore those that condition the composition of cognitive concepts, so-called empirical concepts (spurned, of course, by worshippers of hypostasis, by metaphysicians of all epochs), common or scientific empirical concepts (hypotheses). These categories are non-rigid because they stand together *through* and *in* the performance of their function as criteria-predicates; in other words, they are dialectical (orbiting around each other, as it is usually put). As pure categories, then, they can no longer be cited as values of knowledge—as, for example, 'dialectical laws' (like the Hegel-Engels 'law of the transformation of quantity into quality and vice-versa').[20] Instead, the gnoseological value is the complex that results from the *reciprocal functionality* of predicate and subject (if the subject were not itself functional, it would abdicate to itself, thereby immediately decaying, as we have seen, into subject-*essence*, into hypostasis, and even into Kant's 'thing-in-itself'). We thus discover the complex, the result of their reciprocal functionality (that is, the circularity of deduction and induction), which is the empirical concept (the truly concrete concept), namely

[19] Ibid., p. 190.
[20] Cf. Lenin, 'What the "Friends of the People" Are and How They Fight the Social Democrats', *Collected Works*, volume 1, p. 164.

the judgement of experience, or judgement *tout court*, which is *the sole cognitive value*. We find, for example, not pure quality and the like, but instead 'wooden trunk', and so on. To put it another way, we find not the abstract equation 'pure quantity = pure quality, and vice versa', but instead a particular physical *law* dealing, for example, with mechanical motion. (As I have pointed out elsewhere, Engels himself eventually came to recognize this in regard to economic laws.)

3. Once all this is understood, the question of non-rigid thought becomes the question of scientific law (or necessity of the fact), since scientific law eminently and typically exhibits: a) thought which is dialectical, relational, or truly thought inasmuch as it is functional, directed at things, and therefore productive of perfect truth in the only possible non-dogmatic sense of the word; b) consequently, the *necessity* of the content of this thought—since the latter does not possess the Parmenidean metaphysical fixity of hypostasis, since its determinateness is a result of the discrete-material, the specific condition of the non-contradictoriness of thought itself—is the *contingent* necessity of scientific law in general. Scientific law is therefore correctable, as in the example cited by Engels, or rather *perfectible*, but constitutionally so, and therefore within the continuity of *scientific*, real thought. Ultimately, the continuous constitution and perfecting of law, eminent and ever-open temporal and historical discourse, alone constitutes the true *dynamism* of the dialectic, the *real dialectic* (which is, in fact, the historical dialectic). Any other 'dynamism', including that ascribed to 'dialectical laws', is, in point of fact, the mystified mobility of *abstract thought*, in other words, mystified dialectic.[21]

[21] Nevertheless, Engels himself recognizes, in regard to the three 'laws of dialectics'—'the law of the transformation of quantity into quality and *vice versa*; the law of the interpenetration of opposites; the law of the negation of the negation'—that: 'All three are developed by Hegel in his idealist fashion as mere laws of *thought*: ... The mistake lies in the fact that these laws are foisted upon nature and history as laws of thought and not deduced from them. This is the source of the whole forced and often outrageous treatment; the universe, willy-nilly, is made out to be arranged in accordance with a system of thought which is itself only the product of a definite stage of evolution of human thought.' (*Dialectics of Nature*, p. 26.) Also: 'This [is] mystical in Hegel himself, because the category appears as pre-existing and the dialectics of the real world as its mere reflection' (p. 153). 'What, therefore, in Hegel appears as a development of the thought form of judgement as such, confronts us here as the development of our empirically based theoretical knowledge of the nature of motion in general' (p. 239). 'But the activity of human beings *forms the test* of

'The question', wrote Marx, 'whether objective truth can be attributed to human thinking is not a question of theory but is a *practical* question. Man must prove the truth, i.e. the reality and power, the this-sidedness of his thinking in practice. The dispute over the reality or non-reality of thinking that is isolated from practice is a purely *scholastic* question.'[22]

This famous second thesis on Feuerbach suggests *positively* that one and the same method should be applied in both the so-called physical sciences, which we have been examining so far, and the so-called moral, or strictly 'philosophical', sciences. The same suggestion, this time from a *negative* direction, was implicit in Marx's critique of the Hegelian-Platonic dialectic as mystified dialectic—in sum, in the development and generalization of the materialist critique of a priori thought and the subsequent processes of hypostatization characteristic not only of traditional rationalism in all its forms but also of every variety of idealism and spiritualism. In this second thesis on Feuerbach, then, we find the full fecundity of the *moral Galileanism* of Marx in its positive and constructive, and no longer purely polemical and negative, aspect. It poses the general necessity of a *unification of logic* that abolishes the dualism of epistemology, the logic of the 'sciences' on the one hand, and 'philosophical' or 'general' logic on the other. We must therefore conclude, as Lenin did in *Materialism and Empirio-Criticism*, that 'if what our practice confirms is the sole, ultimate and objective truth,

---

causality. If we bring the sun's rays to a focus by means of a lens and make them act like the rays of an ordinary fire, we thereby prove that the heat comes from the sun' (p. 171). 'Only when natural and historical science has adopted dialectics will all the philosophical rubbish—outside the pure theory of thought—be superfluous, disappearing in positive science' (p. 244). Finally, Engels again, but from another source: 'The reproaches you make against the law of value apply to all concepts, regarded from the standpoint of reality. The identity of thought and being, to express myself in the Hegelian fashion, everywhere coincides with your example of the circle and the polygon. Or the two of them, the concept of a thing and its reality, run side by side like two asymptotes, always approaching each other yet never meeting. This difference between the two is the very difference which prevents the concept from being directly and immediately reality and reality from being immediately its own concept. But although a concept has the essential nature of a concept and cannot therefore prima facie directly coincide with reality, from which it must first be abstracted, it is still something more than a fiction, unless you are going to declare all the results of thought fictions because reality has to go a long way round before it corresponds to them and even then only corresponds to them with asymptotic approximation.' (Letter to C. Schmidt, 12 March 1895, in *The Correspondence of Marx and Engels*, London, 1934, pp. 527-528.

[22] *Early Writings*, p. 422.

then from this must follow the recognition that the only path to this truth is the path of science, which holds the materialist point of view.'[23]

In other words, the method of Galilean science is universal; it consists in the elimination of any idealist, positivist, phenomenalist, or pragmatist misunderstanding. The method of science is the materialist rigour that permits ascertainment of the reciprocal functionality of reason (consciousness) and matter, theory and practice, idea and fact, predicate and subject, and thereby shuns all dogmatic, sterile, and unreal cognitive procedures. In sum, in every field, scientific prediction (hypothesis) must replace metaphysical apriorism (hypostasis). We thus return to the positive gnoseological and logical exigency that arose from Marx's materialist critique of the hypostatizations characteristic of the moral 'dialectic' of Hegel: the instance of the 'specific logic of a specific object'; or, 'philosophy as science'.

It is now no longer difficult to adumbrate the content of this correct, *unitary* gnoseological procedure. (I say *unitary* because it effectively includes scientific law, which is a typically 'specific' conception inasmuch as it is, as we have seen, determinate and non-contradictory, in sum, a materialist conception; and *correct* because its correctness has already been established by the generalized materialist critique of a priori thought, whether dialectical or not, from which this instance acquired its original foundation.)

Let us again consider the philosophy of the state, which will keep us in the domain of philosophic problems that have been subjected to Marx's critique of the aprioristic method and therefore his critique of *generic* concepts. What, then, do we mean by *specific* concepts or criteria? Or better: *how* are such concepts structured? (The materialist critique has already demonstrated that they *are* indeed indispensable for any knowledge worthy of the name.) To begin with, it is obvious from all that has been said thus far that they must be *historic* concepts, for otherwise they would be marred by the result-retribution to which all meta-historical concepts that claim the status of a priori concepts or general, *generic* classes are subject: their content is not really mediated; in other words, they are burdened by a gratuitous, undigested, abstract empirical element (which is aprioristically transcended). This is what prevents them from being *concepts* (or forms) in the sense of genuine syntheses.

---

[23] *Collected Works*, volume 14, p. 161.

But it is not enough simply to say that they must be historical, for to do so would be to run the equivalent risk of a passively accepted empirical, one not properly mediated or rationalized. These concepts, then, must indeed be historical, and therefore genuinely determinate and specific; but they are nevertheless *concepts*, or universals, and therefore genuine criteria. On the other hand, the rational, dialectical instance of unity, which they must satisfy as concepts, must not be satisfied in an illusory manner, the concepts acting as moments of an original unity or meta-historical idea, for such concepts would thereby become hypostases (with the consequent result-retribution). Instead, the concepts must genuinely satisfy this instance as functional elements of a historic, temporal unity or continuity—that is, as functional elements of a rationality common to the most diverse historico-philosophic or ideological systems. It follows that any proper, *scientific* solution of philosophical problems must meet three conditions.

1. To start with, the difficulties, the problems, must be real and determinate, not ambiguous and abstract; they must arise specifically from historical-material (and not meta-historical-material) instances, and therefore as a function of corresponding historical-rational (and not meta-historical-rational) instances.

2. The subsequent formulas devised to resolve these difficulties must derive their *objectivity*—which co-operates in making them resolutive, since it makes them *rational* instances, i.e. instances of unification of the *real* diversity or historic-materiality inherent in the difficulties posed—from their status as a dynamic mean of antecedent historical-rational instances. They must therefore extend their functional resolutive, or unifying, capacity to the problematical difficulties of the time of the actual research and beyond. Hence the rigorous establishment of these formulas as resolutive ideas-hypotheses: the rigour lies in the fact that these formulas, generated by historical-material instances, satisfy them by synthetically reconnecting them with their historical-rational (and not meta-historical-rational, i.e. generic) antecedents. It is this that expresses, in *every science* worthy of the name, the *functionality* of reason, in other words, its actual and authentic rationality. ('The pure ideality of a real sphere could . . . only exist in the form of a science.'[24])

[24] Marx, 'Critique of Hegel's Doctrine of the State', in *Early Writings*, p. 65.

3. These ideas-hypotheses must be genuinely resolutive, which means they must be subjected to *verification* such that *the fallacy of affirming the consequent* is avoided here as well; in short, such that human-social practice, or historical-experimentation, co-operates with the *theoretical* objectivity of the hypotheses to establish a congruence between the historical-rational (or properly resolutive) and historical-material (or properly problematical) instances. They must co-operate in the pure reciprocal functionality of reason and fact—in this case, of *ideology* and *action*—through which the circle of historical-material and historical-rational instances is closed in the active and definitive, non-contradictory *experimental synthesis*. This is the process that generates moral and physical laws alike. The specific logic of a specific object, which we have termed *philosophy as science*, therefore does not and cannot mean anything but the *experimental conception*, the law, wherein lies the solution to philosophical or 'moral' problems no less than the solution to problems of the 'physical' sciences. On this basis, one can only agree with Marx that 'the [hypostatizing] philosophers have only *interpreted* the world, in various ways; the point is to *change* it'.[25] In sum, it is in *practice*, in action, that *theory*, or truth, is *confirmed*, and thereby *affirmed*.

If we keep this methodological schema of the (scientific) solution to philosophical problems in mind, it is perhaps not too difficult to see, for example, how the philosophy of the state should be approached in order to avoid the results-retributions of the metaphysics of law. Indeed, it ought not to be difficult to persuade ourselves that, precisely in order to avoid the crass, surreptitious materialism that results from Hegel's spiritualistic premises, we must travel another road, replacing a priori discourse on the state (whether 'dialectical' or not) with the moral Galileanism of scientific (materialist) sociology. In accordance with the methodological schema we have just outlined, this implies that:

1. A problematic of the state and society must start from *real* difficulties and contradictions, from historical-material instances, and begin to become clear through an *analysis* of the 'fundamental representation' of the 'de facto presuppositions'—in other words, the historical antecedents (economic, social, political, etc.)—of the

[25] 'Theses on Feuerbach', in *Early Writings*, p. 423.

present real situation, however divided and contradictory, from which it arose.

2. Such an analysis must be a dialectical analysis of historical-rational antecedents, or antecedents-values, and therefore a synthetic formulation of the historical-rational development (of institutions, etc.). Out of this emerges a *normative mean*, which is a valid functional *idea-hypothesis* (for example, Marx's seminal concept-model of radical democracy, which was derived from the comparative historical analysis of the medieval and modern representative systems, on the basis of which Marx demystified and purged from theory the hypostatized Prussian and European monarchy of the 1820s with its 'hereditary' High Chamber, and so on).[26] This idea-hypothesis, as such, is interwoven with categories that are gnoseologically productive because they are precisely category-functions and not defective and sterile category-hypostases, like, for example, the categories of *substantiality* and *accidentalness* used aprioristically by Hegel in and for the justification of his hideous anachronisms such as 'born legislators' and the like.

3. This evaluative hypothesis must be verifiable in practice, through the *historical experiment* concretized in specific and exclusive actions and institutions. It is only through this sort of political philosophy as science that ethical and human progress is conceivable and realizable. Why *only*? Because its concrete and dynamic ideas, which correspond to reality, are wholly free of the *conservative* spirit that stems from the *dogmatic* (a prioristic) *universality* of hypostases, which are immobile by definition. (Lenin's general conclusion about *Capital*, with which we will deal below, relates to the possibility of verifying this seminal idea-model of Marx and its social and economic presuppositions.)

Having come this far, we may now legitimately conclude that just as the science of biology underlies the techniques of medicine, so the 'science of history'—that is, history-science and not (metaphysical) history-philosophy—'underlies the techniques of the moralist'.

---

[26] In this regard it is important to keep in mind Marx's entire 'Critique of Hegel's Doctrine of the State' (*Early Writings*, pp. 57-198), the first attempt to lay the methodological bases for a materialist sociology of the state. See also *Per la teoria di un umanismo positivo*, pp. 19-49, 200-202.

Thus, 'from the Marxist point of view, the scientist and the moralist are one and the same'.[27]

To all this, however, it must be added that this specific conception of philosophy as science is synonymous with the 'determinate' or

[27] Roger Garaudy, *Le communisme et la morale*, Paris, 1947, pp. 89, 92. Cf. Lenin, 'What the "Friends of the People" Are', *Collected Works*, volume 1, p. 139: Marxism as 'a strictly scientific approach to historical and social problems'. Cf. Stalin, *Dialectical and Historical Materialism*: 'the science of the history of society can become as exact a science as, for example, biology'. See also, Antonio Gramsci, *Il materialismo storico e la filosofia di Benedetto Croce*, Turin, 1948, especially pp. 98, 142-143. On the question of the relationship philosophy-science-materialism, see: J. Desanti, *Lénine, philosophe nouveau* (in *Nouvelle Critique*, 1949, no. 4, pp. 5 ff.); L. Lombardo-Radice, *Galileo Galilei e la disputa dei massimi sistema* (in *Rinascita*, May 1949, pp. 222 ff.). On the relationship science-materialism-(proletarian) revolution, see: Palmiro Togliatti, 'Sviluppo e trionfo del marxismo', in *Rinascita*, December 1949, pp. 526 ff.: 'the doctrine of Marx, Engels, Lenin, and Stalin . . . forever abandons and *closes* the phase of contemplation, initiates a new period of comprehension of the world that is both a *condition* and *aspect* of its conscious *transformation* by men. The doctrine is therefore both *theory* and *practice*, careful analysis of objective processes and struggle to master them. Its decisive confirmation is in *action*, which, emerging from the very conflicts lacerating a society in its decline, creates the preconditions of a new society and brings it into being.' (See also Togliatti's recognition of the contemporary importance of Marx's 'Critique of Hegel's Doctrine of the State', in *Rinascita*, June 1954, pp. 392-393). E. Sereni, *Scienza, marxismo, cultura* (Milan, 1949) also deals with the relationship science-materialism-revolution (especially pp. 190 ff.). As for Henri Lefebvre's *Logique formelle, logique dialectique* (Paris, 1947), its inspiration is so evidently different from that of the present work that it is impossible to discuss it fruitfully in a footnote. A glance at the formal arrangement of Lefebvre's work is sufficient: it conserves *all Hegel's logical schemata* (which are to be turned upside-down, of course, or so he intends). In any event, Lefebvre himself acknowledges in a subsequent *Autocritique* that, for example, 'this intention to demonstrate the objectivity of human thought theoretically contains a remnant of speculative illusion; for "Man must prove the truth, i.e. the reality and power, the this-sidedness of his thinking in practice" (second thesis on Feuerbach).' (Cf. *La Nouvelle critique*, 1949, no. 4, p. 49.) Of course, such a statement taken in itself, without the reservations required by the scientific-logical tasks and obligations that follow from Marx's methodological critique of the defective procedures of Hegelianism and idealism (a critique of which Lefebvre, like all the others, seems unaware), cannot lead very far and threatens to tumble into a new 'practicist' oversimplification no less sterile than the speculative, or 'theoreticist'. Remnants of Hegelianism and (even scholastic) formalism may also be found in the discussions on logic among W.T. Perry, V.J. McGill, Howard Selsam, and Harry K. Wells, in *Science and Society*, 1948-1949. Even the best of these contributions, 'Dialectics Transformed into its Opposite', by Selsam and Wells, fails, as usual, to realize the *limits* of Hegel's critique of Aristotelian logic, and Aristotle's positive (materialist) instances are therefore overlooked. (This is not the case with the article by Popov cited above.) As for the position of Lukács, an examination of *Existentialisme ou marxisme?* (Paris, 1948, especially pp. 15 ff., 253 ff.) will make clear my differences with him. On the other hand, Ernst Bloch (*Subjekt-Objekt, Erläuterungen zu Hegel*, Berlin, 1951, especially 445 ff.), who begins from a line different from Lukács's Marxistic-Hegelistic approach, stands closer to my position. He writes, for example:

'precise abstraction', the rigorous scientific *abstraction*, which Marx discovered and employed in the particular 'moral discipline' of political economy. He counterposed this determinate abstraction to the 'speculative', generic, or 'forced' abstraction employed by traditional economists, who affirmed that there were 'natural' and eternal economic laws. The most comprehensive presentation of this view may be found in Marx's 1857 introduction to *A Contribution to the Critique of Political Economy*.[28] Let us examine his argument in some detail.

Marx notes, for example, that if we examine the economic category of production in the most general sense, we realize that its apparently general or common character is actually revealed by comparative analysis to be articulated and complex, for it is 'itself segmented many times over and splits into different determinations'. Some of these elements of the category 'production' are common to all epochs, others only to a few. Certain features will be seen to be shared by the most modern and most ancient epochs alike, such that no production would be conceivable without them. But just as the most developed languages have laws and characteristics in common with the least developed—although their 'development' consists precisely in that in which they diverge from the general—so the 'general' features of production must be separated out (*gesondert*) 'from the determinations valid for production as such' in order that the 'essential' or specific difference is not forgotten in the 'unity', uniformity, or generality. (Here Marx indicates that only a rigorous and scientific gnoseological analysis of the general and the particular, one that 'separates out' the general characteristics and avoids confusing them with the particular, can prevent the 'forgetting' of

---

'Materialism, on the contrary, as Engels says, is not only an explanation of the world from itself; it is also, as a consequence of the experimental constitution of the world, a system of dialectically mediated interruption, of non-schematism, of new formation.' (See the review by Nicolao Merker in *Società*, 1955, no. 2.) Finally, more or less polemical approaches to the general problematic of Marxism from various points of view include: E.J. Walter, 'Der Begriff der Dialektik in Marxismus', in *Dialectica*, Neuchâtel, 1948, I, I, pp. 69-70; Augusto Del Noce, *La non-filosofia di Marx e il comunismo come realtà politica*, Milan, 1947; Arturo Massolo, 'Marx e il fondamento della filosofia', in *Ricerche sulla logica hegeliana*, Florence, 1950, pp. 197ff.

[28] The quotations from the 1857 introduction that follow are from the translation by Martin Nicolaus, in Marx, *Grundrisse*, Penguin books in association with *New Left Review*, Harmondsworth, 1973, pp. 83-111; see especially pp. 84-87 and 100-105— *Translator's note*.

the particular because of, or rather in favour of, the general. This 'forgetting', which amounts to the prevalence of the general over the particular, constitutes the abstractly synthetic garb of the a priori, of hypostasis.)

The supposed 'profundity' of those economists who strive to demonstrate 'the eternity and harmoniousness of the existing social relations' consists precisely in this 'forgetting', this dissolution of the particular into the general. They explain, for example, that no production is possible without an instrument of production, 'even if this instrument is only the hand'. There is no production without stored-up, past labour, 'even if it is only the facility gathered together and concentrated in the hand of the savage by repeated practice'. And they explain capital as a 'general, eternal, relation of nature'—which is true if we disregard the 'specific quality' that makes accumulated labour into capital in the modern sense. They thereby tend to 'confound or extinguish all the historic differences' through the formulation of 'general human laws'. Thus, and Marx cites John Stuart Mill as an example, they 'present production . . . as encased in eternal natural laws independent of history, at which opportunity *bourgeois* relations [of production] are then quietly smuggled in [*ganz unter der Hand . . . untergeschoben*] as the inviolable natural laws on which society in the abstract is founded'. They thus continually fall into 'tautologies': 'All production is appropriation of nature on the part of an individual within and through a specific form of society. In this sense it is a tautology to say that property (appropriation) is a precondition of production. But it is altogether ridiculous to leap from that to a specific form of property, e.g. [modern, bourgeois] private property.'

By this Marx means two things. First, the conclusion is ridiculous because it is futile to try to define a specific, historical form of property like bourgeois private property by saying that since it is property (appropriation), it is a precondition of production (appropriation), which amounts to a tautology and a genuine *petitio principii*. Second, this sort of conclusion, tautological and therefore cognitively sterile, is merely the result-retribution of a hypostasis: apriorism imparts reality to the most generic concept of production as appropriation of nature, such that the concept assumes and exhausts within itself modern, bourgeois production, thus transcending the *specific* characteristics of that form of production. In sum, to put it as Marx did, the specific meaning of bourgeois relations of production has been replaced by generic and immutable production, preconceived as an eternal natural law of economic society *in the abstract*. The invalid, incorrect structure of 'metaphysical' economic reasoning therefore lies in the metaphysical interpolation, or a priori substitution, of the generic, or more abstract, for the specific, or more concrete, in the definition of the latter. This kind of structure is now well known to us: it is the mystifying dialectic which, by reducing the specific or concrete to the merely 'allegorical' or symbolic manifestation of the idea or generic, concludes with tautologies or *petitio principii*, which represent the retribution of a specific or concrete that is undigested or non-mediated precisely because it is merely allegorical, transcended in apriorism.

What is needed, Marx continues, is a 'scientifically correct' method. This means above all that we must make abstractions (without which no thought or knowledge is possible) on the basis of the concrete (*das Konkrete*), 'the real subject', which in this case is a specific historical society. (The 'Robinsonades' in which so many bourgeois economists indulge even today, Marx says, are merely 'illusions' inspired by the doctrine of natural law, since 'production by isolated individuals outside of society—something that might exceptionally happen to a civilized man who was accidentally lost in the wilderness and already dynamically possessed the forces of society within himself—is as great an absurdity as the idea of the development of language without individuals living together and talking to one another'.) But although the 'concrete' is indeed the point of departure for observation and conception, it nevertheless appears in our thought as a 'process of concentration', as a 'result' and 'not as a point of departure'. Indeed, the concrete is concrete 'because it is the concentration of many determinations, hence unity of the diverse'.

If, in attempting to explain the social process of production as a whole, we begin with the population of a country as the basis, without correctly taking account of the 'classes' of which it is composed, which in turn are 'an empty phrase' unless we consider the concrete, historical elements on which they rest, 'e.g. wage-labour, capital, etc.'—in other words, if we begin with a 'chaotic conception of the whole' and then proceed, through a gradual analysis, to increasingly simplified concepts—then in so doing we are proceeding from the 'imagined' concrete 'towards ever thinner abstractions' until we arrive at 'the simplest abstractions', such as labour, money, value, and so on. This is the method adopted by bourgeois political economy, a method by which 'the full [concrete] conception is evaporated [*verflüchtigt*] to yield an abstract determination', which, let it be noted, is not at all empty, as Kant's critique of abstract rationalism would have it, but is quite full—of a 'chaotic', confused, undigested concrete, or non-mediated 'unsound empirical'. This 'abstract determination', with its a priori character, is indeed a substantial, and not merely formal or verbal, tautology. The 'evaporation' of the concrete 'full conception' therefore signifies not that the conception has been voided, but rather that its content has been rendered 'chaotic' or 'imaginary'. What is evaporated by the 'abstract' (a priori) determination is the *cognitive value* of the conception and *not its content*. (The *materialist* critique of a priori reasoning is far more profound than the Kantian, and even subjects the latter to criticism.)[29]

But if, having arrived at the simplest abstractions—such as labour, division of labour, demand, exchange-value, and so on—we 'retrace the journey' and return to 'the population again, but this time not as the chaotic conception of a whole, but as a rich totality of many determinations and relations'—in other words, considered in its historical development—then we thereby attain the *correct method*. The 'abstract determinations' (abstract, but no longer a priori, since they are founded on this continuous 'return journey' to the concrete as such, to a 'unity of the diverse') now 'lead towards a reproduction [*Reproduktion*] of the concrete by way of thought'. Hegel erred when he 'fell into the illusion of conceiving the real as the product of thought concentrating itself, probing its own depths, and unfolding itself out of itself'. In fact, 'the method of rising from the abstract to the concrete is the only way in which thought

---

[29] This eludes, for example, the Marxist Hermann Ley, who *Kantianizes*, as follows: 'The unsound abstraction dissolves the whole idea into non-concrete determinations. A procedure of abstraction of this kind would allow the content to be lost in these determinations. The reproduction of the concrete in thought must produce abstract determinations that envelop the entire diversity.' ('Karl Marx Einleitung in die Grundrisse der Kritik der politischen Oekonomie', in *Deutsche Zeitschrift für Philosophie*, Berlin, 1954, no. 3, p. 578.) When a question as decisive as the materialist critique of a priori thought is ignored, the results are quite serious, for all that remains is to toy with mere literary metaphors, which is what such phrases as 'reproduction' (of the concrete), or the much-abused 'reflection' (of reality) become in such a context. A fine materialism that produces! For the *logical* significance of 'reproduction' and similar expressions, see the discussion below, which attempts to analyse the (synthetic-analytic) structure of determinate, or historical, abstraction (particularly note 31).

appropriates the concrete, reproduces it as the concrete in the mind'—the concrete in this case being 'the subject, [the specific] society', since it is the 'presupposition' from which we begin and which 'we must always bear in mind'.

The correct method may thus be depicted as a *circular* movement from the concrete to the abstract and thence back to the concrete, an unbreakable and continuous historical evolution of abstractions, in this case economic categories. The truth of these categories therefore stands in inverse relation to the simplification, or one-sided and forced abstraction, of their content. Money, for example, can and indeed did exist historically before capital, banks, or wage-labour. In this sense it may be said that the 'simplest', most general economic category can express an economic relation 'predominant' in an 'undeveloped' historical social whole (or else the 'subordinate' relations of a 'more developed' whole, since these relations existed historically before this social complex developed in the direction indicated by 'a more concrete category'). Thus it is that 'the path of abstract thought, rising from the simple to the combined, would correspond to the real historical process'. This may be seen quite clearly in the correct scientific elaboration of the fundamental category of *labour*. Labour is 'a quite simple', or general, category. The conception of labour in this general sense—'as labour as such'— is quite old. 'Nevertheless, when it is economically conceived in this simplicity, "labour" is as modern a category as are the relations which create this simple abstraction.' Which means quite simply that this category is indeed an *abstraction*, but *historical* and *not a priori*. In other words, it sums up the economic, practical, and theoretical 'steps forward' taken by the 'industrial or manufacture system', under which the source of wealth was located no longer in the object, in money, but in 'a subjective activity—in commercial and manufacturing activity'. The 'Physiocratic system' marked a further advance, for it posited 'a certain kind of labour—agriculture—as the creator of wealth', while Adam Smith took 'an immense step forward' when he defined it as 'labour in general'. Hence, with 'the abstract universality of wealth-creating activity, we now have the universality of the object defined as wealth', namely, 'the product as such or again labour as such, but labour as past, objectified labour'.

Now, Marx continues, 'it might seem that all that had been achieved thereby was to discover the abstract expression for the simplest and most ancient [economic] relation in which human beings—in whatever form of society—play the role of producers. This is correct in one respect. Not in another'. It is true that 'indifference towards any specific kind of labour presupposes a very developed totality of real kinds of labour, of which no single one is any longer predominant' and that 'the most general abstractions arise only in the midst of the richest possible concrete development, where one thing appears as common to many, to all. Then it ceases to be thinkable in a particular form alone'. On the other hand, if this abstraction of labour as such is not merely the result of a concrete totality of labours, this also means that 'indifference towards specific labours corresponds to a form of society in which individuals can with ease transfer from one labour to another, and where the specific kind is a matter of chance for them, hence of indifference. Not only the category, labour, but labour in reality has here become the means of creating wealth in general, and has ceased to be organically linked with particular individuals in any specific form. Such a state of affairs is at its most developed in the most modern form of existence of bourgeois society—in the United States'.

The 'simplest abstraction, then, which modern economics places at the head of its discussions, and which expresses an immeasurably ancient relation valid in all forms of society, nevertheless achieves practical truth as an abstraction only as a category of the most modern society'.[30] Thus, the 'example of labour shows strikingly how even the most abstract categories, despite their validity—precisely because of their abstractness—for all epochs, are nevertheless, in the specific character of this abstraction, themselves likewise a product of historical relations, and possess their full validity only for and within these relations'. Another example of a fundamental *determinate*, or historical, *abstraction*, or unity of the diverse, would be *capital*.

But this historical evolution of categories (in this case economic abstractions), which embodies the method of the circle *concrete-abstract-concrete*, in no way means that these categories should be accepted 'in the same sequence as that in which they were historically

---

[30] 'It is important to realize', Paul Sweezy has written, 'that the reduction of all labour to a common denominator, so that units can be compared with and substituted for one another, added and subtracted, and finally totalled up to form a social aggregate, is not an arbitrary abstraction, dictated in some way by the whim of the investigator. It is rather, as Lukács correctly observes, an abstraction "which belongs to the essence of capitalism".' (*The Theory of Capitalist Development*, London, 1947, p. 31.)

decisive'. Indeed, it would be 'unfeasible and wrong' to do so. 'Their sequence is determined, rather, by their relation to one another in modern bourgeois society, which is precisely the opposite of that which seems to be their natural order or which corresponds to historical development'. Thus: 'The point is not the historic position of the economic relations in the succession of different forms of society.' And of course: 'Even less is it their sequence "in the idea"', as Proudhon, following Hegel, maintained. 'Rather, their order within [*ihre Gliederung innerhalb*] modern bourgeois society'.

Now, what is the meaning of Marx's rejection not only of the 'sequence "in the idea"' but also of 'that which seems to be their natural order, or which corresponds to historical development'? Why the appeal to their 'order within modern bourgeois society', that is, the order determined '*by* their relation to one another in modern bourgeois society' (which is 'precisely the opposite' of what seems to be the natural order)? I would reply that what is at issue here is the problem of how to reconcile the essential *historical character* of the economic categories with the *non-chronological character* or *ideality* of their order ('precisely the opposite'). Indeed, this problem amounts simply to the consistent development of the methodology of the circle concrete-abstract-concrete. In other words, it is the question of the method of economics as a method of determinate, historical, or exact (not 'forced')—which is to say rigorously *scientific—abstraction*. We may then begin to see the shape of the relation between the *historical* economic categories and *modern* bourgeois society and its categories. (The direction of the research has already been given by the observations about the historical formation of the 'most general' but nevertheless 'quite modern' category, 'labour'; now it is a matter of drawing out all the consequences.)

'Bourgeois society', Marx continues, 'is the most developed and the most complex historic organization of production'. Hence, the categories, or economic abstractions, that 'express its relations, the comprehension of its structure, thereby also allows insights into the structure and the relations of production of all the vanished social formations out of whose ruins and elements it built itself up'. In sum, just as 'human anatomy contains a key to the anatomy of the ape', so 'bourgeois economy thus supplies the key to the ancient, etc. But not in the manner of those economists who smudge over all historical differences and see bourgeois relations in all forms of society' (because of their own hypostases). For it is true that one 'can understand tribute, tithe, etc., if one is acquainted with ground rent. But one must not identify them'. But it is also evident that 'since bourgeois society is itself only a contradictory form of development, relations derived from earlier forms will often be found within it in an entirely stunted form, or even travestied. For example, communal property'. Thus, while it may be affirmed that the categories of bourgeois economics contain elements of the categories of all other forms of society, 'this is to be taken only with a grain of salt. They can contain them in a developed, or stunted, or caricatured form, etc. but always with an essential difference'. For example, in the Middle Ages, 'capital itself—apart from pure money-capital—in the form of traditional artisans' tools etc.' has a 'landed-proprietary character', while in 'bourgeois society it is the opposite', since agriculture 'more and more becomes merely a branch of industry, and is entirely dominated by capital'. In other words, agriculture is ruled by the *predominant* element, 'the social, historically created element'. Hence, ground rent 'cannot be understood without capital. But capital can certainly be understood without ground rent'. Capital, then, 'the all-dominating economic power of bourgeois society', must 'form the starting-point as well as the finishing-point, and must be dealt with before landed property'. In sum, after 'both have been examined in particular, their interrelation must be examined'.

It is thus clear *how* the direction of the relation between the 'historical' economic categories of the past (like medieval landed property and the capital associated with it) and the categories of modern society (ground rent and the capital that dominates it) is dictated by an order that is 'precisely the opposite' of the chronological sequence of the categories (not landed property, then capital; but capital, then landed property). The reversed order of categories, which determines the direction of the 'past-modern' relation, is a result of the *modern, present* necessity to understand and explain the modern phenomenon of ground rent, and towards this end it is fitting that capital should be the starting- and finishing-point and should be explained 'before' landed property. It remains, however, to grasp the *why* of this inversion of the historical and logical sequence. Marx writes: 'The so-called historical presentation of development is founded, as a rule, on the fact that the latest form regards the previous ones as steps leading up to itself, and, since it is only rarely and only under quite specific conditions able to criticize itself [*sich selbst zu kritisieren*] . . . it always conceives them one-sidedly. The Christian religion was able to be of assistance in reaching an objective [non-one-sided] understanding of earlier mythologies only when its own self-criticism had been accomplished to a certain degree, so to speak, potentially. Likewise, bourgeois economics arrived at an understanding [i.e. an objective understanding] of feudal, ancient, oriental economics only after the self-criticism of bourgeois society had begun. Insofar as the bourgeois economy did not mythologically identify itself altogether with the past [through the aprioristic projection of categories into the past and the future, which is what hypostasis amounts to], its critique of the previous economies, notably of feudalism, with which it was still engaged in direct struggle, resembled the critique which Christianity levelled against paganism, or also that of Protestantism against Catholicism. In the succession of the economic categories, as in any other historical, social science, it must not be forgotten that their subject—here, modern bourgeois society—is always what is given [*gegeben ist*], in the head as well as in reality, and that these categories therefore express the forms of being, the characteristics of existence [*Daseinsformen, Existenzbestimmungen*], and often only individual sides of this specific society, this subject, and that therefore, this society by no means begins only at the point where one can speak of it *as such*; this holds *for science* as well.'

Thus far we have been quoting or paraphrasing Marx's 1857 introduction to *A Contribution to the Critique of Political Economy*. If the most suggestive aspects of this text are developed and coordinated with the methodological lessons Marxism-Leninism has drawn primarily from *Capital*, the following conclusions, if I am not mistaken, may be drawn.

1. Political economy can arrive at an objective, non-one-sided, understanding of its own historical antecedents, and therefore of its own consequent problems (ground rent, for example), only if it is capable of self-criticism. In other words, finding itself in crisis, it apprehends that crisis as the dubiousness of its own categories. To do this, however, it must have acquired a *historical* consciousness of the concrete or *given* subject, which is present-day bourgeois society. Once it has acquired this historic consciousness (which is lacking in bourgeois political economy, in the eyes of which, as Marx put it in *The Poverty of Philosophy*, 'there has been history, but not any

more', since it considers its own institutions 'natural' and 'eternal'), it finds itself, like any *science* worthy of the name, solidly established *ab initio*, without apriorism or dogmatism, on the terrain of experience itself, on the terrain of historical-*material* instances.

2. Consequently, this historical consciousness of the present, as consciousness of historical-*material* instances, is itself simultaneously consciousness of historical-*rational-functional* instances (in other words, reason is a function of matter, and vice versa). This is conjointly represented by the two movements of the methodological circle outlined above: *from the concrete to the abstract and back to the concrete*. This is a one- and twofold movement that produces abstractions which, since they are historical and determinate (for example, the category of capital as starting-point), satisfy the *unitary but functional* instance of reason and therefore constitute *hypothetical* normative *means* of *antecedents* and *consequents*, which are the present phenomena, or given problems. (Compare this with the terms used above: as a historical or determinate abstraction, the category 'labour' presupposes and summarizes the economic, practical, and theoretical 'steps forward', etc. This concept of labour, no less than that of capital, is precisely a typical concept-mean in this sense.) On the one hand, this explains why the sequence of the constituent economic categories of such a mean is ordered in a manner opposite to the chronological or *analytic* sequence, since it explains that this order is both rational and synthetic-analytic, a *sequence of means*.[31] On the other hand, it is

---

[31] Cf. the conclusion of the entry 'Dialectics' in the *Grosse Sowjet Enzyklopädie*, Berlin, 1953: 'The *logical* method of Marx in his critique of political economy . . . was but the *historical* method, *only shorn of the historical form* [i.e. chronological sequence] and of any unsettling elements of chance [i.e. irrationality].' To which it should nevertheless be added that the point here is precisely *to reconcile* the substantially historical character of the economic categories (in this case) and their non-chronological character, or ideality, or *rationality*—without, that is, confusing Marx's method with Hegel's, which is entirely too bereft of 'unsettling' historical 'elements of chance', conjured away through a priori, or preconceived, rationality, despite its claim to be a historical dialectical method. In short, it is important to realize that Marx's reasoned history, to use Schumpeter's expression, differs from Hegel's in two respects. 1. In the synthesis, or concept, constituted, for example, by the quite modern abstraction 'labour *tout court*' or 'capital', the various previous historical characteristics of labour or capital become elements of the concept and are therefore transvalued, assuming a unitary or general significance through which they lose their particularist, purely historical-chronological or analytic significance, but without losing their determinateness, or significant analytic character, which is one with their historic *necessity* (since the precedents are not imaginary). The *synthesis* is therefore

now clear that the objective, non-one-sided understanding of antecedents consists precisely and above all in the formulation of historical-rational, and not *meta*-historical-rational antecedents and conditions of the given problems (rent, for example), which is required for the objectivity of the scientific, or non-dogmatic, understanding of things.

3. Since the (objective) normativity of these means is not categorical or absolute but only hypothetical (for it expresses historical-rational and therefore rational-functional instances), this normativity-of-hypothesis can be verified, and thus become *reality-law*, only in and through the historical (non-abstract) materiality characteristic of *practical* economic and social *experience*. This is just what is meant by the second and final movement—the return *from the abstract to the concrete*—that *closes* the methodological circle concrete-abstract-concrete (a circle that is historical, and therefore dynamic, moving from the concrete to the concrete; it therefore affords genuine development).

Thus, Marx's fundamental *hypothesis* of the labour theory of value and the related hypothesis of surplus-value (scientific because produced by the method of determinate or historical abstraction) has acquired the *truth-reality* of *law* since the *practical historical and economic experience* of monopoly capitalism over the past fifty years has confirmed that a phenomenon as serious as crises, for example, could be explained only by the organic contradiction of the

---

also *analysis*. 2. These preceding characteristics of labour or capital become elements of a concept whose formation can be generated only by the historically latest, or *present*, character (of labour or capital), recognized as such; in other words, from their being posited as problems (the problematic of labour as an abstraction belonging to the essence of capitalism, as illustrated by Sweezy in note 30, above, or of capital, which has to be explained 'before' landed property). The (chronological) precedents are thus transformed into (logical-historical) *antecedents*, or preconditions of the *consequents*, and thereby fall into a genuinely historical-dialectical and progressive order ('opposite' to the chronological sequence). This is a rational order that constitutes precisely the *determinate abstraction* described above, the *concept-mean*. This is a true *concrete concept* because, unlike Hegel's, it does not sacrifice the analysis for the synthesis, but reconciles them by bringing together the ideality and historical character of the categories. There is little notion of these problems in 'Das Besondere im Lichte des dialektischen Materialismus' (in *Deutsche Zeitschrift für Philosophie*, 1955, no. 2, pp. 157ff.), by Lukács, who read Marx's 1857 introduction without the key of the materialist critique of a priori reasoning (contained, principally, in the 'Critique of Hegel's Doctrine of the State'). The work of the Soviet philosopher E.V. Ilyenkov is marked by the same deficiency (see note 33 below).

capitalist profit economy, with its social yet anarchic production. This contradiction was *predicted*, along with others derived from it, precisely by the basic *hypothesized* connection between labour-value and surplus-value. And as Lenin notes in *Materialism and Empirio-Criticism* (p. 162), 'inasmuch as the criterion of practice, i.e. the course of development of *all* capitalist countries in the last few decades, proves the objective truth of Marx's *whole* social and economic theory in general, and not merely one or other of its parts, formulations, etc., it is clear that to talk of the "dogmatism" of the Marxists is to make an unpardonable concession to bourgeois economics'; the latter being genuinely dogmatic, since abstract.[32]

It now remains to examine some of the important implications of this scientific dialectic of political economy and to specify once more the mystification characteristic of the defective, speculative dialectic. We may thus more sharply illustrate the contrast between the two and demonstrate the correctness of the former, genuinely materialist, dialectic.

It may already be inferred from the preceding argumentation that the logical and gnoseological structure of Marx's economic law is well symbolized by the methodological circle of concrete-abstract-concrete, the circle of the reciprocal functionality of matter and reason (induction that is deduction and vice versa). In economics, this is embodied in the determinate, historical abstraction that replaces the indeterminate, aprioristic (and therefore defective) abstraction employed by bourgeois political economy. This in turn signifies, *sub specie logicae*, the historical-sociological method of Marxist economics, namely the *critique* of political economy. Leaving metaphors aside, the logical structure of economic law in

---

[32] In support of these conclusions we may recall these observations of Maurice Dobb ('Marxism and the Social Sciences', in *The Modern Quarterly*, New Series, Vol. 3, No. 1, winter 1947-1948, pp. 5-21): 'Marx alone among economists held a picture of capitalism as developing towards the sort of monopoly-capitalism that we now know [a typical example of one of Marx's scientific *predictions* in economics], with its restriction of output and its chronic unemployment and under-capacity working. . . . It is hardly surprising that Marxian political economy should have been a theory *par excellence* of economic crises, whereas non-Marxian economics not only should have treated crises as something quite abnormal (due, e.g. to the presence of frictions or the impact of external influences), but should only very belatedly, and as an afterthought, have produced any theory of crises at all' (pp. 18-19). And: 'Can anyone seriously deny the *substantial* validity of Marx's picture (never mind the detail of his drawing) of economic crises growing more and not less serious, of concentration of industrial control and ownership instead of what Alfred Marshall called "the decline of exclusive class advantages in industry"?' (p. 20).

the Marxist sense consists in: a) the concrete, given problem (the historical-material instance); b) the *hypothesis*, or establishment of a non-absolute normative *mean* of the antecedents or conditions of the given consequent (the historical-rational instance); c) the criterion of *practice*, which validates, or verifies, the hypothesis, thereby converting it into a law (the ultimate instance of the historical reciprocal functionality of fact and hypothesis, matter and reason, induction and deduction).[33]

[33] It is important, of course, to bear in mind not only this *intellectual* aspect of the Leninist criterion of 'practice' as a *technical* criterion (closing the methodological circle concrete-abstract-concrete), but also its indissociable *moral* aspect, emphasized by Sweezy in the following penetrating summation of the method of the critique of political economy: 'To the Marxist, on the other hand, the specific historical (i.e. transitory) character of capitalism is a major premise. It is by virtue of this fact that the Marxist is able, so to speak, to stand outside the system and criticize it as a whole. Moreover, since human action is itself responsible for the changes which the system is undergoing and will undergo, a critical attitude is not only intellectually possible, but it is also morally significant—as, for example, a critical attitude toward the solar system, whatever its shortcomings, would not be—and, last but not least, practically important.' (*The Theory of Capitalist Development*, p. 22.) To this we should add Togliatti's observations (note 27 above) about the relation science-materialism-(proletarian) revolution. And, of course, Marx's highly fruitful methodological declaration in the second thesis on Feuerbach (note 22) must never be forgotten. This problem of the Leninist criterion of 'practice' is touched on only indirectly in the rather interesting essay 'Dialectic of the Abstract and the Concrete in Scientific Knowledge', by E.V. Ilyenkov, (*Voprosi filosofii*, 1955, no. 1, translated in *Critica economica*, June 1955 [the quotations that follow have been translated from the Italian version].) The essay is devoted primarily to the 1857 introduction and its relation to some of the key concepts of *Capital*. Ilyenkov recognizes that 'analysis and synthesis, deduction and induction coincide organically here', but he also speaks of non-scientific abstraction as 'empty'—this even though he has previously admitted that 'Hegel himself, although he imagines that his analysis of law and property, for example, begins from absolutely rational principles,...actually arrives at these principles through the current bourgeois representations of his epoch'. On the other hand, Ilyenkov understands that 'the "universality" of the concept is not...the formal definition of the concept, but the logical characterization of its concept' and that 'the aspiration to discover absolutely simple elements common to every object, the first building-blocks of the edifice, in an attempt thereby to arrive at the comprehension of real objects, is foreign to the [materialist] dialect'. Also: 'when one says that to move from the abstract to the concrete means to rise from the simple to the complex, or more precisely from comprehension of the simple to comprehension of the complex, one has in mind the simplest element of a *determinate object* and not of any object whatever.' He also understands that 'the theory of knowledge, dialectical materialist logic, unlike Locke's gnoseology, does not centre its attention on the single act of generalization *independent of the general course of the logical process*, but considers it precisely as a moment, a step, a degree in this process'. Finally, he grasps that the one-sided analytical method of classical bourgeois economics, i.e. 'the method that consciously proposes to grasp the "constituent parts" of which the object consists, cannot, by its very nature, resolve another, no less important aspect of scientific inquiry: it cannot explain *why* these "constituent parts" are conjoined as

This also means, however, that these three logical aspects are actually common to *any* knowledge worthy of the name, to any cognition as science, and therefore no longer as mere knowledge or contemplation. It means, ultimately, that there is but *one* science, because there is but *one* method, *one* logic: the *materialist* logic of modern, Galilean experimental *science*, purged of the implicit, more or less mathematistic Platonism that has formed the philosophical background of all bourgeois scientists, from Galileo to Einstein. True, the *techniques* through which laws are formulated in physics, the social sciences, and economics certainly vary, for the empirical subject matter, the reality under investigation, varies. For example, mathematical calculations generally represent an essential constituent element in the formation of the laws of physics, whereas they can be employed only occasionally, as an auxiliary element (statistics, for example), in the formulation of the laws of social science, and even in economics. In the case of the latter, for example, the pure or abstract mathematical curve is replaced, in the Marxist approach, by a sort of historicized curve. There is, however, no variation in the *method*, the *logic*, symbolized by the circle concrete-abstract-concrete.

'History itself', Marx wrote in the 'Economic and Philosophical Manuscripts', 'is a *real* part of *natural history* and of nature's becoming man. Natural science will in time subsume the science of man just as the science of man will subsume natural science [i.e., it will adopt its experimental method, and will employ a historical-experimental, and in that sense historical-dialectical, method, within which the third logical moment—point c) above—representing historical-social *practical* confirmation, will correspond to Galilean *experimental* technique]: there will be *one* science'.[34] 'The science of the history of society', noted Stalin, 'can become a science as exact as biology, for example'. And Zhdanov: 'The unique character

---

they are and not in any other way'. Nevertheless, things would be much clearer if Ilyenkov recognized explicitly that the *scientific* abstraction is a *historical* abstraction and that the 'general course of the logical process' of which the abstraction is not independent is the course of history itself (although not the mere historical-chronological course). It is this that explains why the 'constituent parts' are conjoined in one way and not in another, and how we can avoid those abstractions 'in which the *specific* character of capitalism vanishes'. On the 1857 introduction, see Lucio Colletti, 'Il metodo dell'economia politica', in *Critica economica*, June 1954. Alessandro Mazzone's article in *Aut-aut*, November 1955, is also interesting as far as the problem of the 'moral sciences' is concerned.
[34] *Early Writings*, p. 355.

of the development of philosophy resides in the fact that from it, as the scientific knowledge of nature and society developed, the positive sciences branched off one after another. Consequently, the domain of philosophy was continually reduced on account of the development of the positive sciences. (I might add that the process has not ended even up to the present time.) This emancipation of the natural and social sciences from the aegis of [speculative] philosophy constitutes a progressive process, for the natural and social sciences as well as for philosophy itself'.[35]

In other words, the advance of human knowledge itself entitles us to proclaim not only the unity of scientific logic, but also, consequently, the unity of logic *tout court*; no philosophical logic distinct from scientific logic is admissible any longer. Since philosophy has become the 'science of man', in the sense in which Marx uses the term in the quotation above, there is no longer any such thing as 'science' in the thoroughly metaphysical, gratuitous, and illusory sense in which the word is employed in such expressions as 'philosophy as the science of spirit', which amounts simply to 'metaphysics', 'speculation', 'contemplation', and so on. Instead, science exists only in the strict sense of history-science, the (materialist) science of history, of which Marx's 1857 introduction (a methodological preface to the *critique* of political economy) is one of the earliest expositions, developing similar points expressed in *The Poverty of Philosophy* and the 'Critique of Hegel's Doctrine of the State'. This is the scientific gnoseological foundation of economics as a science.

The central point bears repeating: the techniques of research do vary, but there is only *one logic*—the materialist logic of modern science. This may be termed the *moral Galileanism* characteristic of Marxism (that is, the proposition that the 'moral sciences', without exception, are 'science' in the most rigorous sense of the word). I say Galileanism so as to underscore the divergence of Marxism as a method not only from idealism, with its hypostases, but also from positivism, with its idolatry of 'the facts' and its consequent repugnance for 'hypotheses' (not to mention Comte's quintessentially

---

[35] A.A. Zhdanov, 'On Literature, Music and Philosophy', in *On Philosophy* (1947), London, 1950, p. 82. Compare, in *Soviet Studies*, 1949, p. 50, the manifest inability of the illustrious mathematician-philosopher Bertrand Russell, modern adherent of the Enlightenment, to arrive at the same logical conclusions as Zhdanov, even though he begins from the same, apparently obvious, observation. See also Gramsci, *Il materialismo storico e la filosofia di Benedetto Croce*, pp. 98, 142-143.

metaphysical claim that the task of philosophy is to 'synthesize' the 'results' of the sciences). All these conclusions are implicit in the 'scientific dialectic' of economics towards which Marx was striving at least as early as *The Poverty of Philosophy*[36] and which he attained in the 1857 introduction to *A Contribution to the Critique of Political Economy* and in *Capital*. The new method, the method of the materialist dialectic, is both universal and revolutionary.

It is appropriate to add at this point that Engels's profound and illustrative argumentation about what constitutes 'dialectical thought' in 'nature' now appears, in substance—if we keep in mind the scientific-economic dialectic—as necessarily equally applicable elsewhere. It embodies what constitutes dialectical thought in the human, and more specifically historical, world. In other words, it acquires a general methodological significance.

It is therefore legitimate, indeed obligatory, to add to this example of dialectical thought in nature as many other examples as one wants of dialectical thought in the realm of the human, social sciences. These, however, must be of the type of the law of value, for it would be absolutely illegitimate to intersperse any so-called dialectical laws of the Hegelian type, such as the 'transformation of quantity into quality and vice versa', or the 'negation of the negation'. Such 'laws' are merely formulas of *abstract thought*, of a *mystified* and therefore 'falsely mobile' and undialectical dialectic. They are characteristic of static thought (see even Engels's and Lenin's critique of Hegel's triads). Engels's observation about the 'inaccuracy' threatening Galileo's law of falling bodies signifies not only that scientific laws are generally inherently correctable or perfectible and can therefore be replaced by other laws in a *continuity* of scientific, or real, thought. It also signifies that it is precisely this

---

[36] Indeed, in his well-known letter to Jean-Baptiste Schweitzer of 24 January 1865 (see *The Poverty of Philosophy*, New York, 1963, pp. 194-202), Marx explains that in this work he showed 'how little' Proudhon 'penetrated into the secret of scientific dialectics and how, on the contrary, he shares the illusions of speculative philosophy in his treatment of the *economic categories*; how instead of conceiving them as the *theoretical expression of historical relations of production corresponding to a particular stage of development in material production*, he transforms them by his twaddle into pre-existing *eternal ideas*, and in this roundabout way arrives once more at the standpoint of bourgeois economy'. It should be noted that Marx's concluding gnoseological observation—namely that Proudhon, following the defective, twisted path of his Hegelistic, aprioristic, and therefore generic economic conception, finally arrived back at his starting-point, the standpoint of bourgeois economy—recalls the *sterile* results of all a priori reasoning. On Marx's critique of Proudhon, see my *Rousseau and Marx*, pp. 174-185.

continuous, ever-open formulation and perfecting of scientific law, as historical discourse *par excellence, and this alone,* that constitutes the real *dynamism* of the dialectic—of the *real dialectic,* or dialectic of the real. Any other dynamism, including that of Hegel's 'dialectical laws', is merely false, mystified mobility.

Indeed, that this and only this is what Engels means is confirmed in another passage, also from *Dialectics of Nature,* in which he affirms his complete agreement with Marx that induction and deduction constitute a *methodological circle.*

We thus turn yet again to the same central point: the *reciprocal functionality* of induction and deduction, of matter and reason, of fact (or 'accidental') and hypothesis (or 'necessary'). It is the *twofold functionality,* required by the *scientific dialectic,* that produces *determinate* or historical abstractions and thereby laws in the materialist sense; it is symbolized by the methodological circle of concrete-abstract-concrete expounded by Marx in his 1857 introduction and applied with maximum rigour and success in *Capital.* But what we wish to emphasize here is that Marx's application of this methodological circle to one of the 'moral sciences' (economics) marked the first establishment of the *universality* of this scientific-materialist method. It is this achievement that best represents his enormous revolutionary impact in the domain of thought and culture, which can be summed up, let us repeat once again, in this formula: there is only *one* logic, there is only *one* method, that of modern science understood and expounded in the materialist sense, which has nothing whatever to do with any attempted positivist or scientist justification of science. In sum, the 'moral' domain, the terrain of (speculative or contemplative) 'philosophy', has been so narrowed that nothing remains of it, neither in economics, nor therefore in social science, politics, and so on (bear in mind the young Marx's merciless critique of the logical, ethical, and political hypostases inherent in Hegel's 'classical' philosophy of right). We know that this implies a complex of particular gnoseological and methodological problems, with which this book itself is concerned. Here it is sufficient to add that the logical problem of the 'determinate dialectic'—a dialectic in which the instance of 'contradiction', or *unity* of opposites (the dialectical instance in the strict sense), is necessarily reconciled with the instance of 'non-contradiction', or *distinction,* and therefore the 'struggle' and 'exclusion' of opposites—is the problem to which we are inevitably led by Marx's concept of 'determinate' or historical abstraction, namely the concept of 'scientific dialectic'. (Mao Tse-tung, following in the footsteps of Lenin, has in his writings on the theory of knowledge been one of the few to become aware of this problem. Ultimately, it is the problem of a *tauto-heterological identity*.)

But let us proceed to the conclusions with which we are most immediately concerned. There is no better way to complete the concept of the logical structure of Marx's economic law, at which we have arrived through illustrating the major implications of his formulation of the 'scientific dialectic' in economics, than to consider once again the negative consequences of the defective structure of the 'speculative' or 'metaphysical' dialectic in economics to which we have counterposed Marx's scientific dialectic. To conclude, then, let us again examine the capacity for mystification characteristic of bourgeois economic doctrine as the metaphysics of economics, or the aprioristic theorization of historical-economic facts.

Towards this end it is useful to repeat the analysis of the defective structure that produces the result-retribution, the negative consequences, substantial tautologies, and *petitio principii* that have been scrutinized throughout this work. Now, the schema of the defective structure of the 'speculative dialectic' in economics, and in the social sciences in general, may be summarized as follows, in the terminology employed by Marx in his 'Critique of Hegel's Philosophy of Right': a) The universal or idea as such—in other words, the predicate of any judgement—is rendered 'subsistent', is substantified or hypostatized, and thereby illegitimately transmuted into the (logical) 'subject' of the judgement; the universal is thus 'immediately confused with empirical existence', which is the 'real subject'. The 'limited' or 'real' subject is thereby 'taken immanently and uncritically as the expression of the idea', as its 'product', 'manifestation', or 'predicate' (the predicate of the predicate!). Aprioristic thought thus 'renounces the thing', or real subject, in its particularity and specificity and 'lends it [*unterschiebt*], in its limited shape, the opposite meaning of this limitation', from which it follows that the meaning of the particular thing 'is not its own determination, but rather an allegorical, interpolated' (*untergeschobene*) or substituted determination. b) As a consequence of this transformation (*Umschlag*) of the empirical into the speculative, there is a contemporaneous 'transformation of the speculative into the empirical'. In other words, it is that which 'belongs to the exoteric' or empirical side that 'properly advances development'; that is: 'development always proceeds from the predicate', or mystified predicate, which is the empirical 'real subject' and the logical subject (of the judgement) transmuted into the predicate. Hence: 'no content is gained in this manner, but the form of the old content is changed', and indeed, 'development depends in particular on wholly empirical motives, that is, highly abstract, unsound empirical motives'.

In regard to point a), however, it must be recalled that:

1. Precisely because there has been a hypostatization—that is, an actualization of the universal, the idea, the dialectic, the generic concept, or whatever it may be called—the universal, namely the predicate, is 'confused' with the empirically existent, the particular, or the real subject, which is the logical subject of the judgement. The universal as substance-*essence* replaces (or rather claims to replace) the substratum-*matter* that is the real subject or particular, exchanging the reality-immediacy of this subject with its own reality-mediation (and therefore positing itself precisely as hypostasis).

2. The merely allegorical character of the universal or idea which is thereby acquired by the material or real substratum is a consequence of the (defective) character of this metaphysical, or aprioristic, interpolation, since this claims to exhaust the material in the essence, form, or idea such that the material retains only a purely symbolic value.

In regard to point b), however, it must be recalled that:

1. As a consequence of a), namely the 'transformation of the empirical into the speculative', which is hypostatization, or the 'philosophical dissolution of the empirical', there is a contemporaneous 'transformation' of the speculative into the empirical, manifested precisely in a 'philosophical restoration of the empirical'.

2. This restoration—which consists in the fact that the 'development, progress, or articulation of the universal or idea proceeds *from the mystified predicate*', in other words, from the real empirical substratum and logical subject transmuted into the predicate—is both *vitiated* and *inevitable*: vitiated, because it is the restoration of an empirical that is *gratuitous*, since presupposed a priori and

therefore tacitly assumed or *surreptitious*; inevitable, because this empirical is nevertheless the indispensable substratum-*subject* of the judgement, of any judgement or reasoning. It is the 'concrete', the foundations or reasons for which are sought in the judgement and without which *there is no judgement worthy of the name*. The replacement of this substratum-subject by a substratum-*essence* proves to be a pure pretext. (Concepts, judgements, or propositions are never wholly essence, purely formal, or devoid of content—not even the 'abstract definitions' of the most aprioristic rationalism, in which it is not the representative content but the cognitive value of the representation that is evaporated.)

3. This restoration of the empirical (-content) is therefore the restoration of an 'abstract' and 'unsound' empirical, since it is not adequately mediated and is therefore gratuitous and surreptitious, for it is transcended in the apriorism of hypostasis. This restoration-subreption is the specific root of the substantial, and not merely verbal, tautologies and *petitio principii*—in short, the negative (for the advance of knowledge) consequences which are the penalty, the result-retribution, of any philosophical dissolution of the empirical, of any hypostasis. An example of an economic tautology that may be considered classic in its extreme simplicity is the definition of bourgeois private property as an immutable precondition of production.[37]

[37] It is perhaps opportune to note that this *materialist* denunciation of the (substantial) tautologies of bourgeois economic science has a meaning directly opposite to Croce's denunciation of the tautologies of science in general, for Croce's denunciation is based solely on the idealist and mystical prejudice of the pure 'practicity' and therefore untruth, arbitrariness, and defectiveness of the 'pseudo-concepts' and 'pseudo-judgements' of the empirical sciences as such. In other words, he is denouncing their inability to rise to the speculative point of view of the *absolute unity* of the 'pure Concept' (with a capital 'C'), which he holds to be the sole true 'concept' and therefore the sole 'truth'. The materialist denunciation, on the contrary, begins from the anti-idealist drive to restore and extend the dignity of modern science and therefore of knowledge, against all dogmatism, apriorism, or false knowledge. In other words, Croce's denunciation signifies only total faith in the development and accretion of truth through the method of *pure deduction* (while the continuous scientific appeal to a fact that is not 'overcome' or totally dissolved in 'pure' thought or concept seems to him a mere tautology). The materialist, however, has faith only in the reciprocal *functionality of deduction and induction*. For the classical idealist source of Croce's distinction between judgement and pseudo-judgement, etc., on which his conception of the mere 'practicality' and untruth of the sciences depends (cf. the mere 'labels' to which Bergson, the spiritualist and mystical affirmer of a 'fluid', purely 'intuitive' unity of things, reduces the 'static' and 'rigid' concepts of science), see the discussion in chapter III of the present work on Hegel's distinction

Let us now examine several recent attempts to apply this revolutionary historical-materialist critique of apriorism to economics. This will bring the negative, mystifying character of traditional, classical and neo-classical economics into sharper relief and will simultaneously encompass and illustrate more extensive critical material in the logical framework we have outlined. In his *Political Economy and Capitalism* Maurice Dobb writes: 'But in all such abstract systems there exists the serious danger of hypostatizing one's concepts; of regarding the postulated relations as the determining ones in any actual situation, instead of contingent and determined by other features; and hence of presuming too readily that they will apply to novel or imperfectly known situations, with an abstract dogmatism as the result. There is the danger of introducing, unnoticed, purely imaginary or even contradictory assumptions, and in general of ignoring how limited a meaning the corollaries deducible from these abstract propositions must have and the qualifications which the presence of other concrete factors (which may be the major influences in this or that particular situation) may introduce. All too frequently the propositions which are products of this mode of abstraction have little more than formal meaning, and at most tell one that an expression for such-and-such a relation must find a place in any of one's equational systems.' And he adds in a footnote: 'Such pursuits are sometimes defended on the ground that they are "tool-makers" for subsequent analysis. Perhaps it is true that this is their principal use. But even tools are better made when their manufacture is fairly closely subordinated to the uses which they are intended to serve.'[38]

This rigorous methodological analysis of Dobb's is clearly more perspicacious than that of another, nonetheless eminent, English-

---

between the 'judgement' or 'unity of the concept' that is 'truth' and the 'dualistic' 'proposition', which is devoid of truth.

[38] Maurice Dobb, *Political Economy and Capitalism*, London, 1937, p. 130. The following methodological observations by the same author are also noteworthy: '...the categories they [bourgeois economists] use exclude any notion of class exploitation (and I refer to class exploitation not as a moral judgement, but as a factual description of a relationship). Hence, the only definition of capitalism to be found among most contemporary economists is the purely technical one of a system that *uses* a so-called roundabout, or mechanized, method of production (according to which, of course, either a slave society or a socialist one could be "capitalistic" in this sense).' ('Marxism and the Social Sciences', *The Modern Quarterly*, winter 1947-1948, p. 17.) The term 'roundabout' is a reference to the term '*Umwege*' used, for example, by Böhm-Bawerk.

speaking economist, Paul Sweezy. Guided, not always properly, by Lukács and Korsch, he oscillates between two different assertions, which he never mediates—first: that 'Marx was a strong adherent of the abstract-deductive method which was such a marked characteristic of the Ricardian school'; and second, that nevertheless, 'Marx's method, says Lukács, "is in its innermost essence historical"'.[39] Dobb, on the other hand, shows that he has understood the concept of 'determinate' or 'historical abstraction'. Likewise the Italian economist Pesenti, who in his article 'La scienza inutile' (*Il Contemporaneo*, 12 June 1954), emphasizes that '"science" necessarily had to acquire two characteristics which seem contradictory but actually are not: on the one hand an extreme formal abstractness, an extreme unhistoricness, with the result that it expresses pure *tautologies*; on the other hand a meticulous search for the concrete, the casuistic' (the unsound empirical!).

Another Italian economist, Giulio Pietranera, has written as follows: 'Let us take, for example, "labour", this fact that presents itself to us concretely in the *historical* life of a class, or a group homogeneous in its capitalist relations. It constitutes the positive, the concrete, of which science must take account positively and specifically. In the theory of economic equilibrium, however, it appears on the contrary as a "personal capital". The positive "has been salvaged", as Marx would say . . ., but it has become "a medium through which the absolute light shines"—in this case the absolute light of the mathematical laws of equilibrium. It has become a "sign [an allegory] of something other than itself", namely of the *generic* category "capital", which acts as the "absolute light" in this case. Therefore, when it becomes necessary really to speak of labour—and above all when it becomes necessary to perform it in the concrete—this "personal capital" reappears in its full garb as the *labouring* population, afflicted by greater or lesser unemployment, as the mass of wage-workers and salaried employees, such that equilibrium models, ultimately, are indeed full of meaning, but defective and therefore sterile meaning. . . .

'Likewise with the employer, who is posited a priori in the mathematical heavens, so as to be divested of any mundane embodiment (i.e. any historical, sociological, or class determination) and who thus becomes a sort of automaton who establishes, on the basis of

---

[39] *The Theory of Capitalist Development*, New York, 1942, pp. 11, 20.

iso-costs and iso-quantities, the combinations of factors of production. When the equations balance, he does not even make a profit. This employer—who has also become a beneficiary of absolute light—nonetheless soon reappears, with his unexplained (because transcended) mundane historical features, which so resemble those of the "Manchester manufacturer".... Indeed, we find the very same "metaphysical interpolation" in every law of technical-abstract economics.... For example, the equations of economic equilibrium and dynamics are presented as "rigorous" abstractions, but in fact they are only abstractly general (metaphysical interpolations!). Therefore, the aspects of concrete economic life apriorized or transcended in the idea filter through the "rigorously" scientific terms and algebraic expressions, which are still raw, undigested, and unmediated.'[40]

Another example. Discussing the 'temporal' theory of interest (and of profit in the classical sense; cf. Böhm-Bawerk and Fisher) whereby the necessity of profit is explained by the fact that the capitalist and worker exchange goods divided in time, the worker offering a future commodity (the product of his labour), the capitalist reciprocating with a present one (the wage), Pietranera observes as follows: 'In substance, this [theory] abandons the concrete, historical category of production (in the process of which labour-power is transformed into a commodity and through which exploitation gives rise to profit) in favour of the abstract-formal category of exchange (exchange over time, and therefore credit), and then claims to draw consequences of this category in the domain of production (that of the concrete relations of labour). It is therefore an instance of the usual "mystificatory" procedure, which in this case takes the form of an apparently formal paralogism. In other words, the theory of "exchange of future goods" could at most explain a phenomenon like credit or interest, whereas here it seeks to explain a phenomenon that belongs properly to the sphere of production, namely profit. Now interest, according to classical theory and also according to Marx, is part of profit. This doctrine therefore attempts to explain the whole through the part. We have said, however, that the logical deficiency is only *apparently* formal. In reality, the *petitio principii* is one of substance.... In this case, indeed, the theory moves ... from profit to interest, from the concrete to the less concrete. Profit,

---

40 G. Pietranera, *Capitalismo ed economia*, Turin, second edition, 1966, pp. 177-211.

however, implies the entire structure of the "capitalist mode of production", of which it is the motor force, and therefore implies the [concrete, determinate] category of capitalist production. Interest represents a more abstract category, since it is also a feature of mercantile capitalism, and even of pre-capitalism. Concrete capitalist production is thus transcended and "made metaphysical", an abstraction of abstractions, until the pure schema of credit is obtained. Except that then the theory attempts to explain production through this schema.'[41]

[41] 'Marx e la storia delle dottrine economiche', in *Società*, 1955, no. 1, pp. 8-9. In order to highlight the universality of the method of the materialist critique of a priori thought and the scientific dialectic that results from it, let us note that typical examples of the applicability of this method may be gleaned from the most diverse fields, from economics to political philosophy to aesthetics. For instance: 1. The materialist denunciation of the 'crass materialism' or 'unsound empirical' that is the result-retribution of Hegel's idealist abstraction or hypostasis of bourgeois man, from which he deduces absolutely that the citizen, as 'burgher or bourgeois . . . is the composite idea which we call *man*'. (*Philosophy of Right* §190; and cf. the hypostasis of the European monarchies of 1820 as the 'essence of the state'.) 2. The parallel denunciation of the unsound empirical that is the historic 'content' *transcended* and therefore *unexplained*, to the detriment of the very 'form' of the work of art, in the traditional, idealist and mystifying 'critical' interpretation of *Orlando Furioso* and *Don Quixote* (to take the extreme examples of 'fantastic' works, which are therefore more searching). Aesthetic hypostases such as the formula '*Orlando Furioso*, poetic of harmony' or '*Don Quixote*, poetic of the conflict of Ideal against Real' can only produce, as retribution, the surreptitious and therefore crass historicism and philologism to which the idealist critique is compelled to resort in the actual reading of both these works, when it tries to grasp, in their significant determinateness and concreteness (which makes them artistically alive), the figurative abstractions and forms produced by that quality of Ariosto's or Cervantes's *irony*, which is at least as *intellectual* as it is *imaginative*. For a critique of idealist aesthetics, see my *Critique of Taste* [translated by Michael Caesar, NLB, London, 1978].

On the connection between logic and aesthetics, it is sufficient to note: 1. In accordance with the method we have outlined here, the question of art can be approached only on the basis of a historic-scientific re-examination of the classical antinomial instances of aesthetic mysticism and rationalism. The anti-mystical and anti-romantic conception that results, dictated by the experience of historical consciousness embodied in the aporias of post-romantic and decadent aesthetics, must blend together the positive residues (not historically exhausted) of the opposite instances of both 'feeling' (and 'fantasy' and so on) and 'rationality' (and 'veracity' and so on). This must produce a concrete, modern (materialist) aesthetic rationalism. 2. From the standpoint of this aesthetic rationalism, the work of art is an object endowed with a concrete rational structure (matter-reason, image-concept, etc.), exactly like the work of science or historiography. Nevertheless, it presents characteristics of its own, not gnoseologically abstract, but gnoseological-technical, i.e. *semantic* (inherent in its actual construction and therefore indispensable to its real, cognitive-practical value). 3. Because the *semantic* nature of reason or consciousness in general has been disregarded (although not by Marx, who tells us that language is the 'immediate' concrete expression of thought and that the problem of descending from the world of

Finally, to conclude this section of the argument, let us add that Keynesian and neo-classical reformist economics—the ultimate theoretical and practical defence of bourgeois economics—is enmeshed in an implacable contradiction: it still rejects the Marxist sociological method (and therefore masks the class structure of the capitalist economy), while at the same time it attempts to appropriate some of the results of that method, in a purely technical-abstract manner. Its systematization of involuntary unemployment therefore clashes irrevocably with unemployment that is already structural everywhere, both in the most developed and in the backward capitalist countries. Keynesianism is thus a sterile theory, testimony to the disarray of bourgeois economic 'science'. This evidence of confusion and disarray, however, becomes apparent only through the *critique* of political economy; in turn it validates that critique. It is thus an instance of the application of the Marxist-Leninist criterion of practice in its twofold aspect, as technical (the movement that closes the methodological circle) and moral criterion, or criterion of conduct, since the *decisive* confirmation of the doctrine lies in action—if it is true, as Sweezy has said, that human action itself is responsible for the changes in a social system, which is obviously not the case, for example, for the solar system, whatever the observations of astronomy and physics may be.

Thus *determinate abstraction*, the method of economic science, is identical to the specific logic or method of the philosophic sciences. This is demonstrated on the one hand by the fact that they have a

---

'thought' to the real world may be converted into the problem of descending from 'language' to life), the peculiar *semantic*, verbal *organic character* of a poetic text, for example (think of the phenomenon of literary 'style'), has been confused with the metaphysical organic character of the content of the text; hence all the muttering about the 'unreality' of the poetic image and its gnoseological value as pure 'intuition' or 'transcendent' vision of the world, and therefore 'dream', etc. 4. Consequently, the theory of metaphor as (concrete) *concept*, as nexus of images, of a multiplicity, is central to such an approach to aesthetics. On the one hand, this theory necessarily emphasizes the continuous presence of metaphorical nexuses in the most ordinary, and thus less artistic, language; on the other hand, it is capable of explaining the specifically artistic value of a metaphor through the technical-gnoseological character of the semantic, verbal organicity of such a metaphor. Finally, this is an aesthetic of realism, since it is a theory of the (concrete) intellectuality and verisimilitude (truth) of the so-called artistic fantasy, and therefore of its 'typicality'. Cf. *Critique of Taste*; see also: the article of Mario Spinella in *Società*, 1955, no. 4 (an acute recollection of Marx's recognition of the semantic nature of thought) and Armanda Giambrocono-Guiducci, in *Ragionamenti*, 1955, no. 1 (a critical comparison with Lukács).

common premise in the materialist rejection of apriorism and on the other by the fact that both become sociology (the critique of political economy itself is only sociology: materialist sociological economics), in other words, history-science or the (materialist) science of history. In short, both turn out to be experimental conceptions or judgements (tauto-heterological identity). Which means in turn that ultimately there is but *one* science, because there is but one method, one logic; the *materialist* logic of modern *science*.

The symbol of this logic is the circle concrete-abstract-concrete, the circle that betokens the three logical-gnoseological aspects common to any cognition as science, and therefore no longer merely as knowledge or contemplation: a) the problematic fact, or historical-material instance; b) the hypothesis, or historical-rational instance (the establishment of hypothetical resolutive means of antecedents-consequences); c) the experiment, or closure of the circle of the reciprocal functionality of fact and hypothesis, matter and reason (conversion of the hypothesis into law).

We have thus reached the final question in the exposition of this logic: its *scientific* character and its consequent superiority over any other.

The scientific character of this logic is implicit in the entire preceding argumentation. Its criterion—the heterogeneity and the reciprocal functionality of reason (consciousness) and matter, that is, of predicate and subject—is indeed the product equally of induction and deduction. The hypothesis (deduction) is based on rigorously historical *precedents* (induction), as is indicated by the very logical-semantic formulas employed in the course of this book—for example, the 'being of not-being', 'tauto-heterological diairesis', the 'numerical unity' of the material, and so on. All these are ideological formulas, functions of the conclusive hypothetical formula of 'tauto-heterological identity', which contains them as signs of the concept (-mean) and transvalues them. These formulas are therefore no longer Platonic, Aristotelian, etc: on the one hand they are understood in an ideal order that is opposite to their historical-chronological order, dictated by a crude philology; and on the other hand, they are in no way forced into any ideal-abstract order according to a preconceived, a priori dialectic (of philosophical systems). Let us begin with this latter point. A critical examination of the negative historiographic results of the (metaphysical) exposition of a history of philosophic systems dialecticized in the abstract (or hypostatized), the sort of method that underlies Hegel's logic at bottom, will help us to understand the necessity and value of the historic-scientific method on which the present logic rests.

The method by which Hegel conceives the relations between the 'systems' and 'history' of philosophy, and therefore of logic, may be exhaustively summarized as follows, in the words of Hegel himself: 'I maintain that the sequence in the systems of Philosophy in History is similar to the sequence in the logical deduction of the Concept-determinations in the Idea. I maintain that if the fundamental conceptions of the systems appearing in the history of Philosophy be entirely divested [entkleidet] of what regards their outward form [äusserliche Gestaltung], their relation to the particular and the like, the various stages in the determination of the Idea are found in their logical Concept. Conversely in the logical progression taken for itself, there is, so far as its principal elements are concerned, the progression of historical manifestations; but it is necessary to have these pure Concepts in order to know what the historical form contains.'[42] The reason for this sameness of the 'systems' and 'history' of philosophy is that 'philosophies are the forms of the one'. In other words, 'the forms [the systems] are integrated in the integral form' since they are 'the determinations of the original idea'. Every historical system, Hegel explains, is indeed 'singularly determined', but 'it must be added that these determinations are destined to be placed together and reduced to moments', since 'the expansion is followed by contraction, that is, the unity from which they originally emerged'. Hence, 'the temple of self-conscious reason is . . . the sole worthy of the history of philosophy'.[43]

This also means that: 1) Since they must 'leave contingency behind the moment they enter philosophy', their history 'has the necessity of development as the Concept itself and the propulsive force is furnished by the internal dialectic of the forms'. 2) 'Every philosophy has been and is necessary and none is eliminated; instead, all are conserved in philosophy as moments of an affirmative whole.' In sum, 'the principles are conserved', for 'since the most recent philosophy is the result of prior principles, no philosophy is ever confuted'; rather, 'only its [abstract] positions are

---

[42] Hegel's Lectures on the History of Philosophy, translated by E.S. Haldane, London, 1955, volume 1, p. 30.

[43] Jena Introduction 1805-1806, Italian translation by Momigliano, 1925, p. 55.

confuted'.[44] Hence these evident corollaries: a) in philosophy and its history 'we have to do not with any past, but only with thought, with our spirit', and 'there is therefore no genuine history [*keine eigentliche Geschichte*], or there is a history which is at the same time not a history since the thoughts, principles, ideas that we have are something present' (the absolute presence that is self-conscious reason); in other words, 'they are determinations of our spirit'; and thus 'what is historic or past as such is no longer, is dead';[45] b) contrary to the view that 'political relations' and so on should be considered as having 'great influence' on the philosophy of each epoch and therefore on its history, we must examine things 'from a wholly different standpoint', since 'the essential category is unity'. Therefore, 'here we must keep in mind that there is only one spirit, one principle, which is both imprinted on the political state of affairs and manifested in reason, art, ethics, society, commerce, and industry; hence these forms are but branches of a single trunk'.[46]

The conclusions of a logic whose relation to the history of logic, or of philosophy itself, is conceived in this manner have been examined throughout this book; the negative characteristics and corresponding reasoning produced by such a method need not be synthesized here. It is sufficient merely to recall the cardinal systematic and mystified concept of the dialectic as *dialectic of pure thoughts*. This systematic concept of Hegel's is organically linked to: a) the historiographic and philological omission of the self-critical Plato, theorist of a diacritic dialectic, or dialectic of *doxa*; b) the parallel omission of the empiricist and materialist, non-Platonist and more original Aristotle, which omission becomes glaring in Hegel's basic treatment of logical principles, namely his perversion of these principles through an abstract 'totalization' of their meaning, an Eleaticized and Platonized transmutation of their original anti-Parmenidean significance; c) the omission, finally, of what is most original in the modern philosophy of experience, from Bacon to Galileo, from Hume to the Kant of the Analytic of the *Critique of Pure Reason*. From this we may draw two conclusions.

First, the mystified concept of the dialectic goes hand in hand with a generic philological abstraction by which the fundamental concepts of the various philosophical systems are 'divested' of their

[44] Ibid., p. 57.
[45] *History of Philosophy*, volume 1, p. 39.
[46] Ibid.

'application to the particular'. In other words, Hegel *abstracts* from their concrete *historical* articulation (*keine eigentliche Geschichte*). Second, this generic philology, operating with such omissions, far from affording us a universal all-inclusive synthesis or mediation of the history of philosophy and logic (which was Hegel's purpose), instead presents us a historiographic *pseudo-synthesis*, the product of the hypostatization of Plato's system in which this philology properly consists. This process, like any other of its kind, implies a continuous ontological *petitio principii* (in this case concerning the experience and historic reality of the philosophic systems) and is therefore marred by the result-retribution of a merely apparent mediation, a gnoseological sterility. The empirical—in this case the extremely abstract and unsound history (since mediated only in appearance)—is here represented, for example, by Aristotle's disjunctive entelechy, erroneously understood as the principle of individuation in the sense of pure subjectivity, precisely in accordance with the omissions, or generic abstractions, cited above. The meaning of this is that the philosophic systems, precisely because they are historical, are themselves facts, and therefore also repugnant to generic (historiographic) abstractions.

For the rest, even the positive results of Hegel's system—which may be summarized in the gnoseological instance of consciousness of contradiction, or modern tauto-heterology, and are organically linked to the less generic philology of the Platonistic Hegel, for example, with the accurate Platonic philology he did attain (although within the limits mentioned)—again confirm the decisive importance of the nexus of every logic and philosophy with the history of logic and philosophy. They likewise reconfirm the gnoseological necessity of the limitation, namely the insuperable instance of a coherent conception that obeys Hegel's 'speculative-dialectical' thought itself, because and to the extent that it is subjected, despite Hegel, to a (non-formalistic) principle of non-contradiction. This occurs in a gnoseologically positive manner precisely when this thought begins from a non-generic philological contact, with, for example, Plato—that is, with the historical fact he represents. It occurs in a gnoseologically negative manner, when—diverted into Platonism-hypostasis, that is, into a Platonism as substantified philosophical predicate and therefore absolute truth-reality—Hegel inevitably falls into a continual but coherent *petitio principii* regarding the other *facts* that must be explained, which are the *other* philosophical systems (of Aristotle, and so on), and even aspects *other* than those philologically apperceived of the Platonic system itself. The supreme (philosophical-historiographic) hypostasis which is Platonism for Hegel—the reduction of the plurality of philosophic systems to the fixed preconceived unity of one system— thus also reconfirms that even the 'speculative' thought of the *rationalist* Hegel himself is never composed of *empty* concepts, but rather of full ones, for the most part defective and sterile, as may be seen in the mystified systematic concepts described above.

It is thus also confirmed that the (transcendental) logic of a Kant, for example, contains positive instances even after Hegel: precisely since the philology from which the systematic Kant begins is less generic and more faithful to the *facts* than were the preceding philosophic systems. We need only recall Kant's comprehensive criticism of both Platonism and empiricism, his historiographic, philological equilibrium, which is the greatest philosophical lesson bequeathed us by his 'critical' balance, and by 'criticism' in general.

We could continue in the same manner: the most original and vibrant problematics and correlative systematic theses of an Aristotle are organically linked to his correct historical interpretation of his predecessors (Plato, the Eleatics, etc.), just as the problematic and correlative systematic theses of the self-critical Plato are organically linked to his correct interpretation of Parmenides.

This approach therefore rules out the establishment of any logical or gnoseological criteria or philosophic categories on the basis of an 'ideal' or supratemporal history; it excludes, in sum, any philosophy based on a preconceived, abstractly dialecticized history of systems. It therefore remains only to consider more closely the materialist, historic-scientific foundation of the present logic. As is clear, this is a matter of the final application of the logical categories inherent in the concept of historic evolution previously applied to the economic and moral categories. Here, as before, the indeterminate, generic, and forced abstractions or conceptions must be replaced by determinate abstractions, by specific conceptions. As usual, this requires that the historical-chronological, or merely empirical and analytic, sequence of categories (or systems, in this case) be replaced by the precisely opposite sequence, the synthetic-analytic sequence of hypothetical means of antecedents and consequences in which the synthetic instance of reason and the analytic instance of the empirical and material are jointly satisfied: in sum, the general gnoseological instance of the reciprocal functionality of matter and reason, the instance of science, must be satisfied.

It must therefore be kept in mind that: 1) Every concept-mean satisfies reason precisely because it is a mean (synthesis) of the antecedents and consequent, the problematicized object. 2) Every concept-mean therefore satisfies the instance of the empirical as much as that of reason, since it satisfies a present or historical-material instance. 3) In effect, the mean of antecedents and consequents is not categorical and absolute (which would be a hypostasis), but instead hypothetical, since it is made up of historical-rational elements (through a non-generic philology). Such a mean is therefore true only experimentally—in other words, by virtue of its ultimate coincidence with the historical-material, or genuinely problematic instances out of which the research and the concept-hypothesis arise (the usual circle: concrete-abstract-concrete). Hence, although the objectivity and truth represented by this mean, which expresses a sort of *mind of humanity*, is undeniable, it is equally undeniable that such objectivity and truth are purely functional; they are a function of present cultural (philosophical, gnoseological, and logical) experience, of the existing questions and problems (the historical-material instances). In this sense, science is the collective mind of humanity concretely brought to bear in the present; it is the historical, concrete mind of humanity (and not spirit, since science, including the science of logic, is anti-hypostatic by definition).

Let us examine, then, the conclusive concept-mean of the relation between reason and matter. We may comprehend its structure and validity by comparing it above all to Marx's concept-mean of labour, or of capital. We then note:

First, like Marx's economic concept, it is the product of historical conditions, beginning with the manufacturing-commercial system. It is valid as concept (abstraction) because of the determinate or historical character of the abstraction, such that the gnoseological concept is therefore also the product of historical conditions—from the Greek cultural system of the *eidos*, or finitude-perfection (Parmenides-Plato-Aristotle) to the Christian-modern system of the spirit, or infinity-perfection. It is valid as (gnoseological) abstraction precisely because of its determinate or historical character; it is an abstraction that summarizes and indeed transvalues—since it is a genuine *synthesis*—both the Parmenidean and Platonic instances of being as one and as *eidos* and the Aristotelian instances of first substance and matter as numerical unity, etc.; it equally satisfies both Bacon and Galileo's anti-scholastic and Hume and Kant's anti-rationalist instances, both Hegel's anti-empiricist and Marx's anti-Platonic and anti-Hegelian instances, etc.

Second, like the historical-economic concept, it takes shape only in organic connection with bourgeois society and its capacity for self-criticism, and therefore at the point at which bourgeois political economy ceases to identify itself with the past through a process of myth-making. In sum, it takes shape when the bourgeois economic world begins to sense its own crisis and becomes aware of the contradictions and problems of the present. This historical-gnoseological concept (or concrete gnoseological concept) thus takes shape as self-criticism of the Christian-modern (or Christian-bourgeois) ideological system, in and through the crisis of dissolution of idealism and spiritualism as philosophical categories, or supreme categories of the superstructure of the bourgeois economic world in the present (ultimate) phase of capitalism. In short, it takes shape as objective and non-one-sided comprehension of historical (ideological) precedents—as scientific comprehension.

There should be no illusion as to the peculiarity of the (gnoseological) abstraction in question here. If philosophical systems are also facts inasmuch as they possess the historical and determinate character immune to and unattainable by hypostases or generic abstractions, and if, as (ideological) facts, they can be understood only through hypothetical and not categorical or absolute means—in other words, through working hypotheses, historical (experimental) hypotheses—then not only is a science of these systems inevitable, but only this scientificity, as such, will permit their coordination with *other* facts and their respective sciences, and thus maintain the vital unity of the world. It is, then, only on this condition that it is possible rigorously to grasp the interdependence of superstructures (cultural or moral in the broad sense) and (economic and social) structures. The coincidence of certain philosophical and corresponding economic or material categories, for example, will then no longer be merely empirical and extrinsic. The law that caste and class relations of production are concomitant with theological, metaphysical, and spiritualistic conceptions in general may thus be justified. These relations of production coincide with conceptions that deprecate the material world, which is linked directly with the 'inferior' social spheres of manual labour, from the ancient slaves to the modern proletariat.

In this manner Marx's profound observation (in the 1857 introduction) that the development of 'material production' is disproportionate with respect to 'law' and other superstructural phenomena—the disproportion, for example, between ancient Roman law and modern production in the post-Napoleonic bourgeois state (in which this system of law continues to hold sway)—acquires its full significance. Roman law, although it arose centuries before the modern social and economic world, nevertheless remains the cultural expression of a class society and economy (the 'individualism' of private Roman law, etc.). Marx's law as cited above thus accounts for this phenomenon, even if we leave aside the conservatism inherent in the tendency towards dogmatism characteristic of every universalist conception and of every schema and all similar superstructural phenomena. All this acquires real significance in the light of the law of concomitancy. But this law is a law because it is based not on a generic philological but on a specific and historical abstraction; it therefore consists in an articulated or complex unity. Hence, for example, the (logico-semantic) system of the *eidos*, or metaphysical philosophy of Greek caste society, is not confused with the (logico-semantic) system of the spirit, or metaphysical philosophy of medieval caste and modern class society. This law, of course, is but a natural corollary of a materialist logic, namely of the anti-metaphysical, or scientific, philosophy of a classless society, or of a society—contemporary bourgeois society—in the process of transformation from class to classless society. (Non-dogmatic philosophy-science, with its rigorous predictions-hypotheses, is proleptic because it does not enclose the world in the a priori deductions or hypostases of metaphysics, which Hegel represented precisely by the owl of Minerva.)

But all this presupposes, then, that the 'theory of thought', philosophical logic, must be transformed into a 'positive science' and that there can be no more talk of a 'pure' theory of thought, as Engels once put it in contradiction both with himself and with the deeper conclusions of historical materialism. This lesson begins to take form as the methodological conclusion characteristic of the merciless critique of every 'pure theory', which implicitly underlies Marx's analysis of Hegel's processes of hypostatization. The prime task of the methodological investigation of the present book has been to trace the relevant precedents (Aristotle's critique of Plato and Galileo's critique of the scholastics) and the corresponding historical framework of that analysis and to generalize it. Its further and consequent task is to uncover the potential significance of a genuinely material or real dialectic, freed of the last vestiges of the abstract, mystified, falsely mobile dialectic, still teleological and anthropomorphic, if not purely and innocuously metaphorical.

Now, the real and authentic dialect is, in general, none other than the dialectic that 'the scientist performs without knowing it', as Lenin said. But we can come to know this dialectic not through any 'pure theory of thought', but rather through a logic that is itself a positive science; which means, once again, that there is only one logic.

Appendices

Galileo and the
Principle of Non-Contradiction

1

To clarify our assertion that Galileo employed a principle of non-contradiction of a new type, different from both the abstract technical-verbal principle of formal logic and the logical-ontological principle of metaphysics (from Parmenides to the scholastics to Leibniz), we must consider first of all the *pars destruens*, or negative aspect, of Galileo's discourse on method. We begin, then, with his critique of the aprioristic foundations of peripatetic physics.

The following passages seem typical in this regard. Galileo is refuting the Aristotelian-scholastic thesis of the geocentric universe precisely by criticizing the method of 'a priori discourse' employed by Simplicio, the opponent of Copernican theory. Galileo concludes his critique by charging Simplicio with 'an obvious fallacy': presupposing exactly what was to be proved. Galileo's central argument concerns the aprioristic, metaphysical theory of motion: 'With Aristotle', Sagredo says to Simplicio, 'you began by removing me somewhat from the sensible world, to show me the architecture [or 'ideal world', the mathematical models of the heavens and the earth] with which it must have been built. . . . [Next,] as to the explanation of what Aristotle means by simple motions, and how he determines them from properties of space, calling those simple which are made along simple lines, these being the straight and circular only, I accept this willingly. . . . But I resent rather strongly finding myself restricted to calling the latter [circular motion] "motion about the centre" [*the* centre, in the singular, meaning the centre of the earth] (while it seems that he wants to repeat the same definition in other words) and the former [straight motion] *sursum* and *deorsum*—that is, "upward" and "downward". For such terms are applicable only to the actual world [the sensible world] and imply it to be not only constructed, but already inhabited by us. Now, if straight motion is simple with the simplicity of the straight line, and if simple motion is natural, then it remains so when made in any direction whatever; to wit, upward, downward, backward, forward, to the right, to the left; . . . provided only that it is straight, it will be suitable for any simple natural body. Or, if not, then Aristotle's supposition is defective.

'Moreover, it appears that Aristotle implies that only one circular motion exists in the world, and consequently only one centre [namely, the earth] to which the motions of upward and downward exclusively refer. All of which seems to indicate that he was pulling cards out of his sleeve, and trying [tacitly] to accommodate the architecture [the a priori models] to the building [the a posteriori sensible world] instead of modelling the building after the precepts of architecture. For if I should say that in the real universe there are thousands of circular motions, and consequently thousands of centres, there would also be thousands of motions upward and downward.'[1]

It seems evident that Galileo's exposure of surreptitious and qualitative abstract-empirical residues (like 'upward', 'downward', and 'the centre') already implicitly embodies his judgement that the peripatetic premises are defective gnoseologically (epistemologically), and not merely verbally-formally, or formalistically. The organic sterility of any subsequent deduction based on this a priori discourse therefore follows. Referring to the 'construction of the Aristotelian universe', Galileo notes: 'Having very well and methodically begun his discourse, at this point—being more intent upon arriving at a goal previously established in his mind than upon going wherever his steps directly lead him—he [Aristotle] cuts right across the path of his discourse and assumes it as a known and manifest thing that the motions directly upward and downward correspond to fire and earth. Therefore it is necessary that beyond these bodies . . . there must be some other body in nature [the heavens] to which circular motion must be suitable. This must, in turn, be as much more excellent as circular motion is more perfect than straight. Just how much more perfect the former is than the latter, he determines from the perfection of the circular line over the straight line.'[2]

---

[1] *Dialogue Concerning the Two Chief World Systems*, pp. 15-16.
[2] Ibid., p. 18.

Galileo then concludes his case against the peripatetic thesis of the geocentric universe as follows: 'I say that all Aristotle sees of the motion of light bodies is that fire leaves any part of the surface of the terrestrial globe and goes directly away from it, rising upward; this indeed is to move toward a circumference greater than that of the earth. . . . But he cannot affirm that this is the circumference of the universe, or is concentric with that, so that to move toward it is to move toward the circumference of the universe. To do so he must suppose that the centre of the earth, from which we see these ascending bodies depart, is the same as the centre of the universe. Now that is just what we were questioning, and what Aristotle intended to prove. You say that this is not an obvious fallacy?'[3]

It is clear, then, that the following observations may be made about Galileo's truly modern discourse on method.

1. The critique of the abstract, metaphysical rationalism of the scholastic peripatetics is based precisely on the charge that the conceptual system of peripatetic physics is sterile and can produce no advance in knowledge, because the empirical world, to which the facts 'we are questioning' belong, is aprioristically ignored and transcended, and *therewith* 'supposed', which is to say tacitly presupposed and illicitly (surreptitiously) postulated. The sensible world is thereby non-mediated and unresolved.

2. At the same time, Galileo's critique renews and deepens (as surprising as this may seem) Aristotle's most profound and genuine critique of the abstract, dialectical rationalism of Platonic classification (diairesis), namely the critique of the purely dialectical, or tauto-heterological, foundation of Plato's division of the empirical, or 'participating' classes as expounded in *The Sophist* and *The Statesman*. This critique indicts Platonic division on two counts. First, it 'takes the genus instead of the species as the middle term' (that is, 'animal' = reasoning-unreasoning, according to the 'opposition' or 'tauto-heterology' of the 'participating' classes, the 'higher genera'). Second, it therefore falls into a *petitio principii*, since the nature or species of the *definiendum* must be *presupposed* in order to *choose* among the merely 'opposite' differences of the class, under one of which this nature must be subsumed.

3. It is above all in relation to this discovery of the not merely formal

3 Ibid., pp. 35-36.

'paralogism' into which the aprioristic logic of the scholastics falls that Galileo's renunciation of metaphysics and of the ultimate premises of the scholastics acquires its complete foundation and full revolutionary philosophical significance. In a letter written to Roberto Bellarmine in 1615 Galileo expressed this renunciation—together with the consequent methodological imperative of 'saving appearances', in other words, of sticking strictly to observed facts, the *how* of the facts—as follows: 'It is true that to show that the mobility of the earth and stability of the sun conform to appearances is not the same as to demonstrate that such hypotheses about nature are *really* [i.e. absolutely] true. But it is equally, and even more true that if the other commonly accepted system cannot be squared with such appearances, then it is indubitably false, since it is clear that the former system, which does accord perfectly with the facts, can be true; no greater truth can or should be sought in a position than that it corresponds to all the particular appearances.'

4. Consequently, to the dogmatic-expositive and defective method of the scholastics, Galileo could counterpose only an essentially critical method of research. If we subject the structure of this method to rigorous gnoseological examination, we will inevitably find what we are seeking: a new dimension of *the rational*, understood as *non-contradictory*.

2

Indeed, the structural instances of the (experimental-) scientific method that follow from Galileo's critique of scholastic 'a priori discourse' are as follows. To begin with, against Aristotelian-scholastic science, which is formally syllogistic inasmuch as its content comprises the hypostases of the conceptual realism of species-*essences* and the finalism related to it (the 'perfection' of circular motion, for example), Galileo advances a particular type of *deduction*, and more properly a *mode of reasoning*. On the one hand, it effects a mathematical or quantitative *resolution* and 'composition' of the qualitative or empirical (for example, the observed fact of the accelerated motion of falling bodies), through which the *idea* that 'the space covered is proportional to the time of the fall' is formulated as a real *hypothesis* about falling bodies; on the other hand, the proof that this hypothesis is *correct* and may therefore be counted a causal *law* is not sought in the strength of reason itself, in other words, in the replacement of the mathematical concept of function by the physical-metaphysical concept of cause-essence (substance), for such a substitution would blithely dissolve the antecedents of any consequent into the totality of the quantitative *relations* of this consequent, which would in turn give rise to the fundamental difficulty of diverse antecedents or causes of the same effect (plurality of causes) through the self-contained *unity* of the hypothesis (cf. Cassirer and the other neo-Kantians). Instead, confirmation of the truth of the hypothesis must be *specifically* sought in technical experiment. The experiment, by furnishing the *disproof* or *elimination* by one *model fact* of other rival facts purporting to be antecedents of the same consequent thereby enables human reason to surmount this fundamental difficulty, in other words, to avert the *fallacy of affirming the consequent*: the belief that, since if the hypothesis is true certain (related) events must occur, then the hypothesis is shown to be true simply because these events (consequents of the hypothesized antecedents) have indeed occurred (cf. Joseph and Dewey).

We may conclude, then, that Galileo has already posited the indispensable requisite that reason is either functional or it is not reason, i.e. not productive of truth. In positing this instance he implicitly acknowledges a new, non-formalistic and anti-metaphysical, significance of the principle of non-contradiction. This is already implicit in the profound conclusion inherent in the *experimental* instance as described above: that the facts prove, or verify, the hypotheses of reason by *disproving*, or *negating*, other hypotheses. This establishes the *positivity* of elimination, of logical *negation* or *privation*; in short, the 'positive that closes its eyes to the negative' so vehemently rejected (and misunderstood) by Hegel the pure dialectician. Such is Galileo's conclusion, which in this respect accords with the conclusion of Bacon ('*maior est vis instantiae negativae*'; and cf. Joseph).

This, however, is not the end of the matter. Against the inductive science of Bacon, which is distrustful of 'hypotheses' (considered 'premature anticipations' of nature) and is therefore unable to afford them a guiding role in experimental observation (to the point of concluding, as did Auguste Comte, extending Baconian logic to its ultimate limits, that 'really philosophical hypotheses must always present a character of simple anticipations of what experience and reason could have uncovered immediately had the terms of the problem been more favourable'), Galileo advances a type of *induction* that is based on an experience that consists not at all in a Baconian search for empirical constants that reveal the presence or absence of certain 'forms' of corpuscular structure (allegedly the causes of the given sensed properties), but rather in 'the observation of very frequent and palpable accidents' (such as the empirical fact of the accelerated motion of falling bodies). It thus concludes in the 'more adjusted experience' which is the *functional experience* of the experiment.

The experiment can fulfil this role because it is the test—through a typifying model—of an *ideal-hypothesis*. In other words, it provides the disproof, negation, or contradiction by one fact(-type) of other more or less hypothesized facts; negation, discreteness, or analysis is thus a function of affirmation, unity, or synthesis (hypothesis). Hence the affirmation-negation, or exclusive affirmativity, or identity-non-contradiction which is the proper characteristic of Galilean law, of the hypothesis that is true, and therefore is form, only inasmuch as it is experimentally verifiable. In other words, it is no longer Bacon's preconceived or abstract form, which is therefore juxtaposed to and not the mediator of experience, but is instead precisely a mediator of experience inasmuch as it stands in functional reciprocity with it, since we have already seen that the fact, or empirical given, is itself functional; that is, either it is a *fact-type* or it is not a fact, is not productive of effectuality or reality (just as non-functional reason is not productive of truth). 'The man who has lost his reason', Claude Bernard wrote, 'no longer learns from experience.... Experience is therefore the privilege of reason'.

Finally, it should not be difficult to recognize that the 'necessary demonstrations' of Galilean science constitute a *rational non-contradictory* of a new type. The reciprocal functionality of hypothesis and empirical fact establishes a rationality or necessity that is indeed non-contradiction, but it is a non-contradiction that is due no longer to the Parmenidean absoluteness of Aristotelian-scholastic species-essence, but rather, specifically, to the instance of the discreteness (contingency) of the empirical fact, since it is from the experiment (the testing of the hypothesis) that the necessity—of the fact—arises. It is in this sense that we draw the Galilean 'conclusion

[that] is inescapable [since] no worthwhile argument can be produced against it'.[4]

In this regard, the typically contradictory character of the fact as such must be considered that which, grasped in the concrete and therefore as the functionality of the fact with respect to reason, appears as a specific condition of the affirmation-negation or non-contradictory rational which is precisely the necessity of the fact. (This explains the non-absurdity of the negation of the fact, of which Hume and Kant spoke from the standpoint of the logic of essences, derived from the Aristotelian-scholastic-Leibnizian principle of non-contradiction).

This contradictory character of the fact as such did not elude the Galilean spirit of Claude Bernard, when he wrote that some physicians 'as soon as they make observations in the direction of their ideas, . . . refuse to look for contradictory facts, for fear of seeing their hypotheses vanish'.

This contradictory character of the fact, understood in the concrete and therefore in the light of the functionality of the fact or given itself, also explains, for example, that anything that does not result from the intervention of the thyroid gland is excluded in and through the experimental verification of the hypothesis that the thyroid causes the metamorphosis of the tadpole into the frog. This is precisely the non-contradictory rational of a new type, that which constitutes the *necessity of the fact* in the modern sense. It is a rational which, glimpsed by Aristotle himself in his purest anti-Eleatic and materialist instance (the instance of the determinateness of everything that has meaning and being), had to be reconsidered and developed, despite everything, precisely by Bacon the exalter of the '*negativa*' or '*exclusiva instantia*' and Galileo the discoverer of the 'necessary demonstrations' of the 'new sciences'. This reconsideration and development, moreover, occurred through a persistent polemic against the abstract Aristotelianism of Aristotle himself and the scholastics, an Aristotelianism whose basic formula— 'truth, essence is; untruth, the inessential is not'—was merely the formal development of the virtually inexhaustible content of Parmenides's so-called principle of identity: 'being is, not-being is not'.

---

[4] Ibid., p. 185. And cf. *Dialogues Concerning Two New Sciences*, second day: 'true [things], i.e. necessary, or those that cannot possibly be otherwise.'

In conclusion, it should be noted that here we have not demonstrated the other historic and systematic component of this rational non-contradictory of a new type produced by modern science: the dialectical instance already implicit (albeit in a still dogmatic form) in the very first theory of classifying or epistematic thought to appear in the history of philosophy: Plato's gnoseology of diairesis, target of Aristotle's critique. Here it may be sufficient simply to recall the substantial positive lesson bequeathed us by the self-critical Plato (a lesson ignored by Aristotle the analyst, and therefore absent from his analytic instance and not understood by Hegel the dialectician): in the concrete, in real discourse, it is impossible to avoid contradiction without being conscious of it; in other words, without tauto-heterology or dialectic. It is the character of opposition of the differences which, by making the differences equal sections of the (participating) genus, is posited as that criterion—of their assimilation or *unity*—without which these differences would not be parts-*species*; in short, without which there would be no justification for their validity, or for (non-) contradiction as *rational* partition or distinction.

2
Italian Hegelianism: Croce and Gentile

1

The reader of Benedetto Croce's *Logica come scienza del concetto puro*[1] is struck, from the very first chapter, by the disproportion between the author's intentions and his achievements. It is not at all difficult to assess the validity of Croce's claim to have critically re-examined the problem of a priori synthesis, to have gone beyond Hegel's synthesis of opposites. At the very beginning of the first chapter we are told: 'If man was not picturing something, he would not be thinking.' But the same chapter concludes with this 'affirmation of the concept': 'The concept . . . arises from representations as something *implicit* in them that must be made *explicit*' (p. 12). Leibniz again!

All of the *Logica*, indeed Croce's entire philosophy, is but a systematic exhibition of this contrast between critical intentions and dogmatic results. In the sentence just quoted, for example, Croce, however dissatisfied with Hegel he may be, falls back into Hegel's—pre-critical—conception of sensation as implicit, indistinct, and confused thought. Further on (p. 96), we are told that 'the birth of the concept transfigures the representations out of which it arises, and renders them other than what they were: determinate instead of indeterminate, logical instead of fantastic, clear and distinct instead of clear but indistinct'. And this despite Croce's own theory of the autonomy of intuition, of the aesthetic, wherein lies, Croce himself maintains, Kant's 'advance' over Leibniz: the refutation of the theory of the beautiful as confused concept and the recognition of the need for a 'qualitative' distinction between the two spiritual forms.[2]

[1] *Logic As Science of the Pure Concept*, Bari, 1928, fifth edition, p. 3.
[2] *Problemi di estetica*, Bari, 1923, second edition, p.54.

We shall see that Croce's Logic may serve as the basis for an assessment of the validity of his Aesthetics and of his entire philosophy of the spirit as a circle of distinctions. Indeed, does not Croce adopt Hegel's dictum that in every judgement 'all reality is predicated of the subject' and that 'only the totality of predicates, the full concept of the real, the spirit, or the idea, is sufficient'?

But let us examine systematically Croce's treatment, central as it is, of the identity of the defining and individual judgement (or perception).

He begins with the usual good intention: 'Are not those things that are called *contingent* equally as *necessary* as those that are called necessary? With good reason we scoff at those who claim that things could have happened differently from the way they did. In truth, Caesar and Napoleon are just as necessary as quality and becoming.'[3] If we then consider definition in its concrete reality, we will 'always find, if we look with care, the representative element and the individual judgement.'[4] But having stated that 'although the subject in the individual judgement is a representation, it is also true that this representation is not found in it as it would be in an *aesthetic contemplation*; it is instead the subject of a judgement, and is therefore not a *pure and simple representation*, but a representation that is thought—in other words, an instance of logic',[5] Croce then proceeds to the following demonstration that defining and individual judgements are identical.

'Every definition is a response to a question, a solution to a problem.... But the question, the problem, the doubt, is always considered individually.... In reality, each question differs from all others, and each definition ... differs from all others, because the words, even when they seem substantially the same, actually differ according to the spiritual diversity of those who utter them, for they are individuals and therefore always find themselves in individually determined circumstances. "Virtue is disposition towards moral actions" is a formula which ..., every time it is uttered in earnest as a definition of virtue, corresponds to more or less diverse *psychological* situations; in reality, it is not one, but thousands and thousands of definitions.... Every concept exists only to the extent that it is thought and completed in words, that is, to the extent that it is

---

3 *Logica*, p. 133.
4 Ibid., p. 133.
5 Ibid., p. 129-130.

defined. And if the definitions vary, then so does the concept. These are, of course, variations of the concept, which means of identity *par excellence*; they form the life history of the *concept* and not at all of the representation. . . . Once we grant that every thought of the concept, which means every definition, is individually and historically conditioned (from which conditionality arises the doubt, problem, or question to which the definition responds), then we must likewise grant that the definition, which contains the response and affirms the concept, thereby simultaneously illuminates that individual and historic conditionality, that group of facts from which it emerges. To say that it illuminates it is to say that it qualifies it as what it is, apprehends it as a subject by affording it a predicate, judges it. And since the fact is always individual, it forms an individual judgement. In other words, every definition is simultaneously an individual judgement. . . . The logical act, the thought of the pure concept, is unique; it is the identity of definition and individual judgement.'[6]

Three objections to this argumentation may be advanced.

First, it is naively dogmatic to attempt to reconcile the truth of reason with the truth of fact simply by noting that the thought that defines the fact arises under varying *psychological* conditions (spiritual diversity). The threat of *petitio principii* here is constant. We have, for example, a 'problem' that is individual and always diverse *because* it corresponds to 'more or less *diverse* psychological situations', and a 'fact' that is 'individually and historically conditioned' *because* 'the fact is always *individual*'. But how to justify the individual and historic character of the 'definition', inasmuch as it is the 'solution' of that 'problem' and the 'judgement' of that 'fact'?

Second, this naive and defective description of logicality as representation that is thought finds its point of departure and ground in the concept of the aesthetic as 'pure and simple representation', that is, in the typically psychological but nonetheless external and *insufficient* concept of a *pure intuition* (which therefore cannot be a philosophically adequate intuition). See, for example, *Problemi di estetica* (p. 486): 'Given any sensation, if I do not abandon myself to the attractions and repulsions of impulse and sentiment . . . , I find myself in the same disposition as when I enjoy what is usually called a work of art. I live the sensation, but as pure contemplating spirit.'

[6] Ibid., pp. 133-135.

Third, the insistence that the logical act nevertheless possesses the Hegelian character of 'thought of the pure concept', with its unity or (abstract) identity, is but the natural consequence of Croce's failure to perform the *critical* task he set himself when he identified defining and individual judgements. Exactly because Croce psychologizes, in his 'pure intuition', the Kantian 'disinterested aesthetic' that was his starting-point, he is compelled, as we have seen above, to accept the *rationalistic* notion of the aesthetic as implicit concept, and he therefore returns inevitably to the 'pure concept' of the Hegelian type, despite his rejection of synthesis a priori as purely *logical* synthesis a priori (as Hegel's synthesis of opposites). As we shall see, Croce's logical position becomes even worse with his romantic development of aesthetics.

Given these preliminaries, Croce's approach to the problem of the existential character of judgements will not be surprising. He states at the outset that the question of existentiality arises only for the individual judgement, 'within which there is a representative element, something individual and finite'. Indeed, for the individual and finite, 'essence *does not coincide* with existence; mutable at any moment, while nonetheless always universal, only the infinite is adequate to it'.[7] After this admonition—which is substantially correct, provided that what is meant, rigorously, is that given the preceding identification of definition and perception, or individual judgement, the question of existentiality is posed for *every* judgement (but he excepts, with the pure defining judgement, 'which is concept and has existence as concept, i.e. as essence', the defining judgement of pseudo-concepts, 'which is not even thought'!)— Croce proceeds to determine the precise significance of 'existence' and 'existential' by subdividing the *representative* element (which was cited above as characteristically determining the existentiality of the judgement inasmuch as it appeared as wholly identical to its individuality and finitude into the representation 'indifferent' to existence characteristic of the 'intuitive man', of the artist, and the 'no longer indifferent' representation of the 'logical man', who 'cannot judge that which does not exist'.[8] The consequence of this distinction is just this: 'existence, in the individual judgement, is predicated'; it is 'the *concept* of a reality that duplicates itself in both *actual* and *possible* reality, in *existence* and *non-existence*, or mere

[7] Ibid., p. 106.
[8] Ibid.

representability' (hence in the case of aesthetic judgements, 'there is effectuality, reality, the existence of images, having the ineffectual and non-existent as their content'); and, in sum, every judgement requires 'the entirely determined universal ... as essence in the entire extension of this concept, which *includes* existence'.[9] Any distinction between defining and individual judgement thereby vanishes, but this time not in the sense maintained above (however uncertainly); in other words, not in the sense of a conciliation of the two on the basis of mutual determination, but rather in the sense that the former absorbs the latter, or makes it equivalent to itself. This, however, leads straight back to Hegel. (This *reaction* of Croce's to the problem of existence is surely characteristic and instructive.)

Also of typically Hegelian stamp, despite the pragmatist veneer, is the theory of pseudo-concepts (like triangle, rose, and so on) and of the corresponding *pseudo-judgements*, so closely connected to the theory of the existentiality of the individual judgement. A typical negative consequence of the external dichotomy of the representative element, it disparages the empirical and intuitive character and the existentiality of those concepts it dubs merely conceptual 'fictions', the Hegelian purity of which could not be more evident. Thus it is that Croce admits, betraying a confusion that is surely significant, that 'empirical judgements'—those 'practical' fictions—rest, in the final analysis, on existentiality (by which he means 'on the *concept* of existentiality') since 'they do not constitute pseudo-concepts of possibility'![10]

Thus Croce, turning back to Hegel, and even to the scholastics, maintains that existence is only a predicate, a concept, and he dismisses as mere dogmatic realists both Hume, who holds existence to be a 'belief' and thus a 'feeling' or 'sensation', and the Kant of 1763, who affirmed that existence 'is not at all predicated of something'.

Finally, all Croce's uncertainties and weaknesses are manifested, quite naturally, in his formulation of the logical principle: unity-distinction as a circular linkage of distinctions. He accepts the principle of identity and non-contradiction, but not in the sense that 'A is A alone and is not also not-A, its opposite'; for understood in this way 'it leads one directly to posit the negative moment outside the positive, not-being apart from or opposite to being, and therefore

---

[9] Ibid., pp. 109-113, 372.
[10] Ibid., pp. 118.

to the absurd conception of reality as immobile and empty . . . a perversion of the principle'.[11]

In sum, he accepts Hegel's dialectical version of the principle of non-contradiction, with all the historic errors this implies, in opposition to the principle as formulated by Aristotle. In an attempt to escape from the absolute identity of Parmenidean being, Croce asserts a renovated Eleaticism and Platonism in the name of anti-Eleaticism! (At the bottom of all this, of course, lies the careless identification of the traditional scholastic principle of identity—and its formalist-rationalist treatment of Aristotle's principle—with the so-called Parmenidean principle of identity.) And yet Croce, almost incidentally, recognizes that on the contrary it is the 'individual judgement' that 'excludes its contradictory'.[12] On the other hand, although he substantially accepts the principle of identity in its Hegelian version (or rather *perversion*, in this case the term seems justified), at bottom Croce generally does not consider himself a consistent Hegelian, for his critical intentions prevent this. He rejects the 'false extension' of the dialectical principle (the defect of which is 'the complete loss of the criterion of distinction'), convinced that he can philosophically conciliate the two principles through the theory that 'distinctions as such are distinctions and not opposites; and opposites cannot be, because they bear opposition in themselves: aesthetic fantasy bears within itself its opposite, fantastic passivity, which is the ugly; and thus this is not the opposite of thought, which in its turn bears within itself its opposite, logical passivity, anti-thought, the false'.[13]

This is an explanation, but not a justification, given Croce's typically empirical, external, and psychological conception of distinction. Otherwise he would have understood that opposition, the dialectic, conceived in the manner of Hegel, does not tolerate distinctions as such and absorbs everything into its unifying thirst (does he not acknowledge that 'opposites are not concepts, but the *sole* concept itself'?). To resolve the inevitable problem of the transition from one distinction to another, Croce is compelled to concoct a psychological duplicate of the dialectic in the form of a 'law of life as a whole', which is the 'transition' inherent in 'all the existential and

[11] Ibid., p. 63.
[12] Ibid., p. 107.
[13] Ibid., p. 64.

contingent determinations of each of these forms [the distinctions]', such that, for example, 'existentially, a poet becomes a philosopher only if a *contradiction* to his poetry takes shape in his mind, and thus only if he feels dissatisfied with the individual and the individual intuition; and at that moment there is no transition; rather, he is already a philosopher, because to undergo transition, to be real, and to become are synonyms'. On the other hand, he affirms that distinctions, as 'ideal moments', 'do not pass into each other, because they are eternally distinct the one in the other and the one with the other'.[14] It thus seems clear that (here again) he oscillates between a reduction of distinctions to opposites (the ideal moments, which are in each other, and are therefore the *sole* concept that opposites are) and a *petitio principii*: the moments do not pass into the other *because* they are distinct from one another in any case.

It is thus confirmed, in the final analysis, that Croce's approach to the problem of distinctions has from the very outset been compromised by his inadequate—because purely psychological—conception of the autonomy or positivity of aesthetics, for indeed only a genuinely rigorous recognition of sensibility or aestheticity and its 'indispensability' for the 'intellect' (to use Kant's expression) can break the spell of the theory of truth as synthesis of opposites, or pure concept (pure self-consciousness). Ultimately, however, this would require avoiding the plunge into romantic aesthetics in which Croce indulges with his concept of art as '[pure] intuition of a cosmic character'; which concept is replaced, through the psychologistic reduction of aesthetic intuitivity or disinterestedness to ineffability, by the sameness, i.e. uniqueness or singularity, of sensation or intuition with the sameness, i.e. unity or universality, of the idea, and concludes with the possession—in the intuited or ineffable—of the pure (poetic) universal or pure oneness (the very same exchange or mistake that occurs in Bergson's 'intuition', whose distinctive characteristic is 'continuity').

The cardinal consequence of all this is that Croce loses sight of that positivity of intuition which Kant considered the very indispensability of intuition, since it is capable of justifying a non-abstract intelligence. It is this intelligence whose concreteness Croce the romantic, who refuses to accord it the fullness of relations with the intuition (which is said to fuel it, although without in turn needing

---

[14] Ibid., p. 65.

it in order to be intuition), ultimately fails to grasp. Having lost sight of this concreteness, he disregards the concreteness of history itself, of the real world, abandoning himself to the artistic universal, the self-evident and vapid unity which, synonymous as it is with the 'eternal' or supratemporal, amounts merely to the self-evident and vapid unity of romantic mysticism.

It is this *theological* conception of aesthetics that accounts for Croce's falsely concrete rationalism (both his Hegelianism in logic and his more general spiritualism).

2

Giovanni Gentile's *Il sistema di logica come teoria del conoscere* (The System of Logic as Theory of Knowledge) is an attempt to conciliate—but not eclectically, like Croce—the old and the new, the logic of identity and dialectical logic, the principle of non-contradiction and the principle of absolute contradiction. The attempt is made, however, in the framework of Platonic-Hegelian schemata, and despite certain appearances to the contrary, it leaves totally unsatisfied Aristotle's instance that being and truth must be determinate and distinct. It therefore fails to extract us from the predicaments of a defective dialectic.

In this work Gentile strives to abandon his initial conviction, expounded in *L'atto del pensare come atto puro*, §8: 'The principle of identity (or of contradiction), A = A, expresses a necessity of what is called abstract thought—i.e. relative to nature—which by definition is the negation of thought and therefore cannot accept any logic of this sort', since logical necessity is characteristic of the 'real and concrete process of thought, which could rather be formulated, schematically, thus: A = not-A'. Gentile thus sets out to justify the 'old logic' as the theory of that 'thinkable being' which constitutes the response to the Socratic question (*tí estin?*) and is therefore concept, which 'is rather what one thinks it is, and therefore is itself being; but being that is what it is: determinate being having a *particular* content'.[15]

The 'nucleus' of logical thought, then, must be, as Plato and Aristotle maintained, the synthesis or unity of the noun and the verb:

[15] *Il sistema di logica come teoria del conoscere*, third edition, 1940, volume I, p. 175.

'in which the noun (A) is not an unthinkable (natural) being, but that being which is because and to the extent that it is thought through the verb (= A); neither, therefore, can it be detached from it without vanishing from the realm of the thinkable. To attempt to think, then, is necessarily to maintain the noun within the relationship proper to it, with the verb. The latter's function is precisely to duplicate the simple and abstractly identical unity of the noun, such that *identity* is realized in the concrete. It therefore can and must be said that the noun is distinguished from natural being in that through the verb it is realized as identical to itself.'[16]

Moreover, 'although in thought itself we distinguish something that is known as the noun, made a noun by the verb, that is, under the rubric of the concept (an A, which is not yet A = A), this abstract noun, in its *lack of distinction*, turns out to be a pure natural being; it is called sensation or intuition. It is the blind material of our knowledge, which is actually presented to consciousness inasmuch as it is illuminated in the concept, through thought, in virtue of which it, once perceived, remains what it was, except that it is reflected in itself and divides in relation to itself with itself, and thereby is known as what it is.'[17]

If to think is therefore 'to think something, or to think that being which is something', in other words, 'to fix not only the being, but the being identical to itself', then the fundamental law of the logic of that which is thought, or 'abstract' thought, can only be the principle of identity.

And since the 'objective affirmation' of being as being that is thought 'is, we may say, not only affirmation of thought being, but at the same time *negation* of natural being', and since natural being is only the abstract noun, which stands outside its synthesis with the verb, and this is, as the noun's verb, the assertion of being in thought, i.e. its 'transfiguration' in thought being, it is appropriate to say that 'the noun is affirmed of the verb inasmuch as it is negated: affirmed as thought, negated as being. *Omnis affirmatio est negatio.*'[18] This 'negativity of the verb [or thought] relative to the abstract [noun = sensation]', or negativity that is the 'force' or 'logical value' of the affirmation, embodies the significance of the principle of non-contradiction (in which the affirmation, being

[16] Ibid., p. 177.
[17] Ibid., pp. 177-178.
[18] Ibid., p. 180.

posited as the identity of being with itself, is posed as the 'negation of this identity', or negation of that identity which is being in its 'natural immediacy'). It should be noted, however, that being, as the abstract noun of the synthesis, 'does not negate anything, since it has no right to exist; it is absurd'. Furthermore, thought 'consists in the negation of this absurdity and is therefore posed as concept or idea, and no longer as natural being'. And the concept, since it is the concept of this being and must negate it in its immediacy in order to affirm itself, 'is affirmed as the opposite of that immediate being'. Because of this affirmation, 'this being as such, with respect to the concept, is an opposite such that, if it was, the concept would not be, and since the concept is, it is not'. (And it is therefore 'negated as a negative' and 'negates by reflection of the sole real negation, which is that of the concept, in the function of the verb', or predicate.)

Thus, 'if A is A, the being of A consists as much in being A (identical to A) as in not-being not-A (not identical to A)'. But if non-contradiction were really the same as identity, 'affirmation would be pure and simple affirmation without negativity', in which case identity 'would be equivalent to that abstract position of immediate or natural being which is not thought and cannot think'. But it is, on the contrary, thinkable, and differentiates itself from pure primitive being, which 'is accomplished as thought' inasmuch as it 'is not limited to affirming this being (A = A), but also negates and annuls the absence of the same being that is not reflected in itself and is not identical with itself': 'thought can find itself in being as concept, but cannot find itself in natural being, because in reality thought never knows anything but itself.'[19]

How, then, do the two principles, of identity and non-contradiction, 'form a whole, although without merging into each other'? Gentile answers by distinguishing opposition from opposition. 'There is the opposition of the identical and there is the opposition of the opposite. Given A = A, each A, in its own identity, is the opposite of the other; otherwise it would not be identical to the other; in other words, it would not be identical to itself'. Then there is another opposition, under which A is no longer identical to, but is rather the opposite of A: this is 'the immediate and non-resolved opposition of the abstract noun and the natural being which remains outside the identity, absent from thought; the opposition that exists between A

19 Ibid., pp. 180-183.

conceived as external to the synthesis A = A, and A as element of the synthesis'. And precisely 'the negated opposition of any affirmation is not the opposite, as identical, but the absolutely opposite. Whose being is the not-being of its opposite and whose not-being is the being of its opposite'. Hence, from this unity of identity and non-contradiction emerges the principle of the excluded middle: 'A is either A or not-A; where the either/or expresses the mutual exclusion of the two opposites as such, A and not-A'.[20]

Nevertheless, although the principle of the excluded middle means that 'there is no third term between the being and the not-being of a concept, such that if a concept is shown to be false, namely non-existent, its negative will be true', this principle also acknowledges that 'the false . . . has no place in the logic of the objective *logos*, except as the immanent negativity of the true'. The false, indeed, is 'the negative whose positivity is a reflexive positivity, because it consists in the negativity of the positive, which the positive itself (the concept) confers on it as other than itself, or its negative opposite'. Therefore: 'not-A is within A; and A as identical to not-A is within A as identical to A: as it is identical in falsity, so its negativity is attributed by truth with respect to A or A = A. There is no false without truth: given falsity, the truth must emerge'. Any concept, as 'negation of its negative', is therefore affirmed with 'a circularity that makes the concept a closed system'.[21]

It is commonly held that logical thought can exit from this circularity 'in such a way that there would be another mode of thinking both the concept and its not-being, provided that once its not-being is thought, the concept is no longer thought'. ('In this is alleged to consist the mutual exclusion of opposites as dictated by the principle of the excluded middle.') Contrary to this common belief, however, it must be noted that 'this mutual exclusion, through which the negative becomes the positive and negates its negation, is the reflection into itself of the negation characteristic of affirmation'. In short, the third principle, the difference of which from the other two 'consists in the unity between affirmation and negation that it demonstrates', may be recapitulated in the following formulation: 'Either being or thought: being is the negation of thought, just as thought is the negation of being. But this cannot mean that one can

[20] Ibid., pp. 184-185.
[21] Ibid., pp. 186-187.

choose indifferently between the two, provided that one renounces being, having chosen thought. There is indeed not-A, but as posited of the A that negates it. And not-A therefore cannot be true except in the sense that it is an unreal hypothesis, incompatible with the being of thought'.[22]

Although this modification of the traditional logical principles of thought or content (or multiplicity) of thought reduces the excessively gnoseological-metaphysical features (as compared with the excessively *logical*-metaphysical character of Hegel's treatment), it remains typically Hegelian and therefore subject to the very same difficulties. For it also reduces Aristotle's principle of distinction, the fundamental dianoetic law of identity and non-contradiction, to a principle of *unity*, a *rational* law of contradiction. We may note in particular Gentile's effort to preserve the difference between the second and third principles on the one hand and the first on the other, a worthy effort inasmuch as it is intended to show, correctly, that the second and third principles constitute the necessary integration and development of the first, which is also a principle of determination. But the effort rests on the distinction of two sorts of opposition, which collapses immediately with the enunciation of the second, 'immediate' or 'absolute' opposition between not-A, or 'natural' and 'immediate' being, and A (= A), or thought which is also dialectical, like the first A = A (intended, according to our Hegelian, to correct, precisely through its own dialecticity, vacuous Eleatic identity). The end-result is that not-A—not-being, or multiplicity, or natural being—is only a mere reflection into itself of the negation characteristic of affirmation ('of the thought'). In sum, it is an unreal hypothesis incompatible with being (or thought)! It is thus clear that the Aristotelian exigency of the incompatibility of contraries makes its appearance (in the supposed immediate or absolute opposition of not-A and A) only to vanish immediately in the absorbing 'dialecticism' of being or thought and not-being or natural being.

Let us examine the principal consequences of this dialectical reduction of the traditional logical principle.

To begin with, let us see exactly what Gentile means by the circularity and identity of what is thought. There is, he tells us, 'no

22 Ibid., pp. 188-189.

answer' to the problem of why A = A, not because the principles are undemonstrable, as Aristotle thought, but 'because the thought of the abstract logos is *always* undemonstrable, for it is ever revolving within the circle in which its principle consists'.[23] Sextus Empiricus's traditional critique of the syllogism is therefore 'highly accurate'. He held that if from the universal 'every man is an animal' one attempts to conclude the particular 'Socrates is an animal', while the universal is founded on particulars through a process of induction, then one is caught in a vicious circle, attempting to extract 'the universal from the particulars by induction, and the particular from the universal through the syllogism'.[24] This criticism, 'although it strikes at the Aristotelian syllogism, which claims to be a process leading from one judgement to another, does nothing if not clarify the essence of the logical force of the thought that is thought'. Hence: 'This diallelon, which has always been the bugbear of thought, will be—nay is—the death of *thinking* thought; but it is the life, the fundamental law, of *thought* thought, without which it is impossible to conceive of thinking thought'. And as for the syllogism, 'it is marked by the same diallelon as the highly solid living organism of thought in its logical mediation'.[25]

Now, 'we have already had occasion to refer more than once to the circularity of thought, which can only be that system which is closed among certain terms, each of which leads to the other. . . . Thought is *determined* through terms, each of which terminates, or limits, thought, repelling it from itself to the other term. And therefore it is closed, and as such *identical* to itself; and it is not pure natural being'. Consequently, 'either one thinks, . . . or one does not think; but when one thinks, thought is such as to link to itself the thought that it thinks: it is a thought that is being, the sole that exists (inasmuch as one is thinking), therefore *universal* and necessary'. By virtue of the law of circularity or identity, 'all the thinkable . . . is itself, for the simple reason that it is *all* the thinkable'. And finally, 'matter, all the matter, of thought, is the concept that is mediated in a closed system, within which it is true because infinite. There is nothing apart from it, to which it must adjust itself. Even error, like its negation, lies within the circle of the system, as immanent

[23] Ibid., II, p. 71.
[24] Ibid., I, pp. 249-250.
[25] Ibid., pp. 250-251.

negation of affirmation, since it is infinite, since it links the thought that thinks it'.[26]

It is striking that in this argument the concept of the circularity of thought does not serve to suggest the fruitful concept of the circularity of induction and deduction, which is inherent in the sceptics' criticism of the syllogism, from which this argumentation correctly began (in order to broach the problem of the undemonstrability of that which is thought). Instead this suggestion fades from view, and circularity becomes identical with the concept of system, winding up with a complete misunderstanding of the nature of that which is thought (or multiplicity), namely of the discreteness and determinateness signified by its identity; hence this thought or concept is proclaimed 'infinite', which means indeterminate! And of course, since circularity and identity are synonyms of systematicness and dialecticity, it must inevitably be concluded that thought—and what is thought—is infinite and 'unique' in the sense that it is 'universal', the universal or the one itself, and is 'logical mediation' or the truth itself. What has then become of the *undemonstrability* of what is thought (which is connected to determinateness)?

Naturally, Gentile is convinced that in his concept of the circularity of thought as system, he can make use of the most precious teaching of the concept of circularity as a circle of induction and deduction. But an examination of his theory of judgements, and of his consequent attitude to the problem of the truth of fact and reason, and of induction and deduction, decisively confirms what we have observed above.

Every judgement, he holds, is a de facto truth 'by virtue of the subject [A, as terminated term]; just as it is a truth of reason by virtue of the predicate [A, as terminating term] under which the subject is assumed',[27] since he holds, critically, that 'every judgement has a sensation for a subject'.[28] On the other hand, however, he immediately loses the advantage of this critical acceptation of the concept of subject (of the judgement) by subsequently asserting that the nature of sensation or intuition is 'indistinction', i.e. indistinct 'unity'.[29]

---

26 Ibid., pp. 250, 256, 257, 279.
27 Ibid., p. 231.
28 Ibid., p. 234.
29 Cf. *Filosofia dell'arte*, p. 230: 'Beyond the thought that varies it [unity] in its multiplicity; beyond the feeling that constrains this multiplicity in its unity, there is no residue.')

Hence, once again falling into line with Hegel and with all idealism, into the pre-critical concept of the aesthetic as indistinct or confused thought, and thus obliterating Kant's cardinal critique of Leibniz, Gentile considers it legitimate to affirm that 'the same sensation, to the extent that we talk about it, to the extent that it is perceived, i.e. illuminated by the light shed upon it by the predicate'. He then concludes without further ado that 'the colour, the first colour (as first sensation of colour that I experience), since I see it, perceive it, and since it is like A = A, like *that* colour, it is no longer the natural fact of my sensation, but is already the reflection into itself of this fact: it is perception or thought, and therefore universal'.[30]

In the light of this frustration of the positive character of the aesthetic, it is understandable that Gentile also considers it legitimate to regard 'true induction' as 'precisely that induction which refers the judgement to it itself, thus resolving itself in the same syllogism', namely in the *system*.[31] We can fully gauge the abstract-rationalistic sense of this conception if we remember that Gentile is determined to affirm it both against Leibniz's principle of sufficient reason ('the same motive that inspired Hume in his search for a principle to justify the synthesis that takes place in the judgement of causality') and against Kant's basis for the inadmissibility of existence as a predicate. Thus Gentile writes: 'since thought itself is truth in fact *because* it is truth in reason, there is no need, if there is thought, for the principle of sufficient reason in order to pass from absence to existence. Which [thought], as judgement, is, in its analysis, the terminating term, but it is above all terminated term: in other words, that which, being in its immediacy, would be if it was not already invested by thought and was not therefore itself made thought. Without this there would be that intuition of the given which Kant, polemicizing against the ontological argument, denied could be considered the mark of a concept, namely simple existence'.[32]

It is likewise on the basis of the denial of the positivity of the aesthetic that Gentile is constrained to emphasize the unity of the terms of logical thought, to the detriment of their *distinction*, as, for example, when he says that the thought 'the straight line is the shortest distance between two given points' is a true and objective thought 'only if what is thought as a straight line is the same thing that is

---

[30] *Sistema di logica*, I, pp. 233-234.
[31] Ibid., p. 261.
[32] Ibid., pp. 231-232.

thought as the shortest distance between two points . . . , such that the thought of what is the shortest distance between two points must indeed be *different* from the other, enough to serve as a point of support to thought, which would think nothing of the straight line (thus identified with what marks the shortest distance between two points), if it did not have such a point of support; it must be different, but in order *to be identical to it*.[33]

It is thus clear that his conception of the circularity of thought as system, rather than as circle of induction and deduction, namely synthesis or circle of 'heterogeneities' (Kant), compels Gentile to elude the distinction of the terms of thought, of subject and predicate; then, in order to account for it, he ultimately resorts to that extrinsic—even illegitimate—factor of the necessity for a point of support, or of departure, so that thought may discourse, or be thought.

If we now compare the 'logic of the abstract' to the 'logic of the concrete', we find that 'between the synthesis (A = A) and the synthesis of terms in which the act of the concrete logos is explained and concentrated (I = not-I), there is a *radical* difference, since the one is essentially thought as fact, the other thought as act'. Moreover: 'the synthesis, . . . is fact, because the thought that knows it is a result, the process of which eludes thought itself'.[34] We already know what is meant by thought in this context. We know that this difference between thought, or multiplicity, and thinking, or unity, does not exist, or has not been demonstrated by Gentile. We know that the 'fact' reduced to 'system' is no longer fact. Likewise, when we read that 'this identity of A and not-A, which the logic of the abstract rejects as contradiction, is the immanent law of the concrete logos',[35] we recall the dialectical identity of A, or thought, and not-A, or natural being, demonstrated above with regard to the second and third principles (within which identity returns willy-nilly to Hegel's elimination of the 'singular which is meant', or the aesthetic *Aufhebung*, since for Gentile himself natural being coincides with sensation).

Likewise, in 'that obscurity . . . called sense or temperament or nature . . . , being itself illuminated by thought itself which corresponds to the first term of the first formula (I = I), which expresses the

[33] Ibid., p. 221.
[34] Ibid., II, pp. 70-71.
[35] Ibid., p. 53.

conception or transcendental thought or thinking thought',[36] we recognize the same 'sensation' as 'terminated term' of the thought that is thought. And Gentile, precisely sensing the need to persuade us that to say 'that the I is equal to itself is not intended in the same sense as A = A', justifies himself by allowing that the second 'is objective identity, which reproduces in the relation of terms the immediacy characteristic of abstract being' and that the former 'is subjective identity, which is not posited, immediate, with respect to a possible object, but is generated, posits itself'.[37] Gentile thereby commits a *petitio principii* in regard to the very foundation of his philosophic logic: namely thought 'as object of itself', or 'thinkable', which 'renews in thought the positing of being that is pure being',[38] and which is distinct from thought that is not 'object to itself'.

His logic of the abstract thus fails to achieve its aim: to account for 'thinkable' and therefore 'determinate' being, or being having 'a certain content'. And this failure also demolishes his logic of the concrete, which is thereby converted into the doctrine of the pure thinking thought, or pure unity, since there can be no *logic* of pure unity, but only, strictly speaking, its mystique.

Gentile's entire philosophy may thus be assessed. It is a philosophy that, since it is focused on the concept that 'the synthesis makes the thesis possible, creating its own antithesis, in other words, creating itself',[39] remains enclosed within the Platonic-Hegelian dogma of truth as dialogue of the soul with itself, or self-consciousness. It is consequently blind not only to the most profound discoveries of Aristotle, but also to those of Kant, not to speak of others.[40]

[36] Ibid., p. 55.
[37] Ibid., p. 52.
[38] Ibid., I, p. 175.
[39] *L'atto del pensare come atto puro*, §18.
[40] At this point we may say a few words about Ugo Spirito, perhaps the most noteworthy contemporary legatee of Italian Hegelianism, and of Gentilism in particular: in the sense that his 'problematicism', namely his rejection of the 'synthesis' and his remaining within the antinomy, leads us to the ancient-sceptical origins of Hegelianism, to that classical scepticism about the intellect common to all those who counterpose it to modern (or critical) scepticism about absolute reason. Spirito, of course, views classical scepticism through the prism of modern romantic idealism. Thus it is that on the one hand he repeats, with Sextus Empiricus, that 'reasoning', the intellect, 'deceives', in other words, leads us into insoluble antinomies or perennial 'problematicities'; and on the other hand, while accepting the substance of the Hegelian conviction that (ancient!) scepticism, by rendering the 'rational' finite and therefore

antinomic, in effect creates the 'scab' of 'dogmatism', of 'limitation', in order to be able to 'pick it', he thinks that this operation can occur only through cosmic sentiment (life as 'love') and not through reason. In sum, he is indebted to *Romantik*, concluding in a neo-aestheticism and secular mysticism. This reconfirms, if there was any need, our analysis of the ancient-sceptical origins of Hegelian idealism (and thus of the ancient source of Hegelianism in *Outlines of Pyrrhonism* and *Parmenides*) and of the cardinal historic-systematic distinction between ancient and modern scepticism (the believer Pascal came close to the former with his 'Pyrrhonism'; the same is true of all mystics, thanks to their initial scepticism about the world and therefore about the intellect).

3

On Logical Positivism

The major difficulty in arriving at a proper comprehension and complete critical assessment of the modern formal (or rather, formalized) logic championed by logical positivism lies in its dual character as theory of thought and of language. Once the theory of thought is examined, and its inability to serve as a valid logic, philosophical or otherwise, is demonstrated (for, as we shall see, it leaves the problem of scientific law unresolved), there remains the theory of language, particularly of semiotics, associated most closely with the name of Rudolf Carnap. Excessively abstract and partial, this theory, with its peculiar obsession with 'correct' language, or the language of 'truth', turns a merely technical language (of a mathematical type) into a dogma and thus fails as a general, truly philosophical theory of semiotics (or semantics).

Let us begin with the most general principles of the neo-positivist school, the so-called Vienna Circle, which are intended to provide us the foundations of an 'anti-metaphysical' logic. These principles, as expounded by W.H. Werkmeister, may be summarized as follows.

1. Knowledge is knowledge only in its form; in any cognition, only the form is important, while all the rest is inessential (Moritz Schlick).

2. A proposition has meaning only to the extent that it can be verified (Schlick), and to verify a proposition means only to find out whether or not it accords with the rules established to govern the connections of that proposition in a given language.

3. Knowledge is always empirical, based on that which is given directly (Schlick); moreover, the sense-data of sensation, which lie at the foundation of the edifice erected by this school (the fundamental

architecture of which was devised by Ernst Mach), are afforded by protocol propositions—primary, or elementary, propositions that are not debatable.[1]

4. The logical analysis of language demonstrates that all metaphysical propositions are pseudo-propositions wholly devoid of meaning (Carnap).

5. All fields of research are based on a single science: physics (Neurath, Carnap); hence the doctrine of physicalism.[2]

6. The propositions of logic are tautologies (Wittgenstein). Hence: 'In logic process and result are equivalent. (Hence the absence of surprise.)' And: 'Proof in logic is merely a mechanical expedient to facilitate the recognition of tautologies in complicated cases.'[3]

7. Mathematics is a logical method (Wittgenstein); all mathematical concepts can be derived from the fundamental concepts of logic (Carnap).

The logic embodied in these principles has been theorized especially by Bertrand Russell, Alfred Tarski, and Carnap, who have given it perhaps its most extensive development. The theory of *material implication* in particular is presented as the most rigorous modern contribution of the new logical formalism. Let us, then, begin with that concept.

The expression 'material implication' denotes an implication or deduction that does not posit any conceptual or formal connection between the premise and the consequent in the traditional, Aristotelian syllogistic sense. (In this traditional sense, the true proposition 'Socrates is mortal' is indeed implied by the true proposition 'Socrates is a man', but because it can be deduced from this proposition by means of the general proposition 'Man is mortal'.) What is of concern to the new formal logic, then, is the truth or falsity of single

[1] Cf. Ludwig Wittgenstein, *Tractatus Logico-Philosophicus* (London and Henley, 1961, reprinted 1978), 5: 'A proposition is a truth-function of elementary propositions. (An elementary proposition is a truth-function of itself.)' Examples of elementary, or atomic, propositions: '*A* is red'; 'the segment AB is congruent with the segment CD', etc. They are so named because they cannot be divided into other *logical* values—in other words, into other propositions.

[2] 'The correct method in philosophy would really be the following: to say nothing except what can be said, i.e. propositions of natural science—i.e. something that ha nothing to do with philosophy . . . ' (Ibid., 6.53.)

[3] Ibid., 6.1261 and 6.1262.

(elementary) propositions, independent of any reference to their (conceptual) content. The focus of interest is the truth or falsity of the connection-implication of these propositions in their entirety or unity, what Tarski calls the 'truth of the whole implication'; in short, the value of consistency, or pure logicality.[4]

A new logical technique necessarily follows, one that is not truly formal, like that of syllogistic logic, but rather *formalized* or formalistic (and the extreme logical formalism is represented, strange as this may seem, precisely by material implication, as Russell himself has warned). The technique of this logic can only consist in a sort of *sentential calculus*—in other words, a calculus of the combinations of truth or falsity of the connections-implications of propositions that are simply assumed to be true or false, independent of their conceptual content. 'The fifth proposition of Euclid', Russell writes in *The Principles of Mathematics*, 'follows from the fourth; if the fourth is true so is the fifth, while if the fifth is false, so is the fourth. This is a case of material implication'.[5] Tarski gives us four typical examples of connections-implications, composite (or molecular) propositions containing the logical constant 'if-then' (other logical constants are 'not', 'and', 'or', 'all', 'some', etc.):

> 'if 2·2 = 4,   then   New York is a large city;
> 'if 2·2 = 5,   then   New York is a large city;
> 'if 2·2 = 4,   then   New York is a small city;
> 'if 2·2 = 5,   then   New York is a small city.'[6]

He then notes that only the third proposition is false (although nevertheless 'meaningful'), while the other three are true, as well as meaningful. The reason only the third is false is that a tacit postulate of logical experience, known as the postulate of consequentiality, tells us that 'it never happens that the antecedent is true ['2·2 = 4', in this case] while the consequent ['New York is a small city', in this case] is false'.[7] The other three are true in accordance with two similar tacit postulates: first, 'a false proposition p implies all

---

[4] 'By proposition is meant, in their view [the view of modern logicians], *any expression of which it can be said that it is either true or false*. They thereby exclude from consideration as propositions any assertion for which no truth criterion has been given.' (Ludovico Geymonat, *Studi per un nuovo razionalismo*, Turin, 1945, p. 61.)

[5] Bertrand Russell, *The Principles of Mathematics*, London, second edition, 1937, reprinted 1979, p. 14.

[6] Alfred Tarski, *Introduction to Logic*, New York, 1965, third edition revised, p. 26.

[7] Ibid., p. 24.

propositions q, whether true or false'; second, 'a true proposition q is implied by all propositions, true or false'.[8] These two postulates were accepted as rules of 'pure material consequence', in medieval terms.[9]

To clarify the spirit of the three typical true implications listed above, Tarski playfully cites an expression of ordinary language that illustrates the false implication: 'If you solve this problem, I shall eat my hat'. He then observes: 'The tendency of this utterance is quite clear. We affirm here an implication whose consequence is undoubtedly false; therefore, since we affirm the truth of the whole implication, we thereby, at the same time, affirm the falsity of the antecedent; that is to say, we express our conviction that our friend will fail to solve the problem in which he is interested. But it is also quite clear that the antecedent and the consequent of our implication are in no way connected [in the traditional, syllogistic sense of conceptual content], so that we have a typical case of a material and not of a formal implication'.[10]

This alone makes clear, and justifies within its limits (which are those of a new, comprehensive formalism of both kinds of implication), the general *ad hoc* technicism of the logical constants[11] and variables of molecular propositions, or propositional functions (for

[8] Geymonat, *Studi per un nuovo razionalismo*, p. 71. Cf. Russell, *The Principles of Mathematics*, p. 35, and J.M. Bocheński, *The Methods of Contemporary Thought*, Dordrecht-Holland, 1965, p. 80: 'In particular a false statement implies every statement and a true statement is implied by every statement.' This is immediately preceded by the following description of implication: 'Implication holds between two statements—an antecedent A and a consequent B—when either A is false or B is true or both. It follows from this definition that implication fails to hold in one case only, namely when the antecedent (A) is true and the consequent (B) false; in all other cases, whatever A and B may be, there is an implication.'

[9] By Strode, Ockham, Buridan; cf. Ernest A. Moody, *Truth and Consequence in Medieval Logic*, Amsterdam, 1953, p. 74: 'He [Strode] gives just two rules for material consequences: (1) An impossible proposition implies any proposition, and (2) A necessary proposition is implied by any proposition.' In a note Moody then observes: 'Ockham . . . gives these two rules, and then remarks: "But such consequences are not formal, so that those rules are not much used[!]".' And he concludes, pp. 77-78: 'It should be emphasized, at the outset, that the medieval theory of consequence is not a logical calculus, not a system of formulas expressed with variables and logical constants. It is, rather, a system of rules governing logically valid inferences to or from sentences of conditional form.' See also Philotheus Boenher, *Medieval Logic*, Chicago, 1952, p. 29; also p. xv: 'the Stoics developed the hypothetical syllogism with a clear insight into material implication and its theorems'.

[10] Tarski, pp. 26-27.

[11] The *logical constant* is also called 'propositional functor'. See, for example, Jan Łukasiewicz, *Aristotle's Syllogistic*, Oxford, 1951.

example, the molecular proposition 'if *p* then *q*' can be considered a propositional function of the variables *p* and *q*[12]): the ever more complex symbolism, the various rules, and finally the truth tables, which are sorts of synoptic tabulations of the typical combinations of truth and falsity obtained from the propositional calculus. ('In what', writes Geymonat, 'does the truth table of the [molecular] proposition *f(p, q)* consist? It is a table whose first two columns record all the possible cases of truth or falsity of the atomic propositions *p* and *q*, while the last column records the corresponding value of truth or falsity of the propositional function *f(p, q)* in the cases in which *p* and *q* assume the values indicated, in the same row, from the first two columns'.[13])

Moreover, we must also bear in mind this warning by Russell: 'Two kinds of implication, the material and the formal, were found to be essential to every kind of deduction.'[14] But without overlooking Tarski's reservation: 'every meaningful and true formal implication is at the same time a meaningful and true implication, but not vice versa' and that therefore the 'concept of formal implication [which is 'not, perhaps, quite clear'] . . . is narrower than that of material implication'.[15]

The problematic character of the following remarks by Russell must also be kept in mind. 'For the technical study of Symbolic Logic, it is convenient to take as a single indefinable the notion of a formal implication, i.e. of such propositions as "*x* is a man implies *x* is mortal, for all values of *x*".'[16] 'Our [propositional] calculus studies the relation of *implication* [simple or material] between propositions. This relation must be distinguished from the relation of *formal* implication, . . . How far formal implication is definable in terms of implication simply . . . is a difficult question, . . . What the difference is between the two, an illustration will explain. The

---

[12] Russell, *The Principles of Mathematics*, p. 13: 'I shall speak of propositions exclusively where there is no real variable: where there are one or more real variables, and for all values of the variables the expression involved is a proposition, I shall call the expression a *propositional function*.' See also, p. 38: 'It is to be observed that "*x* is a man implies *x* is a mortal" is not a relation of two propositional functions, but is itself a single propositional function having the elegant property of being always true. For "*x* is a man" is, as it stands, not a proposition at all, and does not imply anything; . . .'

[13] Geymonat, p. 63.
[14] Russell, p. 33.
[15] Tarski, p. 26.
[16] Russell, p. 11.

fifth proposition of Euclid follows from the fourth; if the fourth is true, so is the fifth, while if the fifth is false, so is the fourth. This is a case of material implication, for both propositions are absolute constants, not dependent for their meaning upon the assigning of a value to a variable. But each of them *states* a formal implication. The fourth states that if *x* and *y* be triangles fulfilling certain conditions, then *x* and *y* are triangles fulfilling certain other conditions, and that this implication holds for all values of *x* and *y*; and the fifth states that if *x* is an isosceles triangle, *x* has the angles at the base equal. The formal implication involved in each of these two propositions is quite a different thing from the material implication holding between the propositions as wholes; both notions are required in the propositional calculus, but it is the study of material implication which specially distinguishes this subject, for formal implication occurs throughout the whole of mathematics.

'It has been customary, in treatises on logic, to confound the two kinds of implication, and often to be really considering the formal kind where the material kind only was apparently involved. For example, when it is said that "Socrates is a man, therefore Socrates is a mortal", Socrates is *felt* as a variable: he is a type of humanity, and one feels that any other man would have done as well. If, instead of *therefore*, which implies the truth of hypothesis and consequent, we put "Socrates is a man implies Socrates is mortal", it appears at once that we may substitute not only another man, but any other entity whatever, in the place of Socrates.[17] Thus although what is explicitly stated, in such a case, is a material implication, what is meant is a formal implication; and some effort is needed to confine our imagination to material implication.'[18]

[17] On page 34 of *The Principles of Mathematics*, Russell notes: '. . . only a vulgar prejudice in favour of true propositions [in the syllogistic sense] stands in the way of replacing Socrates by a number, a table, or a plum-pudding.'

[18] Ibid., p. 14. The following passages from *The Principles of Mathematics* should also be noted: '. . . wherever, as in Euclid, one particular proposition is deduced from another, material implication is involved, though as a rule the material implication may be regarded as a particular instance of some formal implication, obtained by giving some constant value to the variable or variables involved in the said formal implication' (p. 34). 'The point to be emphasized is . . . that our *x* [in '*x* is a man implies that *x* is a mortal'], though variable, must be the same on both sides of the implication, and this requires that we should not obtain our formal implication by first varying (say) Socrates in "Socrates is a man", and then in "Socrates is a mortal", but that we should start from the whole proposition "Socrates is a man implies Socrates is a mortal", and vary Socrates in this proposition as a whole. Thus our formal implication asserts a class of implications, not a single implication at all. We

'We require, then, in the propositional calculus, no indefinables except the two kinds of implication'.[19] 'This brings me to the notion of *such that*. The values of x which render a propositional function ϕx true are like the roots of an equation—indeed the latter are a particular case of the former—and we may consider all the values of x which are *such that* ϕx is true. In general, these values form a *class*, and in fact a class may be defined as all the terms satisfying some propositional function.'[20] 'Such instances make it plain that the notion of a propositional function, and the notion of an assertion, are more fundamental than the notion of *class*, . . . It seems to be the very essence of what may be called a *formal* truth, and of formal reasoning generally, that some assertion is affirmed to hold of every term; and unless the notion of *every* term is admitted, formal truths are impossible. The fundamental importance of formal implication is brought out by the consideration that it is involved in all the rules of inference. This shows that we cannot hope wholly to define it in terms of material implication, . . . '[21]

---

do not, in a word, have one implication containing a variable, but rather a variable implication. We have a class of implications, no one of which contains a variable, and we assert that every member of this class is true. This is a first step towards the analysis of the mathematical notion of the variable' (p. 38). Cf., in regard to the 'theory of types': 'The technical essence of the theory of types is merely this: Given a propositional function "ϕx" of which all values are true, there are expressions which it is not legitimate to substitute for "x". For example: All values of "if x is a man x is a mortal" are true, and we can infer "if Socrates is a man, Socrates is a mortal"; but we cannot infer "if the law of contradiction is a man, the law of contradiction is a mortal". The theory of types declares this latter set of words to be nonsense, and gives rules as to permissible values of "x" in "ϕx". . . . In the older conventional logic, it was customary to point out that such a form of words as "virtue is triangular" is neither true nor false, but no attempt was made to arrive at a definite set of rules for deciding whether a given series of words was or was not significant. This the theory of types achieves. Thus, for example, I stated above that "classes of things are not things". This will mean: "If 'x is a member of the class ϕ' is a proposition and 'ϕx' is a proposition, then 'ϕx' is not a proposition, but a meaningless collection of symbols"' (p. xiv). Finally, on the same theory: 'Every propositional function $\phi(x)$—so it is contended—has, in addition to its range of truth, a range of significance, i.e. a range within which x must lie if $\phi(x)$ is to be a proposition at all, whether true or false. This is the first point in the theory of types; the second point is that ranges of significance form *types*, i.e. if x belongs to the range of significance of $\phi(x)$, then there is a class of objects, the *type* of x, all of which must also belong to the range of significance of $\phi(x)$, however ϕ may be varied; and the range of significance is always either a single type or a sum of several whole types. The second point is less precise than the first, and the case of numbers introduces difficulties; . . . ' (p. 523).

[19] Ibid., p. 15.
[20] Ibid., p. 20.
[21] Ibid., p. 40.

Apart from differences between Russell and Tarski (and others) on the relation between formal and material implication (and here I would share Russell's view), it is interesting to note their agreement (indeed, nearly everyone's agreement) on the definition of the notion of 'class' as established in conformity with none other than the first figure (*dictum de omni et nullo*) of the categorical syllogism, expressed by Aristotle with letters symbolizing the variables.[22] Indeed, Tarski considers 'a sentential function with one free variable, for instance: $x > 0$'. He then notes that if 'we prefix the words *the set of all numbers x such that* to that function, we obtain the expression: *the set of all numbers x such that $x > 0$*. This expression, he continues, 'designates a well-determined set, namely the set of all positive numbers'.[23] This is 'the set having as its elements those, and only those, numbers which satisfy the given function'. He then concludes that in logic, 'to every sentential function containing just one free variable, say "x", there is exactly one corresponding class having as its elements those, and only those,

[22] In his edition of Aristotle's *Prior and Posterior Analytics* (Oxford, 1949, p. 29), the eminent historian W.D. Ross made this general observation: '[Aristotle] by taking propositional functions denoted by pairs of letters, not actual propositions about particular things, makes it plain that validity depends on *form*, and thus becomes the originator of formal logic.' Ross endorses (p. 30n), the following idea of the 'modern logician' J.W. Miller: 'that it is ... proper to interpret a class as meaning "those entities which satisfy a propositional function, provided that there is at least one entity which does satisfy the function and at least one entity which does not satisfy the function"; and that Aristotle's system, which adopts this interpretation (though in fact the condition "and at least one entity which does not satisfy the function" is not required for the justification of Aristotle's conversion of "all B is A"), falls into place as one part of the wider system which modern logic has erected on its wider interpretation of "class".' In his *Aristotle's Syllogistic* (p. 8), Łukasiewicz recalls the commentator Alexander, in the following terms: 'It was Alexander who first said explicitly that Aristotle presents his doctrine in *letters*, στοιχεῖα, in order to show that we get the conclusion not in consequence of the matter of the premises, but in consequence of their *form* and combination; the letters are marks of universality and show that such a conclusion will follow always and for any term we may choose.' He also recalls the commentator Philoponos, 'who is also fully aware of the significance and importance of variables', etc. And he associates himself with Ross: 'I am glad to learn that Sir David Ross ... emphasizes that by using *variables* Aristotle became the founder of formal logic.' I cannot resist adding that Łukasiewicz's general assessment of the *Prior Analytics* sounds strange indeed, to say the least, in view of these comments: 'This purely logical work is entirely exempt from any philosophic contamination' (p. 6).

[23] The entire second part of Tarski's *Introduction to Logic*, pp. 155 ff., is devoted to 'Applications of Logic and Methodology in Constructing Mathematical Theories'. In this regard he recalls the 'epochal work' of Russell and Alfred North Whitehead, *Principia Mathematica* (three volumes, 1910-1913, second edition 1925-1927).

things *x* which satisfy the given function. We obtain a designation for that class by putting in front of the sentential function the following phrase, which belongs to the fundamental expressions of the theory of classes: *the class of all things x such that*. If we denote further the class in question by a single symbol, say "C", the formula *x*ε*C* will—for any *x*—be equivalent to the original sentential function'.[24] Finally, he acknowledges—in contradiction to his previous assertion (p. 19) that 'the old traditional logic forms only a fragment of the new, a fragment moreover which, from the point of view of the requirements of other sciences, and of mathematics in particular, is entirely insignificant'—that the 'most important laws of traditional logic are those of the categorical syllogism, which correspond precisely to the laws of the theory of classes that we stated above and named after them'.[25]

Thus far we have examined, in extremely narrow compass, one aspect of symbolic logic: the theory of the *propositional calculus* in its immediate and partial connection with the theory of *classes*. We have ignored all other aspects of the latter theory, especially that of their internal development and all that goes with it. Nevertheless, this brief sketch is sufficient to ground an equally brief examination of the linguistic or semantic theory implied by symbolic language. That theory was applied, and indeed culminates, in Carnap's 'logical syntax of language'. Russell himself, before Wittgenstein (with whom we are not concerned here), was cognizant of linguistic exigency as the need for a 'correct' method of thought, which he regarded as indissociable from the need for an equally correct *technical* language and related grammar. 'Logical constants', he noted, 'therefore, if we are to be able to say anything definite about them, must be treated as part of the language, not as part of what the language speaks about'.[26] This anticipates Carnap's distinction between 'logical language' and 'object language' and the entire problematic of 'levels of language' and 'metalanguage'. This may be seen, in particular, in the outline of 'philosophical grammar' (= logic) presented in chapter IV of *The Principles of Mathematics*, where Russell discusses 'the terms of a proposition', in other words the 'subjects about which the proposition is'.

He writes: 'It is a characteristic of the terms of a proposition that

[24] Tarski, pp. 69-70.
[25] Ibid., p. 76.
[26] *The Principles of Mathematics*, p. xi.

any one of them may be replaced by any other entity without our ceasing to have a proposition'. In regard to adjectives, or predicates (concepts-classes), he notes: 'With the sense which *is* has in this proposition ['Socrates is human'], we no longer have a proposition at all if we replace *human* by something other than a predicate'.[27]

We may immediately observe that the title 'philosophical grammar' is clearly inappropriate to a grammar like this, *formalized* to such an extent that 'the subject is treated here only because it is essential to any doctrine of number or of the nature of the variable'. Indeed, its 'bearings on general philosophy, important as they are, will be left wholly out of account'.[28] Naturally, a grammar so formalized that it can serve as a technical, scientific language, one precisely quantified in the content of the sign (general or particular), is inherently foreign to the rules of the 'natural' language which, before philosophy, is the language of art and history. Moreover, any claim to bestow the name philosophical language on 'artificial' semiotics and on the special language into which the substance of the syntactic-logical-symbolic doctrine dissolves creates great confusion in the field of semantics. This has been noticed, to some extent, even by one of the worshippers of formal logic itself, J.M. Bocheński. In his book *The Methods of Contemporary Thought*, he expounds the theory of 'syntactic categories' (cf. Russell's grammar), as follows:

'A class of expressions of a language, each of which can be exchanged with any other of the same class in a meaningful statement without depriving the statement of meaning, is called a "syntactic category".' He then cites some examples. The 'proper names constitute a syntactic category in English; in any meaningful English statement—e.g. "Fritz drinks"—one proper name can be replaced by another, without depriving the statement of meaning. In the example quoted, "Fritz" can be replaced by "John", "Eva", "Napoleon", or even "Everest", and the statement will still be meaningful (perhaps true, perhaps false, but still meaningful). On the other hand, a verb, for example "sleeps", belongs to a different syntactic category; if we were to put "sleeps" in the place of "Fritz" in our statement, the result would be a nonsensical statement: "sleeps drinks".'

27 Ibid., p. 45.
28 Ibid., p. 43.

After his exposition of this theory, however, Bocheński notes that the 'imprecise' expressions that his theory strives to eliminate (in favour of the clarity and precision of scientific language) nonetheless contribute 'to the beauty of language' and are 'valuable poetically' even if they detract 'seriously from the precision and clarity of language'. He then concludes that the 'supporters of the logical positivist school' have used such instances of imprecise language to try 'to show up the whole of philosophy as meaningless. They have, however, mistaken syntactic nonsense for something quite different, namely semantic nonsense. [Think, for example, of the semantic nonsense involved in treating *as a variable* in the manner of 'Fritz' in the example above, the name of some historical or poetical person. This sort of nonsense, once corrected, leads us back to a proposition, historic or artistic, which is both meaningful *and* true and not at all 'meaningful and true or false'.] With the passage of time it has become clear that they have gone much too far'.[29]

As for Carnap, his attempt to place 'semantics', and more properly 'pure' logical 'syntax' (or the theory of 'truth' as the theory of 'logical deduction') in the service of the 'so-called theory of knowledge and the methodology of mathematics and of empirical science' is of undoubted interest, especially since he considers semantics of 'great importance' for these two sciences.[30] It is of interest because Carnap, more than other authors, exhibits the positive, as well as the negative, significance of the natural limits of symbolic logic as modern *formal* logic: what it contains or can contain (which the traditional, syllogistic formal logic did not contain), and not merely what it excludes.

'From our point of view', Carnap writes in 'Formalwissenschaft und Realwissenschaft', 'the study of logic, of the logic of science, must be considered the logical syntax of scientific language. As an example of a problem of the logic of science, let us recall the study of the relation between the two principal fields of science: formal science (logic, including mathematics) and real science (including the empirical sciences: physics, biology, psychology, sociology, history, etc.). The problem must be considered *logical*-scientific. . . . Although the two fields present no essential difference from the psychological

---

[29] Bocheński, pp. 44-47.
[30] Rudolf Carnap, *Introduction to Semantics*, Harvard University Press, 1948, p. viii. And on page 9 Carnap writes: 'And if, finally, we abstract from the designata also and analyse only the relations between the expressions, we are in (logical) syntax.'

point of view [but Carnap reduces gnoseology itself to mere psychology!]..., there is, however, a precise and fundamental difference in relation to logic. It is founded on the syntactic difference between *analytic* and *synthetic* formulations.

'To establish how the distinction between formal and real science should be understood, let us suppose that the necessary syntactic structure of language for unified science has been established. This requires a system of syntactical rules: first of all the *formal rules* that determine what forms of propositions are admissible, second the *transformation rules* that govern the conditions under which a proposition can be a consequence of other propositions....

'In relation to the transformation rules, we can distinguish the propositions according to their syntactic character: 1. We shall call *analytic* those that are valid unconditionally in accordance with the transformation rules, whether the propositions at issue are true or false. 2. We shall call *contradictory* a proposition that is unconditionally invalid. 3. We shall call *determinate* an analytic or contradictory proposition. 4. We shall call *synthetic* a proposition that is neither analytic nor contradictory. We may arrive at a different classification of the propositions ... in relation to the symbols. 1. We shall call *logical symbols* those that have a logical-mathematical significance, like "0", "every", "not", "3". 2. We shall call *descriptive symbols* those that have an extra-logical significance, like "big", "house", "anger".... By *logical proposition* we mean any proposition that contains only logical symbols; by *descriptive proposition* any proposition that contains at least one descriptive symbol. It should be noted that since the synthetic propositions are descriptive, but not vice versa, the field of descriptive propositions is wider....

'The use of synthetic and analytic propositions in scientific language is as follows. The practice of real science establishes synthetic propositions: for example, particular propositions to describe observed facts, or general propositions posited as *hypotheses* to be used in experiments. From these propositions other synthetic propositions can be deduced, for example in order to lay down *predictions* as to what should be verified. Now, the analytic propositions will function as *auxiliary propositions* for the indicated *synthetic reasoning*. Considered from the standpoint of a unified scientific language, all of logic, including mathematics, is merely a *calculus serving an auxiliary function in the manipulation of synthetic propositions.*

'Formal science in itself has no importance; it is an auxiliary instrument introduced in language for technical reasons, and only facilitates effectuation of the linguistic transformations necessary for real science. . . .

'A particular observation about the problem of syntax is necessary. The propositions of a language L-1 can be described and classified. If we now formulate pure syntax propositions about the forms of propositions of that language (for example: "a proposition of this or that form is analytic in L-1", "two propositions of this or that form are incompatible in L-1"), the formulation of these *pure syntax propositions* regarding L-1 will generally be made in another language, L-2. In that case, the syntax stands outside the schema of L-1; it is found, however, in the logico-mathematical part of the language, L-2. . . . The assistance rendered real science by formal science introduces *no new objective field*, contrary to the belief of many philosophers, who counterpose the "formal", "spiritual", or "ideal" objects of formal science to the "real" objects of real science. *Formal science has absolutely no object*: it is a system of auxiliary propositions, divorced from any object, devoid of any object, and devoid of any content.'[31]

In his *Introduction to Semantics*, Carnap writes as follows: 'Suppose that a certain physical theory, formulated as a class of laws K_1, is investigated and compared with another theory K_2. There are many questions which are beyond the scope of a merely logical analysis and require factual observation; e.g. the questions to what degree the particular laws belonging to K_1 or their combination are confirmed by the available evidence, whether K_2 is confirmed to a higher or lower degree than K_1, etc. On the other hand, there are questions of another kind, usually called logical questions, whose answers are not dependent upon the result of observations and therefore can be given before any relevant observations are made. These questions involve L-concepts. Examples of answers which might be given to logical questions concerning two theories, K_1 and K_2, as results of logical analysis (formulations in our L-terminology are added in parentheses): 1. The law S_1 in K_1 does not have any factual content but is merely analytic ("S_1 is L-true"); hence it is unnecessary to look for a confirmation of S_1 by the observation of facts, since S_1 is in accordance with all possible facts; it follows that the

---

[31] 'Formalwissenschaft und Realwissenschaft', in *Erkenntnis*, 5, 1935.

simplified theory K'_1 obtained from K_1 by omitting S_1 asserts just as much as the original theory K_1 ("K'_1 is L-equivalent to K_1"). 2. The law S_2 in K_1, although it has factual content ("S_2 is not L-true"), follows from another law S_3 in K_1 ("S_2 is an L-implicate of S_3"); hence the omission of S_2 in addition to S_1 leads to a theory K_1 which is likewise not weaker than K_1 ("K''_1 is also L-equivalent to K_1"). 3. The laws S_4 and S_5 in K_2 contradict each other, are logically incompatible with each other ("S_4 and S_5 are L-exclusive"); hence K_2 contains a contradiction, is inconsistent ("K_2 is L-false"); therefore there is no purpose in looking for a confirmation of K_2 by observation, because such a confirmation is impossible. 4. The three theories K_3, K_4, and K_5 constitute an exhaustive set of competitive theories; that is to say, for merely logical reasons at least one of them must hold ("K_3, K_4, and K_5 are L-disjunct with one another").'[32]

Here it is sufficient to note two points.

1. The four 'examples', cases of application of logical analysis to questions of method in a physical science, are of positive interest from the philosophical and gnoseological point of view. This is especially true of the third example, which illustrates this profound Galilean truth: without the full development of the foundations of reason—that is, without its formal structures, albeit only in an 'auxiliary' capacity—experience tells us nothing and confirms nothing, because without the formal structures of reason it is impossible to manipulate the synthetic propositions comprised of idea-hypotheses. It is the latter that make experience speak, that make it say 'yes' and 'no'. ('Experience is only half of experience', said Goethe.)

2. On the other hand, there is a negative side to these examples of 'logical analysis': they lack any gnoseological explanation, since they are maintained in a rarified logical-formal atmosphere, so to speak, and are referred only indirectly (in order to highlight their logicist validity by contrast) to their 'physical' use (although this, in itself, is interesting from the gnoseological standpoint, for Carnap's need to do this, although involuntary, is significant).

Carnap himself implicitly recognizes this deficiency when he immediately acknowledges that his explanation of the significance

[32] *Introduction to Semantics*, pp. 61-62.

of the L-terms and of the manner in which he intends to use them is 'rather vague', since 'we have not said what, exactly, we mean by "logical reasons" for truth as against factual reasons'. This lacuna, however, is quite organic, strictly dependent on his 'semantic' concept of 'truth', which is identical to Wittgenstein's, as Carnap himself notes in *Introduction to Semantics*. Here are three relevant passages:

1. 'Wittgenstein has emphasized the point of view that the truth conditions of a sentence constitute its meaning' (p. 28).

2. 'Among the possible groups of truth-conditions there are two extreme cases.

'In one of these cases the proposition is true for all the truth-possibilities of the elementary propositions. We say that the truth-conditions are *tautological*.

'In the second case the proposition is false for all the truth possibilities: the truth conditions are *contradictory*.

'In the first case we call the proposition a tautology; in the second a contradiction.'[33]

3. 'The truth-conditions determine the range which is left to the facts by the proposition. Tautology leaves to reality the whole infinite logical space; contradiction fills the whole logical space and leaves no point to reality. Neither of them, therefore, can in any way determine reality.'[34]

We thus encounter the greatest difficulty of this logic of science: its radical (abstract) empiricist foundation and its consequent logical atomism render it completely impotent precisely when faced with the problem of scientific *law*, for the solution of this problem requires an adequate conception of the problem of *induction*. But this logic cannot elaborate such a conception, since it has renounced, as a matter of principle, the positing of the corresponding logical problem of synthetic propositions[35] or idea-hypotheses and the corresponding models through which the formal structures of reason

---

[33] Wittgenstein, *Tractatus Logico-Philosophicus*, 4.46.

[34] *Introduction to Semantics*, p. 107. Carnap is here paraphrasing Wittgenstein, *Tractatus Logico-Philosophicus*, 4.463.

[35] What I mean here is that synthetic propositions constitute a logical problem as much as analytic propositions; logical positivism, however, relegates them (in contradiction, unless I am mistaken, to the fact that they are 'manipulated' through analytical or necessary propositions) to the sphere of 'history', 'psychology', and

mediate the discrete or factual, reducing it to fact-type, and, once having been confirmed, in turn regulate or unify the facts, confirming them.

This difficulty presupposes and indeed subsumes all the others, from the solipsism to which the basic atomic propositions lead (Mach and Avenarius, predecessors of the neo-positivists, were charged with solipsism by Lenin, who observed that if 'bodies are "complexes of sensations", as Mach says, ... it is impossible to arrive at the existence of other people besides oneself: it is the purest

---

'pragmatics'. In short, they are banished from logic and their verification therefore has no logical value and thus, properly, no truth. See, for example, Carnap's *Introduction to Semantics*, p. 28: 'It is especially to be noticed that ... the semantic concept of truth is fundamentally different from concepts like "believed", "verified", "highly confirmed", etc. The latter concepts belong to pragmatics and require a reference to a person [!] ... Let us consider the following example. "The moon has no atmosphere" (S_1); "S_1 is true" (S_2); "S_1 is confirmed to a very high degree by scientists at the present time" (S_3). S_2 says the same as S_1; S_2 is, like S_1, an astronomical statement and is, like S_1, to be tested by astronomical observations of the moon. On the other hand, S_3 is a historical statement; it is to be tested by historical, psychological observations of the behaviour of astronomers. Wittgenstein (*Tractatus*, 4.024, 4.46) has emphasized the point of view that the truth-conditions of a sentence constitute its meaning, and that understanding consists in knowing these conditions. This view is also connected with his conception of logical truth (compare quotations given at the end of 18A).' (These quotations are the ones cited above.) The conclusions of Giulio Preti are different, and superior. He, having well understood Galileo's conclusions about 'models', vehemently maintains that 'the "secret" of induction lies precisely in these models', since 'through them the supposed infinite variety of the facts disappears, the indiscernibility of one fact from others, fixed in well-determined schemata'. Thus, the models reduce the mass of facts to 'a limited number of "standard" facts', or fact-types, 'to which correspond determinate sets of propositions forming a well-defined system'. ('It is thus that the facts, which otherwise would constitute a mere multiplicity of disconnected fragments, acquire "meanings", and it is thus that ... the deviation of the spectral lines of the light from faraway galaxies can signify "the expanding universe".') We therefore must conclude 'an existing heterogeneity among general propositions, which stand with their consequences in a merely syntactical relation, and the consequences themselves that are F-verifiable [i.e. verifiable from the facts], and therefore, if this is the case, F-true'. He thus concludes that a sort of 'metabasis of genera' (the logical and the factual) is the 'constituent problem of structure itself, as a law of the constitution of scientific knowledge'. (*Linguaggio comune e linguaggi scientifici*, Milan, 1953, pp. 61-63.) This is a conclusion with which I can only agree (cf. my own circle of heterogeneities), but it implicitly brings Preti the logician-epistemologist into serious conflict with Preti the logician-formalist. For Geymonat's partial disagreement with Carnap, see, for example, *Studi per un nuovo razionalismo*, p. 444: '[Carnap] does not analyse ... the act of thought. ... For fear of falling into psychology, he winds up remaining on the surface of the "radical conventionalism" to which his entire thought leads.' For a critique of Russell, see John Dewey, *Logic—The Theory of Inquiry*, pp. 154 ff.

solipsism'[36]) to the 'danger', sounded by Russell himself, 'that logical positivism could become a new variety of scholasticism and, by concerning itself unduly with linguistics, could forget the relation to the facts that makes an assertion true'. This would represent the 'danger of a technique that conceals problems instead of helping to resolve them'.[37] A warning well pronounced indeed.

Here I shall not dwell on other, equally dangerous consequences of the improper linguistics of the neo-positivists. An example would be the problem of artistic language, which, like ordinary language (and as we have seen, there is no reason why this should be considered an exception by the logical positivists) should allegedly be composed of 'meaningful', 'intelligible', and 'reasonable' propositions, but which 'does not communicate knowledge', just as 'What time is it?' or 'Let's get going' do not communicate knowledge.[38] From which it is clear that it is quite improper to reduce 'truth' to 'mathematical' or purely scientific truth.

Finally, to conclude, it must be recognized that within the limits of a modern formal, or abstract, logic, symbolic logic does represent an advance over traditional formal logic, because it replaces the study of qualitative, syllogistic formalism with the study of quantitative, mathematical formalism, which is a constituent of the rational, deductive structures of the physical sciences. In sum, it has discovered, or more sharply identified, the type of propositions, different from the usual subject-predicate propositions (or *premises* of Aristotelian logic) that may be called functor propositions, defined by logical constants ('if-then', 'or', 'and', 'not', 'all', etc.) and the related variables; these properly constitute the 'principal (logical) stock of every scientific theory'; but nevertheless, unlike the other sort of propositions, they 'cannot be immediately confronted with the facts', as Lukasiewicz reminds us in his *Aristotle's Syllogistic* (p. 132), in a challenge to the dear departed Kant, one-sided theorist of subject-predicate judgements, his analytic and synthetic judgements.

But it is also true that the final question posed by Lukasiewicz in this regard—'how are true functoral propositions possible?'—can never be answered by an abstract, formal logic, a logic without

[36] *Materialism and Empirio-Criticism, Collected Works*, vol. 14, p. 34.
[37] Bertrand Russell, 'Logical Positivism', in *Actas del primer congreso nacional de filosofia*, Mendoza, 1949, II, pp. 1218-19.
[38] G. Preti, 'Grammatica e logica', in *Studi urbinati*, 1955, 1.

gnoseology. For to respond to this question requires discovery of the logical principle, or common root, that underlies both sorts of propositions: empirical and qualitative (since formal) propositions, which can be immediately confronted with the facts (such as the 'premises' and 'conclusions', the subject-predicate constituents of the traditional Aristotelian syllogism), and functoral propositions, which do not immediately confront the facts. This in turn requires a truly general theory of logic, as free as possible of any tacitly accepted presuppositions, and therefore a logic-gnoseology that tells us, for example, the meaning of 'factuality' and 'fact' as compared to 'logicity' and 'reason'. And it so happens that the neo-positivist formalist, because of the very coherence of his formalistic discourse, is compelled despite himself (like the formalist-dialectician Hegel) to resort to an actual use of the principle of non-contradiction quite different from and much more concrete than that theorized by him in terms of the 'tautological' or 'contradictory' character of mere molecular or *analytic* propositions. (Just as, again despite himself, Hegel actually used a determinate and therefore non-contradictory dialectic quite different from his theoretical use of a pure tauto-heterology or dialectical unity of 'pure thoughts', 'considered in and for themselves' apart from experience, with its necessity of distinction and lack of contradiction.) But to do this, of course, it is necessary to pose the logico-gnoseological problem of the relationship between thought and reality, which means the relationship between reason and matter, and not to disregard, for fear of metaphysics, this and other problems that are no longer, if indeed they ever were, the province of metaphysics. It is, in fact, difficult to deny that such problems properly belong to the domain of any philosophy worthy of the name: philosophy as a science which, through the most anti-dogmatic method possible, seeks to eliminate and resolve the greatest possible number of presuppositions or otherwise unexplained facts and thus to arrive at the greatest possible unity of things.

It seems clear that the materialist critique of a priori reasoning is the method that can broach these problems with the greatest protection against dogmatism, whether logical-metaphysical or logical-formalist, whether old or new. If only because any other 'method', whether idealist, neo-scholastic, spiritualist, vulgar materialist, existentialist, or whatever, contains so many gratuitous presuppositions of its own that it is unable to confront with critical efficacy the presuppositions—admitted with the understanding that they do not impugn it, since they are of *extra-logical* order, namely ontological, gnoseological, epistemological, etc.—of the highly compromised modern formal logic, or pure logic of science, that symbolic or mathematical logic claims to be. Even apart from the fact that the proclaimed *neutrality* of this logic with respect to extra-logical questions facilitates the alliances forged by its followers not only with idealism and existentialism, but even with Catholic spiritualism (Bocheński, Boenher, etc.).

In actual fact, it is only in appearance that the followers of Carnap doubt and reject 'logical' problems, as in the case of the necessity of distinguishing the logical from the factual meaning of truth. This, as well as Preti's excessively self-evident transition from logic to epistemology as far as scientific laws are concerned, are symptoms of an internal philosophical torment that can be critically apprehended primarily, if not solely, by the modern materialist who acknowledges only scientific knowledge (physical and 'moral') and is therefore interested exclusively in the philosophical foundation of this knowledge, with no reservation whatever.

That is why only the materialist genuinely senses the *limits* of this pure logic of modern science and, while not lumping things together indiscriminately, and therefore while not confusing it with any of its crude predecessors, like Machism, objectively and critically denounces its philosophical insufficiencies.

Index

Printed in the United States
by Baker & Taylor Publisher Services